SIX PILLARS

SIX PILLARS

Introductions to the

Major Works of

SRI AUROBINDO

Edited By Robert A. McDermott

WILSON BOOKS

1974

WILSON BOOKS are published for the Liberal Arts by
Conococheague Associates, Inc.
From the Campus of Wilson College,
Chambersburg, Pennsylvania, 17201.

Copyright © 1974, by Robert A. McDermott
All rights reserved. No part of this book may be reproduced or utilized in any form
or by any means, electronic or mechanical, including photocopying, recording, or by
any information storage and retrieval system, without permission in writing from the
publisher. For information, address Conococheague Associates, Inc., On the Campus of Wilson College, Chambersburg, PA 17201.

L.C. Number: 74–77411
I.S.B.N. 0–89012–001–3

Quotations from the works of Sri Aurobindo, the Table of Contents of the Birth
Centenary Library, and the photographs of Sri Aurobindo are reproduced with the
kind permission of the Sri Aurobindo Ashram.

BL
70
1870
.G4
.G4
S59
COPY 2

PREFACE

DURING THE FOUR YEARS from 1971 until the publication of this volume, numerous volumes by and about Sri Aurobindo were either published or made available in America for the first time. The most significant publication of the Sri Aurobindo Ashram distributed in America is the thirty-volume Sri Aurobindo Birth Centenary Library. During this same time, the Ashram has published many other editions of Sri Aurobindo's writings and many studies and symposia by disciples. For Aurobindo studies in America, however, the more significant impetus came from scholarly journals and American commercial publications, particularly new paperback editions. As the Guide to Further Reading indicates in detail, a brief list of recent publications in America includes: Sri Aurobindo's *The Mind of Light* (1971), a full-length philosophical study (1971), extensive writings by and about Sri Aurobindo in three scholarly journals (1972), and *The Essential Aurobindo* (1974). Another anthology, *The Future Evolution of Man*, and two full-length studies by distinguished disciples, will be published within the year.

The present volume represents an advance on previous publications in that it offers novel interpretations of Sri Aurobindo's major works by scholars who approach Sri Aurobindo's works with both sobriety and receptivity. The editor invited precisely those contributors who are distinguished in the field of Indian and comparative religious thought and yet have not been associated with Aurobindo studies. The two exceptions to this policy are John Collins, whose essay on *Savitri* is based on his dissertation, and the editor, who has been publishing on Sri Aurobindo since 1971; these exceptions were necessary because it would be absolute folly to write on *Savitri* or *The Life Divine*, Sri Aurobindo's masterpieces, without previous familiarity with these works.

00404

Disciples and others who have made a lifelong study of Sri Aurobindo's teachings will perhaps find much to criticize in these essays, but the editor decided to take that risk in order to present essays which are manifestly free of the parochialism generally characteristic of writings by devotees. The editor and contributors have proceeded on the premise that even though these essays will be dismissed by some as mental verbiage entirely lacking in the spiritual experience requisite for a sound interpretation of a mystical yogi such as Sri Aurobindo, intellectual and scholarly exercises such as these help to bridge a gnawing gap between the academic community and the increasingly conspicuous community of spiritual seekers. While the contributors do not necessarily exclude themselves from the latter community, the essays in this volume are presented as works of scholarship and intellectual discernment rather than as treatises based on privileged experience. To some degree at least, each author seems to assume the legitimacy of claims for Sri Aurobindo's privileged experience, but each attempts to interpret the implications of that experience in terms acceptable to the academic community— or at least to segments of that community not entirely closed to the riches and mysteries of spiritual experience.

The editor is grateful to each of the contributors for having held other obligations in abeyance in order to write, and in most cases rewrite, these lengthy essays. They endured with patience the editor's suggested revisions of their work, and generously have not reminded the editor that he continued to struggle with *The Life Divine* long after their essays were ready for press.

The work of preparing the manuscript for publication was greatly facilitated by Eric Hughes of Matagiri, who served this volume in his double capacity as an expert on Sri Aurobindo and as copy editor. The editor and other contributors who have worked with Harry M. Buck during his years as Executive Director of the American Academy of Religion (1956–72) wish to express their enthusiasm for his publishing projects and gratitude for the opportunity to number in the excellent series of scholarly volumes which will carry the imprint of Wilson Books.

Each of the six authors has dedicated his contribution to the person who has helped him to see intellectually and, presumably, beyond.

"For where there is no vision, the people perish."

Proverbs

For

FRIEDERICH ENGEL-JANOSI, teacher and friend—T.B.

PHILIP H. ASHBY, teacher and friend —J.C.

ROBERT C. POLLOCK, mentor and guide —E.F.

NORVIN J. HEIN, initiator and guide —T.J.H.

MIRCEA ELIADE, mentor and exemplar —J.B.L.

JOHN J. McDERMOTT, brother and teacher —R.McD.

CONTENTS

A NOTE ON THE TEXT

All references to Sri Aurobindo's writings are to the Sri Aurobindo Birth Centenary Library (BCL, 30 volumes), Pondicherry: Sri Aurobindo Ashram, 1970–1973. Page references to the title work of each essay are in parentheses. References to volumes in the BCL other than the title works are listed in footnotes according to BCL volume and page.

Except for technical terms set off by parentheses, Sanskrit words have been printed without diacritical marks and accents, and have been romanized throughout.

Introduction

ALTHOUGH THE SIX ESSAYS in this volume are exclusively concerned with but one subject—Sri Aurobindo's written account of his intellectual and spiritual experience—they forcefully exhibit both the differences of perspective between authors and the extraordinary range of Sri Aurobindo's major works. These six works include *Savitri*, a 700-page epic poem; *The Foundations of India Culture*, a volume of essays on the aesthetic, spiritual, literary and sociopolitical aspects of Indian culture; *Essays on the Gita*, a detailed interpretation of the most significant text in the Indian spiritual tradition; *The Synthesis of Yoga*, an 800-page exposition of his integral yoga system; *The Human Cycle*, a philosophical and psychological study of human evolution; and *The Life Divine*, a 1,000-page systematic metaphysics of spiritual experience. The six essays on these six major works reveal the range, depth and contemporary significance of Sri Aurobindo's writings.

Savitri

> Nature shall live to manifest secret God,
> The Spirit shall take up the human play,
> This earthly life become the life divine. (29:710–711)

These lines, and countless other passages from *Savitri*, well serve as a keynote not only for *Savitri* and for John Collins' essay, but equally for the entire corpus of Sri Aurobindo's writings. *Savitri*, after all, poetically expresses the theme with which all of Sri Aurobindo's works are essentially concerned, namely, the spiritualization of earthly life. *Savitri* is the poetic expression, as *The Life Divine* is the philosophical expression, of this transformation. In both cases, the media—poetry and philosophy, respectively—are utilized and transcended in order to express the outer reaches of Sri Aurobindo's experience of the spiritualization process.

As *Savitri* marked both the beginning and the end of Sri Aurobin-

1

do's literary career, it could equally well serve as either introduction
or culmination of this volume; it has been placed first in the hope
that it will establish at the outset the scope and intensity of the
spiritual experience and vision which provides the context for Sri
Aurobindo's other writings. In varying ways, the other essays and the
books with which each is concerned, develop variations on John
Collins' summation of *Savitri:* "that the task of spiritual fulfillment
must be accomplished here on earth by a humanity open to the
Divine and prepared for the descent of the Divine into all aspects
of earthly life."

The Foundations of Indian Culture

While *Savitri* represents the spiritual transformation of earthly
life, *The Foundations of Indian Culture* emphasizes the role of the
spiritual in the case of India, principally with respect to Indian
aesthetic, literary and sociopolitical traditions. In Aurobindo's view,
India plays a particularly significant role in historical and spiritual
evolution because for centuries it has been a self-conscious manifestation of shakti, or the divine force in history. It is this emphasis on
the divine play in Indian cultural life, and the privileged place of
India in world culture, which leads Thomas Berry to characterize Sri
Aurobindo as a "spiritual romanticist"—spiritual in that his understanding of Indian culture is determined by his perception of
spiritual energy in the historical process, and romanticist in that his
study emphasizes the subjective or interior view of Indian and world
history. This view presupposes the individual and collective transformation prescribed in his yoga system.

Essays on the Gita

The middle two essays in this volume are concerned with Sri
Aurobindo's integral yoga system, including his own experience, his
theoretical and practical revisions of classical yoga traditions, and the
role of his yoga system in the larger task of spiritualizing earthly life.
Thomas J. Hopkins traces Sri Aurobindo's effort to show the complementarity of karma yoga (or the discipline of selfless action),

jnana yoga (or the discipline by which to realize that the self and the world are one with Purusha or the Supreme Self), and bhakti yoga (the discipline of devotion to the Divine Being). But the final goal for both the Gita and Sri Aurobindo is "a mutual effort by God and man: man moves along paths to God, and God reveals the secrets that guide him by revealing Himself to man as Avatar and Teacher." As *Savitri* and *The Life Divine* poetically and philosophically describe the play of the divine in the world, *Essays on Gita* concentrates on the role of the Avatar, or the divine personality in human form, and the means by which the whole of humanity can realize the Avatar's at-one-ness with the Supreme Being.

The Synthesis of Yoga

As J. Bruce Long explains in his essay on *The Synthesis of Yoga*, Sri Aurobindo's integral yoga system combines elements from Vedanta, Samkhya and Patanjali's raja yoga system, the threefold yoga of the Gita, a blending of Tantrism and an element of scientific realism from the West. Just as *Essays on the Gita* moves beyond the three yogas of the Gita in proposing a theory of divine-human reciprocity, *The Synthesis of Yoga* develops the yoga of self-perfection, according to which "an individual private discipline of body, mind, will and spirit, in due course, 'becomes a part of a collective yoga of the divine nature in the human race.'" Thus, Sri Aurobindo's 800-page systematic treatise on integral yoga concludes with a thesis which is supported by his *Essays on the Gita* and anticipates *Savitri* and *The Life Divine*, namely, "the supramental time vision" by which the integrally realized soul can hold in consciousness "the timeless Infinite" and "the Infinite deploying itself in time." Sri Aurobindo contends that by virtue of the special force and logic of the supermind, the polarity of infinite timelessness and temporality are "only coexistent and concurrent status and movement of the same truth of the Infinite" (852). The success of this reconciliation, however, is precisely what Professor Long questions in the conclusion of his essay. In addition to a detailed exposition of *The Synthesis of Yoga* and a set of insightful questions concerning the viability of Sri Aurobindo's system, Professor Long has also supplied an extremely useful topical index to *The Synthesis of Yoga*.

The Human Cycle

In his "pragmatic approach" to *The Human Cycle*, Eugene Fontinell offers a positive comparison between Sri Aurobindo's account of historical evolution and the pragmatists' emphasis on a processive and open universe. Originally entitled "The Psychology of Human Development," *The Human Cycle* developed in historical terms the central themes of Sri Aurobindo's other major works. As Eugene Fontinell explains: "The central and recurring theme of *The Human Cycle* is the processive divinization of the human race." This process of divinization consists in three overlapping cycles, each of which is detailed in *The Human Cycle* and summarized in this essay: Spirit; infrarational-rational-suprarational; and the five psychological stages.

After outlining these three complex cycles, Professor Fontinell develops a series of convergences between Sri Aurobindo and the position developed by the two most representative pragmatic philosophers, William James and John Dewey. Specifically, he compares Sri Aurobindo's and the pragmatist's positive attitudes on life and experience, their agreement on the necessary, if limited, function of institutions, and their agreement on the need to reconcile the conflicting claims of individuality and collectivity. These similarities are less complete concerning their respective theories of intuition, the Absolute and the future course of evolution—the principal difference in each case being Sri Aurobindo's contention that spiritual experience has disclosed levels of knowledge and reality above the normal, and that these supramental levels reveal a continuing process of spiritualization. Though they are less dramatic than one might have expected, the differences between these two philosophies of history are nonetheless as significant as are the similarities. But neither the similarities nor differences are so significant as the open-minded, open-ended dialogue between these and other major philosophical options. As Professor Fontinell wisely concludes, a dialogue between the pragmatic and Aurobindonian positions "may not only enrich the respective traditions but might make them more widely accessible, thereby enabling them to contribute more fully to the processive realization of the future of humanity."

The Life Divine

While *The Human Cycle* lends itself to comparisons with Western philosophers such as the pragmatists, who are concerned with the meaning and direction of human history, *The Life Divine* begins where *The Human Cycle*—and most Western philosophers—leave off. Although, as Professor Fontinell indicates, there are some convergences between Sri Aurobindo's spiritual vision of history and the pragmatists' concerns for the metaphysical foundation of the historical process, it is nevertheless the case that the differences between Sri Aurobindo and Western philosophers generally widens as the comparison becomes more metaphysical. In both *The Human Cycle* and *The Life Divine* it is metaphysical issues which most dramatically exhibit the impact of Sri Aurobindo's spiritual experience and vision. It should be noted, however, that although Sri Aurobindo develops a philosophical system which both issues from and seeks to advance spiritual experience, this spiritual basis and intent does not detract from the clarity and cogency of most elements in his philosophical system.

Although this essay acknowledges that *The Life Divine* can and will be read simply as a work of the philosophical intelligence, it is at pains to prepare the reader for other aspects of Sri Aurobindo's philosophical system—e.g., the overmind and the supermind, and the emergence of the gnostic being—which are ordinarily regarded as extraphilosophical speculation. These rather occult themes are included in this introductory essay, but the three topics with which this essay, and most of *The Life Divine*, are concerned are evolution, transformation and the delight of existence. Each interpreter must establish one's own criterion for philosophical admissibility, but it is worth noting at the outset that this essay, like *The Life Divine* itself, begins and ends by describing the capacity of the physical world to disclose spiritual and divine content. Sri Aurobindo obviously saw his entire system from blunt matter to the timeless infinite as a symphonic whole, and the need of interpreters to set artificial limits to such a system would seem to speak volumes about the failure of philosophical vision in our time.

—*Robert A. McDermott*

ONE

SAVITRI

Poetic Expression of Spiritual Experience

by John Collins

Thus shall the earth open to divinity
And common natures feel the wide uplift,
Illumine common acts with the Spirit's ray
And meet the deity in common things.
Nature shall live to manifest secret God,
The Spirit shall take up the human play,
This earthly life become the life divine.

—Savitri

SRI AUROBINDO'S LITERARY ACTIVITY begins and ends with poetry. As a student at Cambridge he wrote lyric poems on a variety of subjects.[1] When he returned to India to become first a teacher, then a politician, and finally a yogin, he continued in each situation to use poetry as an effective means of expression. He wrote poetry which attempted to teach the ancient wisdom of India in a contemporary way,[2] he used poetry extensively as a political weapon as he attempted to raise the nationalistic consciousness of the Indian people,[3] and from the time of his first experience of a spiritual nature until the end of his life he regarded poetry as the more appropriate and effective means of expressing his spiritual experiences.[4] *Savitri: A Legend and a Symbol,* upon which Sri Aurobindo labored for many decades and upon which he worked most intensively during his last years, is both the culmination of his poetic creativity and the most extensive and profound of his attempts to express his spiritual experiences and realizations. Well over three-fourths of this poem, perhaps the longest in the English language, is devoted to the detailed description of the spiritual practices and experiences of the two principal characters—Book I, Cantos 3–5, and Books II and III for Aswapathy, and Books VII, IX through XI for Savitri. The rest, though still containing extensive use of spiritual symbols, narrates a story of life's struggle with death which generally follows the Savitri legend of the Mahabharata.

The purposes of this essay are: (1) To discuss Sri Aurobindo's understanding of the special nature of *Savitri* and to clarify his intention in writing it. This is done in the first section, which deals with the problems of describing spiritual experiences, and in the second section, which introduces the reader to what Aurobindo maintains to be a revolutionary vehicle of literary expression, viz., overmental poetry. (2) To enable the reader who is not already acquainted with the Savitri legend to follow more easily the development of the narrative. Thus the third section is a summary of the original story. (3) To introduce the reader to some of the more

1. A. B. Purani, *The Life of Sri Aurobindo* (1964), p. 24. Purani claims that writing poetry and participating in a nationalistic Indian cultural group were the only activities that really interested Aurobindo during this period. These first poems were published originally in *Songs of Myrtilla* (Baroda, 1895) and later, with many others, in Sri Aurobindo, *Collected Poems and Plays* (1942).
2. Prema Nandakumar, *A Study of Savitri* (1962), pp. 53–55.
3. *Ibid.* pp. 55 f.
4. Purani, *op. cit.,* pp. 62–63, 98–99, 114–115.

important aspects of Aurobindo's spiritual experience and realization. This is done in the last three sections, which discuss the setting
of the spiritual life, the characteristics of the ideal yogin, and the
ultimate goal of spiritual discipline as understood by Sri Aurobindo.

The Expression of Spiritual Experience

In speaking with the author of one of his biographies, Aurobindo
expressed skepticism regarding the possibility of giving a significant
account of his life in the usual biographical manner.[5] Biographies
usually deal with external events. They describe the political, literary, military and other discernible activities of the subject. They may
also attempt some evaluation of the significance of these activities
with regard to their effect on the development of human history and
culture. But Aurobindo did not consider the external activities of his
life to be of primary importance. He insisted that the meaning of
his life was to be found in the internal experiences and realizations
which could not be explored by a biographer. Moreover, he pointed
out that any valid attempt to evaluate the contributions of his life
to society could be made only many years in the future. The truths
which he was realizing in his inner experiences were not fully manifested in the present, and their total impact could not now be seen.
For these reasons any biography would necessarily be only partial
and misleading.

However, it is fortunate for those who wish to explore the spiritual
dimension of Aurobindo's experience that he has attempted in *Savitri* what would be impossible for anyone else, viz., a poetic record
of his inner life. In order to demonstrate just how closely *Savitri* is
related to the inner spiritual life of its author, three important factors
will be considered.

1. THE UNUSUAL ATTENTION GIVEN
TO THE WRITING OF SAVITRI

As one might expect, Sri Aurobindo devoted far more time and
effort to the writing and revising of *Savitri* than he did to any of his

5. Sri Aurobindo, *Sri Aurobindo on Himself and on the Mother* (1953), pp. 351–
352, and Purani, *op. cit.*, p. 209.

other works. The main reason for this is that his spiritual experiences changed, and so he had to alter *Savitri* in order to take these changes into account. In many respects the evolution of the poem parallels the evolution of his spiritual life. Just as his spiritual development may be divided into three distinct stages, so the major revisions of the poem fall into three stages. The poem was first written around the beginning of this century.[6] At that time it represented an attempt to treat a popular Indian story in a modern way and in this respect was not significantly different from a number of other poems which Aurobindo wrote during this period before he began the practice of yoga.[7] What is important is the fact that he decided to revise *Savitri* and none of the other poems after his initial experiences as a yogi (728).[8] This second stage of *Savitri*'s development reflects his spiritual progress from 1904, when he began the practice of yoga, until his experience in 1926, when as a result of "the descent of the overmind" his inner life assumed a distinctively different character.[9] After this radically different experience, *Savitri* was completely revised again. Efforts toward this revision continued, sometimes with sustained intensity and sometimes sporadically, until his death in 1950. Although the entire poem was not to be revised under this new inspiration, most of it was completely changed; and many sections, especially those which are important to this introduction, were extended significantly.

2. THE SPECIAL WAY IN WHICH SRI AURO-BINDO USES THE LEGEND

The ways in which Aurobindo altered the original story will be discussed in some detail below, but at this point some of these alterations will be mentioned in order to support the proposition that he intended *Savitri* to be primarily a description of his spiritual

6. Nandakumar, *op. cit.*, p. 65. The exact date of this first draft is not given. The poem was not published until 1946 in its final, though still incomplete, form.
7. *Ibid.*, pp. 46–65.
8. Numbers in parenthesis refer to *Savitri* (BCL, 28, 29). In this edition the poetry ends on page 724. Pages 727–816 contain comments which Sri Aurobindo made on *Savitri* from time to time. These comments attempt to clarify the meaning and intention of the poem in general and of certain key passages which were misunderstood by Aurobindo's readers.
9. Purani, *op. cit.*, pp. 214–220.

experiences and realizations. At certain critical points he greatly expands the story. For example, Aswapathy's eighteen years of austerities, which are covered in ten lines in the Mahabharata, are expanded to over ten thousand lines. This description of Aswapathy's experiences in the inner worlds makes up half of the entire poem and was revised completely by Sri Aurobindo after his overmental experience in 1926. Similarly, the story's brief description of Savitri's three-night fast became in the poem a "Book of Yoga," which runs to over three thousand lines and which focuses on the spiritual experiences of the heroine as she is prepared for the encounter with Death.

3. SRI AUROBINDO'S COMMENTS ABOUT HIS INTENTION

That there is a conscious intentional relationship involved between the events described in *Savitri* and the spiritual experiences of the author is further supported by Sri Aurobindo's own statements about this matter. When the first section of *Savitri* was published in 1946, it received some criticism from those on the one hand who judged it to be inferior poetry and from those on the other hand who felt that it was inferior philosophy (733–816). In responding to these criticisms, Aurobindo did not choose to defend his work on either philosophical or literary grounds. Rather, he answered almost every objection by saying in one way or another that the critics had missed entirely the purpose of his work by looking at it as ordinary poetry or philosophy. He makes it clear in each case that *Savitri* was not intended to be an ordinary epic poem or a philosophical treatise but was written as a response to the experiences of the spiritual life. In a typical response he says:

> I have not anywhere in *Savitri* written anything for the sake of mere picturesqueness or merely to produce a rhetorical effect; what I am trying to do everywhere in the poem is to express exactly something seen, something felt or experienced; . . . *Savitri* is the record of a seeing, of an experience which is not of a common kind and is often far from what the general human mind sees and experiences. (794)

And when one of his critics accused him of misusing philosophical abstractions which have no real meaning in the poem, he replied with the following:

> The Inconscient and the Ignorance may be mere empty abstractions and can be dismissed as irrelevant jargon if one has not come into collision with them or plunged into their dark and bottomless reality. But to me they are realities, concrete powers whose resistance is present everywhere and at all times in its tremendous and boundless mass. In fact, in writing this line[10] I had no intention of teaching philosophy or forcing in an irrelevant metaphysical idea, although the idea may be there in implication. I was presenting a happening that was to me something sensible and, as one might say, psychologically and spiritually concrete. . . . The mystic feels real and present, even ever present to his experience, intimate to his being, truths which to the ordinary reader are intellectual abstractions or metaphysical speculations. . . . To the mystic there is no such thing as an abstraction. Everything which to the intellectual mind is abstract has a concreteness, substantiality which is more real than the sensible form of an object of a physical event. . . . The mystical poet can only describe what he has felt, seen in himself or others or in the world just as he has felt or seen it or experienced through exact vision, close contact or identity and leave it to the general reader to understand or not understand or misunderstand according to his capacity. A new kind of poetry demands a new mentality in the recipient as well as in the writer. (735–736).

This point has been dwelt on at considerable length because it is very important that the reader of *Savitri* be very clear about Sri Aurobindo's purpose in this work. According to his understanding, there is no speculation here; neither is there any attempt at pure aesthetics. In this poem Aurobindo is describing what he understands to be his experience. To him the events are actual, the images are realities. Of course, all of this is experienced in the inner spiritual self, but to Aurobindo this makes it even more real and more true than those things which are experienced by the physical and mental self only. Whether or not one agrees with Aurobindo on this point,

10. He is referring to the following lines:
"A nameless movement, an unthought Idea
Insistent, dissatisfied, without an aim,
Something that wished but knew not how to be,
Teased the Inconscient to wake Ignorance." (1–2)
("Inconscient" is a term which Aurobindo coined to refer to that state of existence in which no form of consciousness appears to be manifest.)

the reading of *Savitri* will be much more valuable to one who always keeps in mind the author's intention.

The Medium: Overmental Poetry

In order better to understand the process by which Sri Aurobindo has transformed the ancient story into an intricate complex of symbols, it will be useful to consider briefly some of the characteristics of overmental poetry. It is neither possible nor appropriate to attempt here an exhaustive description or an extensive criticism of this "new medium of communication," but it is hoped that the following comments will help the reader to appreciate more fully Aurobindo's attitude and poetic technique.[11]

Sri Aurobindo suggests that men can be most appropriately divided according to the types of consciousness by which they are dominated. He suggests that there are four basic types of consciousness: material, vital, mental, and spiritual; and that every man expresses a mixture of these but is usually dominated by one of the four in a given situation. According to his analysis, all previous poetry has been written from the perspective of mental and vital consciousness. He does concede that all really good poetry has in it some inspiration from the higher spiritual consciousness but points out that this level of inspiration is never sustained throughout a work and is never the conscious intent of the author. This is, however, not the case with *Savitri*. The spiritual man, the yogin, has continual access to the highest realms of consciousness, which are only occasionally touched by ordinary men. According to Aurobindo, only a yogin, only one who has opened himself to the inner spiritual realities and has lived for some time in the presence of these realities, can be the vehicle for overmental writing. Whereas the spiritual consciousness is reflected sometimes here and there in the great literature of the world, *Savitri* is permeated by the creations of this higher type of consciousness. Aurobindo admits that not every line is overmental—indeed neither the "Book of Death" (561–565) nor the "Epilogue" (715–724) was revised under the overmental inspiration—but he also insists that throughout the work the presence of the spiritual realm can be felt by one who is open to it (743 ff.).

---

11. For further discussion see Sri Aurobindo, *The Future Poetry* (1953); Nandakumar, *op. cit.*, pp. 336 ff.; and Sri Aurobindo, *Savitri*, pp. 733–742.

The overmental poet does not work; he "waits and listens." He cannot go up to the higher realms in order to seize the inspiration and bring it down into the normal consciousness; he must be still and await the coming of the inspiration. When it comes he receives it and records it. Sometimes the spirit will come as a flood of revelation; often Aurobindo dictated hundreds of lines without interruption. But just as often the inspiration will come very slowly or not at all for several hours or days. This is why the overmental revision of *Savitri* took so long (1926–1950). Aurobindo says that he could not determine when it would be written, he could only open himself to the spiritual levels of consciousness and wait for whatever would come (730–731).

At this point the relationship between the lines of poetry given in this way and the spiritual experiences of the author should be more closely examined. The lines given by overmental inspiration had meaning to Aurobindo only because his previous mystical experiences had given him the insights by which these lines could be understood and interpreted. If the lines were not consistent with the revelations given in these experiences, they were rejected, and he had to wait for a further inspiration. Sometimes this came quickly, and sometimes it did not; but he was not satisfied until the proper lines—that is, those which adequately expressed the truths which he had realized earlier—had been given.

Since the lines of *Savitri* were received differently from other poetry, one should approach the reading of this poem with different expectations than for other poetry. For example, the reader should not expect any kind of logical order or structure. The lines have not been written with the thought of fitting into any type of normal poetic structure. Often there will be rapid transition from one idea or theme to another where there is no apparent connection between the two. Then there are other places where the same idea seems to be repeated over again and again (740, 745). Aurobindo recognizes that this might be confusing and even disturbing to the normal reader who has come to expect a certain logical flow of ideas or connections between ideas, but he insists that the reader must break this pattern of expectation if he wishes to appreciate *Savitri* fully. That which is given in *Savitri* is necessary to the adequate expression of the experiences and realizations which he has received, and it is this factor which determines the structure of the poetry. What may appear to the mind to be disorderly and confused is easily understood by the overmental consciousness because of the spiritual interrelatedness of things which it is able to see. Aurobindo insists that *Savitri*

is a continuous flow of overmental inspiration and suggests that if
the reader wishes to understand fully its meaning and significance,
he must approach the poem with this in mind.

This might appear to present insurmountable difficulties to the
normal reader. Does this imply that one who does not have particularly keen powers of spiritual intuition or who has not had the
experience of the yogi should not attempt to read this highly esoteric
poem? Indeed in many of his comments to his critics, Aurobindo has
pointed out that *Savitri* was not written for anyone but himself. He
tells us that he wrote it out of spiritual experiences (734–735).
However, rather than being discouraged by Aurobindo's insistence on
the unique nature of Savitri, one should see that it is this very
uniqueness which most highly recommends *Savitri* to the reader. Of
course, the reader must keep in mind the fact that there will always be
some barriers which will prevent complete understanding of all the
experiences. Nevertheless, what he learns and feels for himself as a
result of reading *Savitri* may be of great value. To the student of
religion *Savitri* offers a rare opportunity to explore the mind of a
mystic; to the student of literature *Savitri* is aesthetically and intellectually stimulating; to the skeptic *Savitri* presents a challenging statement of spiritual philosophy by a highly articulate contemporary; to
the believer *Savitri* is a strong affirmation of religious faith in which to
participate and for which to rejoice.

The Mahabharata Story

In the Mahabharata the story of Savitri is told by Markandeya to
Yudhishthira in order to show the deposed king that others have
suffered as much as he and his family without the loss of virtue.[12]
The principal characters of the story are Savitri, her father Aswapathy, and her husband Satyavan. Aswapathy was a king of exceptional
virtue and exceeding generosity, but as he grew old he became more
and more despondent because he had not been blessed with children. Hoping to remedy this, he undertook, for a period of eighteen

---

12. This story is called "Pativrata-Mahatmya," or "The Tale of the Exaltedness of
One Who Is Devoted to Her Husband." It is found in the Vana Parva of the
Mahabharata, sections CCLXLII CCLXLVIII. For an English translation, Pratap
Chandra Ray, trans., *The Mahabharata* (Calcutta: Bharata Press, 1889), II: 865–
888.

years, a series of very strict religious practices. He subjected himself to various austerities, recited over again and again prescribed mantras, and offered tens of thousands of sacrifices. Finally, at the end of this period, he was rewarded by the goddess Savitri with the birth of a daughter. When the child reached the proper age, he sent her out to look for a husband. She returned after some time to announce that she had met and chosen Satyavan, the noble son of a famous exiled king. Aswapathy was well pleased with his daughter's choice until he learned from the seer Narad that fate had decreed that Satyavan would live for only a year. Upon hearing this tragic news, the king tried to persuade his daughter to change her mind and seek another husband; but she insisted that she must marry the doomed man. She maintained that, once her decision had been made, it could not be changed, and once her pledge of love and devotion had been given to one man, it could not be transferred to another. So the marriage took place and was followed by a year of happiness, which was marked by the flawless virtue and extreme self-sacrificing attitude of Savitri. As the end of the year drew near, Savitri undertook three nights of fasting as a means of preparing herself for the fatal day. When Yama, the god of death, finally came to call Satyavan to his fate, Savitri met him, refused to let her husband go alone and declared that she would accompany him no matter where Yama might lead. At this point the story becomes a dialogue between Yama and Savitri. In this dialogue the god did all he could to convince Savitri that what she was attempting was both futile and dangerous. He pointed out that as a mortal she had no power over fate and should not tempt the anger of the gods by interfering with their decrees. Savitri readily admitted that her mortality rendered her powerless before the gods and the law of fate. But, at the same time, she maintained that the vow of devotion which she had made to her husband would not allow her to abandon him at this critical time, no matter what the results might be. Yama was so moved by Savitri's virtue and devotion and the simple wisdom which grew out of her deep, unyielding love that he finally allowed Satyavan to return to earth with Savitri to live a long and fruitful life. The point of the story, then, is to show how human virtue, in this case the virtue of wifely devotion, is potentially powerful enough to change even the decrees of fate. We will see now how Sri Aurobindo has used this story.

The Spiritual Setting: The Symbol Dawn

Sri Aurobindo's poem generally follows the chronology of the ancient story.[13] But there is one significant exception to this—his beginning is radically different. He opens his poem not with a description of Aswapathy's difficulties but with a section entitled "The Symbol Dawn." This section describes the dawn of the day on which Satyavan is appointed to die—an event which comes much later in the story. This change is at first very puzzling, especially since it is virtually impossible for the reader to understand what is happening in this section without some previous acquaintance with the story. But as in all other cases it can be assumed that this alteration was made out of some inner necessity. One can assume that beginning in this way was necessary for the adequate expression of spiritual experience. This introduces the tone of the entire poem; it sets the stage on which the action will take place. Hence, in order best to understand Aurobindo's meaning here, one should look for spiritual rather than logical or aesthetic factors. Specifically, one should consider the various dimensions of meaning which are suggested by the symbol dawn, because this is the best way to get at Aurobindo's primary intention.

1. DAWN: THE BEGINNING TIME

The most obvious meaning which can be attached to the dawn stems from its position at the beginning of the day. Since light is preferred to darkness, the beginning which dawn announces is not neutral. With dawn there is renewal or re-creation; dawn is the stimulator of hopeful anticipation. It is appropriate for Sri Aurobindo to begin with dawn, for to him it represents more than the beginning of the day in which the action of the story is to take place.[14] For him the beginning of *Savitri* is the beginning of a new

13. For a comparison of the chronology of the two stories see Nandakumar, *op. cit.*, pp. 296–298.
14. Nandakumar, *ibid.*, p. 69. maintains that Aurobindo is merely following the pattern of the classical Greek epic by beginning his poem with the dawn of the day on which the action of the story is to take place. There is no reason to disagree with this suggestion as long as one does not take this to be Aurobindo's only consideration in beginning this way.

kind of poetry. Both the poem itself and the medium by which it is presented and the inspiration which has created it are new. For the first time a vehicle is given which will allow communication between the levels of higher and lower consciousness. This is the beginning of a new revelation, an outpouring of spiritual truth, a more complete vision of the world than has ever before been possible. Finally, this dawn announces the beginning of a new stage in the evolution of man and the world. On this day Savitri, the Divine descended to earth, will defeat the enemy of progress and begin the spiritual transformation of all earthly existence.[15] It is clear that all of these together—the opening of the day in which the action will take place, the first creations of a new kind of overmental poetry, the proclamation of a new revelation of truth and vision of reality, and the first phase of a new stage of evolution—are to be taken as the meaning which Aurobindo intends in the symbol dawn. Throughout the poem the symbols used are multidimensional, and all the various nuances of meaning must be taken into account if one wishes to get the full impact of the dramatic power of this poem.

2. DAWN: THE MIDDLE TIME

Another characteristic of dawn, which is perhaps more important to Sri Aurobindo, is its situation as a time in the middle between contraries. In the immediacy of the dawn time the announcement of a new day is not yet a certain dogma; it is still only a vision and a hope which is shrouded in mystery of lingering night. In the dawn time the proclamation of a brighter future is not yet confirmed by experience; it is still the confession of faith expressing its highest aspiration in spite of the surrounding, uncertain shadows. In itself, then, the dawn time is a "shadow time," a "time between," a "middle instant," which has an existence of its own, but which is dependent upon both of its extremities. During the dawn time there

15. Dawn as a symbol of the beginning is used extensively in Book XI (671–712). In his discussion of Usha, the Vedic goddess of dawn, Aurobindo refers primarily to this meaning. See Sri Aurobindo, *The Secret of the Veda* (BCL, 10), pp. 118–125 and A.B. Purani, *Sri Aurobindo's Vedic Glossary* (1962), pp. 28–29. Dawn as the symbol of a new beginning is also found extensively in the works of Aurobindo which deal with contemporary Indian culture; see especially *The Renaissance in India*, in *The Foundations of Indian Culture* (BCL, 14). Sisirkumar Mitra in *Resurgent India* (New York: Allied Publishers, 1963) applies this symbol to Aurobindo's life.

is neither complete darkness nor complete light. Or to put it another way, darkness and light are so mixed that neither dominates the scene. Dawn is equally the father of the day and the child of the night. It is neither light nor darkness but the "middle sister" between the two.[16]

It is this characteristic of the dawn as the "between time," as it is described in the first section of *Savitri*, which indicates to the reader Aurobindo's understanding of the nature of the situation in and out of which spiritual experiences arise. This first section begins with a time of total darkness when "a fathomless zero occupied the world" and ends with a time of light when "the common light of earthly day" appears (1, 6). Between these two comes the timid and tenuous half-light-in-shadow of the dawn. The dawn as it is described here is more than a short qualityless interval between day and night; it has a force, a power, a reality of its own. Consider the following description of night's yielding to the dawn:

> Then something in the inscrutable darkness stirred;
> A nameless movement, an unthought Idea
> Insistent, dissatisfied, without an aim,
> Something that wished but knew not how to be,
> Teased the Inconscient to wake Ignorance,
> A throe that came and left a quivering trace,
> Gave room for an old tired want unfilled,
> At peace in its subconscient moonless cave
> To raise its head and look for absent light,
> Straining closed eyes of vanished memory
> Like one who searches for a bygone self
> And only meets the corpse of his desire. (1–2)

Thus, dawn comes with a sense of hope combined with despair. It feels the light but cannot liberate itself from darkness. Dawn is a time of looking backward as well as forward. It is a time of neither a beginning nor an ending, but of a motionless middle ground which

16. In his studies of Vedic literature, A.B. Keith found that dawn is often regarded as the sister of both day and night. Moreover, he found that dawn is not always the ally of light and the enemy of darkness; sometimes it is represented as the adversary of light which delays as long as possible the coming of day. Sir Arthur Berriedale Keith, *The Religion and Philosophy of the Veda and Upanishads*, Harvard Oriental Series, Vol. XXXI (Cambridge: Harvard University Press, 1925), p. 120. Another discussion of dawn's dual role is found in Ananda K. Coomaraswamy, *The Darker Side of Dawn*, Smithsonian Miscellaneous Collections, Vol. XLIV (Baltimore: The Lord Baltimore Press, 1935), pp. 1–18.

endures for a while and feels itself pulled in both directions but does not know which way to turn.

3. DAWN: THE SPIRITUAL SYMBOL

Dawn as the symbol of the "between time" represents to Sri Aurobindo the time in which man's spiritual experiences are born and develop. From this point of view, the entire section of "The Symbol Dawn" refers symbolically to the nature of human existence which makes the spiritual life a possibility and a reality. This reference to human existence is felt more strongly when he changes from the use of the third person to the use of the first. In one particularly revealing passage he says, while still speaking of the dawn time:

> Air was a vibrant link between earth and heaven;
> The wide-winged hymn of a great priestly wind
> Arose and failed upon the altar hills;
> The high boughs prayed in a revealing sky.
> Here where our half-lit ignorance skirts the gulfs
> On the dumb bosom of the ambiguous earth,
> Here where one knows not even the step in front
> And Truth has her throne on the shadowy back of doubt,
> On this anguished and precarious field of toil
> Outspread beneath some large indifferent gaze,
> Impartial witness to our joy and bale,
> Our prostrate soil bore the awakening ray. (4–5)

This dawn time, this time of "half-lit ignorance" and shadowy truth, this time when motion stirs in the eternal stillness, when life turns upward, and when consciousness breaks into the domain of the unconsciousness, is a time of spiritual birth. It is a time when the inner self is moved to activity and the inner light begins to break through the covering ignorance. It is a time when man's faith in life and his aspiration toward fulfillment in the day stand opposed to his sense of finitude and despair born of his affinity with the night. Here in this dawn time the extremities of human existence are dramatically revealed. Life, knowledge, success, etc., are in apparent contradictory opposition to death, ignorance, failure, etc; and man stands in the middle. The dawn time, then, is the time of being fully human, the time of facing human existence as it really is, and thus a time of spiritual vision, aspiration and experience.

Normally man cannot endure for very long the tension and uncertainty of the dawn time. He looks forward to the full light of day and feels comfortable and secure only after the ambiguous shadows of the dawn have been fully illuminated by the rays of the risen sun. For those of ordinary dreams and aspirations this critical time between contraries passes after an inspiring but frustrating instant, and there is rejoicing that dawn has yielded to the promised day (5–6).

But the expulsion of dawn by the light of day, which for ordinary man is an occasion for celebration, is for the spiritual man an occasion for lamentation. For with the passing of dawn there passes the time in which spiritual experience is a possibility. Spiritual man does not rejoice in the full light of day nor does he return to the despair of night. He must remain in the dawn time. Savitri, the representative of spiritual man, does not share the joy which others experience with the opening of dawn into day. The dawn time has become for her the occasion for a vision of higher joys than the temporal pleasures of life; she has heard a call and has begun a spiritual pilgrimage from which she cannot retreat; she knows that she must affirm the reality of both the darkness and the light, of both death and life, of both the unyielding law of fate and constant passion of her love. She must not leave this time of tension, for it is here that the struggle she faces must take place. While those around her begin their daily tasks with renewed vigor and promise, she withdraws into her inner self.

> No part she took in this small happiness;
> A mighty stranger in the human field,
> The embodied Guest within made no response.
> The call that wakes the leap of human mind,
> Its chequered eager motion of pursuit,
> Its fluttering-hued illusion of desire,
> Visited her heart like a sweet alien note.
> Time's message of brief light was not for her. (6)

Because the dawn time is so ambiguous and dependent it might appear to be a rather unstable platform for the launching of a spiritual pilgrimage. But in this case its weakness becomes its strength. It is important to note that Sri Aurobindo calls dawn, not the day, the "omniscient Goddess." Usually the light is associated with seeing and knowledge and the darkness with blindness and ignorance; but Aurobindo points out to the reader that dawn sees and understands more than light. It is only from the perspective of being in the middle between contraries that all realities can be observed and understood. Light sees only light; darkness is immersed in itself; but dawn sees both at the same time. It is because of this that the dawn time is the only appropriate place for the yogin. As we shall see in more detail later, the yogin must experience all realities and be taught their separate truths. But he must also integrate all these realities and their partial truths into a harmonious union. This can be done only from his position of being in the middle.

Before leaving this discussion of the dawn, it is worth noting that, according to Aurobindo, one of the most adequate ways of viewing all reality is to see it as a dawn time. He insists that all realities are to be affirmed—spirit and matter, life and death, good and evil, the absolute and the changing, Nirguna Brahman and Saguna Brahman —both sides of all apparent contraries are real. He suggests in *The Life Divine* that the cardinal error of most previous philosophy has been to affirm some aspect of reality while denying its apparent opposite.[17] But each must be affirmed for its own particular truth because the world is an integral harmony of all.

The Archetypal Yogin: Aswapathy

In the Mahabharata legend Aswapathy's role is necessary but rather minor in terms of the central drama of the story. He is described as a leader of men who has persisted in justice and righteousness throughout his life, who is deeply honored by his subjects and respected by the wise men of his time, who has accomplished many good deeds of personal and social significance, and who, having arrived at old age, becomes acutely aware of the implications of dying without leaving an offspring. Although he has been successful as judged by all the norms of his society, he realizes that his life's work will become empty at his death since he has no posterity to whom he can entrust its continuance. He feels that, unless he has a son to succeed him, all his righteousness will die with him. So as a good man he sets his case before the gods, undertakes the appropriate austerities and performs the accepted rituals. He is faithful to his spiritual discipline as he has throughout his life been faithful to the

17. Sri Aurobindo, *The Life Divine* (BCL, 18, 19), pp. 1–24; see below, ch. VI.

rigorous demands of righteousness, with the expectation that his faithfulness will require some response from the gods. The issue here is one of the most persistent in all religious literature; that is, the question raised by a good man when it appears that his righteousness will come to naught. If the fruits of one's righteousness do not somehow extend beyond the finite life of the individual, then right- eousness is empty in the face of death. In this case the position that the righteous man will always be vindicated is supported by the eventual response of the goddess Savitri,[18] who is so moved by Aswapathy's sincerity and persistence that she promises to send him a daughter who will fulfill his desire to see righteousness continue.

In Sri Aurobindo's poem Aswapathy is still the good man who seeks perpetuation of righteousness; but he is also the "world's desire," the individual desire for progeny. Thus the continuation of the righteous life is transformed into the desire of the cosmos to realize some culmination to all its labor. Aurobindo's Aswapathy is not just a good man whose life is an example of rigorous persistence in righteousness; he represents the persistence of cosmic process. For Aurobindo the issue here is the ultimate purpose and goal of all cosmic movement of which human righteousness is a small but significant part. He claims that all the activities of the world— physical, vital, mental and spiritual—are directed ultimately toward the evolution of the world through various stages. In the past, these activities have resulted in the evolution of life out of matter, and mind out of matter and life. Mind, as presently embodied in man, is the highest product of all previous evolution. Throughout eon after eon the cosmos has labored in strict faithfulness to its task to come finally to this pinnacle, but even after all this there is the awareness that the ultimate meaning of the process has not been discovered. The purpose of the world's work is still hidden. Accord- ing to Aurobindo, the present state of the cosmos is like that of an old man who has lived a life of faithfulness to the good but who

18. The reader of the Mahabharata would not confuse Savitri, the goddess who answers Aswapathy's prayer, with Savitri the daughter, who is, out of gratitude, named after the goddess. However, in Sri Aurobindo's poem the two are the same; the woman is the goddess descended to earth. Savitri's origin as a mythological figure is not clear; but it is suggested that it may have been derived from the personification of the gayatri mantra—verses addressed to the sun god Savitri, which has been given a very special place in Indian religious tradition. At any rate, Savitri appears as divine daughter and wife in many stories in the Mahabharata. See Monier Monier-Williams, *A Sanskrit-English Dictionary* (Oxford: The Clarendon Press, 1960), p. 1211.

comes to his own death without a sense of fulfillment, without an understanding of the purpose of his life, but with a sense that much more must be done, and with no clear perception of what the next step must be. He claims that evolution is now at a crisis point. The means by which previous progress has been made will no longer be useful; further development can take place only after there is a radical transformation of the present state. The desire of the world, which has always been within cosmic motion urging and guiding all that has been done, now reaches out for something beyond itself, as an old man reaches out for the promises of progeny. Sri Aurobindo claims that his spiritual experiences and realizations have shown him that this present cosmic desire will be fulfilled, not by the slow process of evolution, but by the descent of the divine spirit into this material realm. Subsequent progress will depend on the response of the spirit to the world's present need. Therefore, whereas Aswapathy of the legend asks for a favor for himself, Aswapathy of the poem asks for a favor for the entire cosmos. He insists that the spirit must descend to earth in order that there might be a final culmination to the life of the cosmos which cannot be accomplished in any other way. The world now awaits this descent as Aswapathy waited for the birth of Savitri. This descent, and the resulting transformation of matter, life and mind, is, according to Aurobindo, inevitable.

The drama of Aswapathy's experience in the poem corresponds to the various dimensions of the meanings of Aswapathy as an archetypal yogin. Aswapathy, who represents Aurobindo, also represents spiritual man, man as yogin. He has been faithful to his spiritual task and now awaits the further action of the Divine to vindicate his righteousness. Finally, he is the cosmos which has followed its own prescribed path to union, i.e., its own yoga, and now awaits the final culmination of its work in the descent of the spirit to earth.

The specific characteristics of the yogin and the experiences and realizations which are received through the practice of yoga as understood by Sri Aurobindo are given most clearly in Book I, cantos 3–5, Books II and III, which describe the development of Aswapathy's spiritual life, and in Book VII, cantos 2–7, which describe the yoga of Savitri. The fact that these together make up well over half the entire poem indicates the importance which Aurobindo gave to the description of the yogin and his experiences, especially when it is pointed out that these 413 pages, which contain over 13,000 lines, have been expanded from less than twenty lines in the Mahabharata story. It will not be possible here to discuss all the characteristics of the yogin, nor all the experiences of the spiritual life as they are described by Aurobindo.[19] But the following themes are particularly important: (1) the surrender to the inner call, (2) the odyssey through the kingdoms of inner reality, (3) the realization of integral truth and harmony, and (4) the vision of transformation.

1. THE SURRENDER TO THE INNER CALL

According to Aurobindo, every person—indeed, as has been suggested by speaking of evolution as the "yoga" of the cosmos, one should add all existence—is a potential yogin. There is within each man the call of the Divine, which continuously urges him toward higher realization and fulfillment. The intensity of this call and receptivity of the moving is more pronounced in some than in others; but among those who want to follow the call some are able to surrender completely, while most are able to make only a partial or temporary surrender. Sri Aurobindo insists that a total surrender is necessary for success in the spiritual life. Very soon after he first undertook the practice of yoga he said of his own surrender:

> The only thing that can be stated for the moment [i.e., at the very beginning of his practice] is that henceforward I am no longer my own master; I will have to go like a puppet, wherever the Divine takes me; I shall have to carry out like a puppet whatever he makes me do. . . . but I am no more free, [sic.]from now onwards, you will have to understand that all that I do does not depend on my own will, but is done according to the command of the Divine.[20]

To submit to the divine call and follow the divine will means to renounce all preconceptions of the spiritual life and all expectations regarding the fruits of one's surrender. Sri Aurobindo understood his submission to the Divine to be of this nature and says that it became for him:

> a seed force, to which I kept unswervingly and increasingly till it led me through all the mazes of an incalculable yogic development bound

19. For a fuller account of Sri Aurobindo's yoga, see the introductions to *Essays on the Gita* and *The Synthesis of Yoga* in this volume.
20. Purani, *Life*, p. 92.

by no single rule or style or dogma or shastra to where and what I am now [this is in 1932 after many years of yoga and after his most significant spiritual experiences] and towards what shall be hereafter[21]

In one sense the surrender, though motivated by the inner call of the Divine, is the responsibility of the individual yogin. If one can make the initial response by giving oneself entirely to the inner call and by expressing this surrender through the consistent and sincere practice of spiritual discipline, then the inner worlds, the realms of spiritual reality, will be opened to him. Those who are not surrendered to the voice of the Divine within them experience only the external reality of things which is accessible through the five empirical senses. But to one who has submitted himself, the other side of reality, the inner worlds of spiritual and subtle forces and powers, is revealed. The surrendered man is allowed to experience both the inner and the outer character of things and is also shown how the inner and outer worlds are connected and related to one another by a universal scheme of cause and effect. Sri Aurobindo insists that there can be no spiritual progress for the individual until his consciousness is opened to the experience of these inner realms. As long as one's conception of reality is limited to the external alone, i.e., to what is usually referred to as the "natural" world, there can be no true spiritual awakening. In the first stage of spiritual development one becomes aware of these inner worlds; and, if one wishes to progress in the spiritual life, one must accept the reality of the existence and power of these worlds and must continue to seek further knowledge of their meaning and value through increasingly more intimate contact with them.

2. THE ODYSSEY THROUGH THE KINGDOMS

In Book II, "The Book of the Traveller of the Worlds," Sri Aurobindo gives one of the most systematic and detailed descriptions in all mystic literature of the experiences of the yogin to whom the inner realms have been opened.[22] Aswapathy journeys through

21. *Ibid.*, p. 111. For similar passages on the need for complete surrender see pp. 357–358 and 540.
22. See a similar description of Savitri's experience p. 474ff.

the kingdoms of matter, life and mind, and into the kingdom of the spirit. Just as the cosmos has progressed through these stages, so the consciousness of the yogin must experience these separate but inter-related realities each in its proper turn. In this way his odyessey recapitulates all previous cosmic evolution and previews what is yet to come. His experiences are an assimilation of all experiences, at least of the inner spiritual meaning of those experiences, which have preceded him. His vision is a picture of the future experience of the world. This recapitulation and assimilation is a necessary part of the yogin's development because each reality must become "his" reality in the sense that he has come to realize the truth and power of their separate natures.

In the kingdom of matter the yogin is first made aware of the persuasive power of matter's external characteristics. He experiences matter's tangibility and concreteness, the ordered strength of the unconscious mechanical law by which matter operates, and the implication for cosmic life of an endless process which seems to have no ultimate purpose. If this were the whole truth, if the external face of matter were the only reality, then the odyssey would end here and the ultimate futility of the spiritual quest would have been revealed. But the yogin is made to realize that these external characteristics represent only part of matter's total truth. He experiences the presence of a consciousness which is behind and within the motion of matter; he sees that concretization and mechanical law are in reality the instruments by which the inner spiritual guide is working out its eternal purpose.

Passing through the kingdom of matter, the yogin finds himself in the kingdom of life, where the truth and power of the vital dimension of reality are revealed to him. He is struck by the awesome energies displayed by the creative and destructive forces which provide the momentum for motion of the world's evolution. He sees clearly the agonizing struggle of life as it tries to maintain itself permanently on the everchanging base of unconscious matter and feels in turn both the solemnity and the futility of the battle. Carried forward by life's insatiable passion, he descends into the abyss of hell, where the emptiness of all that man values is revealed to him. He then soars to the opposite extreme of the kingdom, where he is shown the "glory of life." In this vital heaven he experiences life free from the bonds of matter in an eternally peaceful state. In hell his soul is almost consumed with despair; in heaven it is almost over-whelmed with delight. But his journey is not over, for he moves on to the kingdom of mind. He first encounters "little mind"—the power of logic and reason to give order and structure to man's life in an otherwise chaotic world. He sees that this function of mind is valuable to man's life because it provides some security and some limited knowledge of the meaning of human existence. But he sees further that the scope of rational knowledge is limited, that the security which it brings is tenuous and that it tends to enslave rather than to liberate.

In another part of the kingdom the reality of "higher mind" is revealed to him as he is made aware of mind's ability to conceive the ideal when it is free from the impediments of life and matter. Here the close relationship between mind and spirit is clearly seen in the ability of mind to separate itself from the lower realities and project itself into a pure ideal state. This ability is the source of man's spiritual longing—of his desire to know and to live within the mysteries and bliss of the spirit. In the kingdom of spirit Aswapathy experiences the touch of spiritual reality. He learns that indeed the soul can be released from matter, life and mind and can move in ecstasy among pure spiritual beings. Here the soul experiences such delight that one would expect the journey to be over, the spiritual task to be complete; but for Aswapathy this is not the case. What would have been seen as fulfillment for previous yogas is only a first stage for Sri Aurobindo.

3. THE REALIZATION OF INTEGRAL TRUTH

It is significant to the understanding of Aurobindo's idea of the role of the yogin to note here that not only is it necessary for Aswapathy to experience each of the realities separately, but it is necessary that he be tempted by the particular claim of each that it is the only reality. At every stage of his journey the yogin is told that he has reached his final goal—he has discovered the true source of all existence. In the kingdom of matter he is persuaded by the appeal of the gospel of "material monism," which claims that matter alone is ultimately real and that everything else is only illusory or transitory. This gospel is not rejected until it has been experienced and understood. Then what it affirms, viz., the reality of matter, is accepted as true and valuable, while what it denies, viz., the nonreality of everything nonmaterial, is rejected. Likewise, in the kingdoms of life and mind Aswapathy is tempted by gospels which must be experienced, understood and accepted as partially valid. But he again rejects as a final goal the bliss of pure spiritual existence, which is free from the struggle and frustrations of the lower realms. Although his total surrender allows him to be opened to all possible types of experience, and allows his soul to be led to the extremes of all the kingdoms of reality, he never surrenders to any one particular reality or one limited and partial truth. For him all these experiences, all these separate realities with their persuasive but limited gospel, must be assimilated and integrated into some harmonious unity.

If we return again to the symbol of the dawn as a time of being in the middle, it can be seen that in his journey through the kingdoms Aswapathy is drawn away from the dawn into various kinds of "light" in order that he might experience the full impact of the claims of each separate dimension of reality. His total surrender calls forth ultimate risk at every turn. But no matter how powerful the call of some particular truth, no matter how totally lost in darkness or consumed in light his soul might be, he always returns eventually to the posture of the dawn. Only from the middle perspective of the dawn can all of these separate truths be properly integrated.

This insistence on returning to the middle reveals a distinctive quality of Sri Aurobindo's yoga. According to him, previous yogas were based on a partial method and partial concept of reality; each seized one limited aspect of reality and human potential and followed that to its highest development.[23] Thus, hatha yoga used the material energy, raja yoga used the mind, jnana yoga used reason and mental vision, bhakti yoga used emotional and aesthetic powers, and karma yoga uses man's will and urge to action. In each case a limited aspect of human nature is used as an instrument for spiritual development. By contrast, Sri Aurobindo calls his path an "integral yoga," which takes each of these yogas for its own particular power and combines them into a harmonious whole. This integration is accomplished by a continuous extension from and return to the dawn as the proper place in the middle where all the various experiences can be united.

23. See Sri Aurobindo, *The Synthesis of Yoga*, (BCL, 20, 21), pp. 28–31, 568–71 and below, ch. IV.

4. THE VISION OF TRANSFORMATION

Sri Aurobindo emphatically contrasts his yoga with previous systems in terms of their respective visions of ultimate fulfillment. He claims that all the old paths are based on a vision which aims at the release of the soul from matter. Their final goal is liberation; they hope to achieve a freedom of the soul from matter, life and mind. In contrast to this Aurobindo sees his path as seeking not liberation but transformation. The ascent of the soul to spiritual heights must be only a first stage in the process of bringing the spirit into matter, life and mind. Once the experience of liberation has been achieved, the work of transformation can begin. To realize the ultimate goal, the yogin cannot permanently leave the realm of body, life and mind; by remaining in intimate contact with these realities he can be the instrument of their spiritual transformation, when the Divine has descended to earth. Hence Aswapathy's odyssey does not end with his soul's resting at peace in some high spiritual bliss. All his experiences have suggested to him that something more must happen. The goal of existence will not be achieved by the separation of the various aspects of reality but by their ultimate harmonious union, which will be achieved through the descent of the Divine to earth.

Savitri: The Divine Descended

As one would expect, the most complex of the characters in the poem is Savitri. Like Aswapathy, she is a yogin. As she prepares for the momentous confrontation with death, she must begin by offering herself in total surrender to the will of the divine voice within her. Her reluctance to do so in the beginning exposes her human qualities; but her eventual total commitment to her task reveals the divine nature within her (474–477). As a result of her surrender and commitment, her consciousness is opened to the inner worlds. She is described as passing through the "kingdom of reality" in order that she might experience the truth of each realm and integrate these truths into her own being (477–485, 491–500, 503–550). Like Aswapathy, she is given a vision of a world which has been transformed by the union of spirit and matter (485–487). But it is important to note that her relationship to this vision is different from that which is experienced by Aswapathy. In his odyssey through the kingdoms,

Aswapathy is led by a power which is external to himself. For the most part, he is the passive observer—the receiver of revelation and spiritual insight. He is shown what must be done, but he realizes that he does not have the capacity to accomplish the task. He must call upon something outside himself to fulfill the vision which he has received. But throughout the poem, Savitri draws her strength from within herself. She is sufficient unto herself because she embodies Aswapathy's vision of transformation. She is the instrument by which the Divine will transform this world of matter, life and mind. Her humanity and her divinity, her body and her spirit, her mind and her spiritual intuition are complementary forces in the process of cosmic transformation.

1. SAVITRI: THE HUMAN WOMAN AND THE DIVINE FORCE

Her unique character is clearly seen when she is compared to Savitri of the Mahabharata story. Awakening on the day on which Satyavan is fated to die, Savitri of the story insists on going into the forest with her husband so she will not be separated from him. She has no plan by which to prevent death from accomplishing his task; she is overwhelmed by a sense of profound hopelessness and power-lessness. Nevertheless she does her duty as a faithful wife because she feels she must. This individual woman, who is helpless in face of the inevitability of human fate, becomes in Sri Aurobindo's poem a cosmic force which awakens to its eternal evolutionary labors and moves toward fulfillment. The woman in the Mahabharata story who remembers with joy the year she has shared with her husband in the bliss of conjugal love becomes in the poem the cosmic life which reviews its endless ages of progress and looks forward to greater accomplishment. Savitri of the poem is the energy of cosmic motion, the momentum of evolution; her passion is the vital breath of all life. The woman of the story symbolizes wifely love; Savitri of the poem is the embodiment of divine love for the world.

Similarly in the story Satyavan, the husband of Savitri, is pre-sented as the ideal man, but there is no suggestion that he should be thought of as anything more than human. The marriage in the story is the marriage of the ideal man and woman. But although Savitri and Satayavan of the poem are given human characteristics, this is only one of the necessary dimensions of their total being; they are cosmic male and cosmic female, Purusha and Prakriti, Shiva and Shakti, Krishna and Radha, Yin and Yang. Their marriage is the union of eternal cosmic forces which create and sustain the life of the cosmos; their separation would mean the end of all motion, all evolution, all life. Thus the struggle of Sri Aurobindo's Savitri with Death is much broader in scope and more fundamental in implication than the encounter between Savitri and Death in the ancient story. Should Aurobindo's heroine fail, then the vision of the transformation of matter, life and mind by the embodied presence of spirit in the world would not be accomplished. The death of Satyavan would mean the defeat of all divine intention for the world, extinction of all life and the end of all human hope.

2. SAVITRI: THE INSTRUMENT OF DEATH'S TRANSFORMATION

Savitri of the story does not defeat death. She is promised progeny and long life for both Satyavan and herself; but after four hundred years she will face death again. Savitri of the poem does not defeat death either; she possesses the divine wisdom to see that death is not her enemy. In the poem the true nature of death is exposed. Death is not the enemy of life, anymore than matter is the enemy of spirit. Death is one of the instruments by which the Divine has brought forth the evolution of the cosmos. But when the final phase of evolution is completed by the descent of the Divine, death will no longer be useful to the Divine purpose in the world. Since Savitri knows this, she does not fear death. Moreover, she does not attempt to escape a world which appears to be under death's sovereign. She knows that the world of matter is the place where the divine work will be accomplished. So in spite of the many tempting alternatives which are offered her—alternatives which Savitri of the story would have gratefully accepted—she insists on returning to earth with Satyavan. This is the key to the meaning of *Savitri* and to Sri Aurobindo's conception of the spiritual life: viz., that the task of spiritual fulfillment must be accomplished here on earth by a humanity open to the Divine and prepared for the descent of the Divine into all aspects of earthly life.

TWO

THE FOUNDATIONS OF INDIAN

CULTURE

Its Contemporary Significance

by Thomas Berry

The right remedy is not to belittle still farther the agelong ideal of India, but to return to its old amplitude and give it a still wider scope, to make in very truth all the life of the nation a religion in this high spiritual sense. This is the direction in which the philosophy, poetry, art of the West is, still more or less obscurely, but with an increasing light, beginning to turn, and even some faint glints of the truth are beginning now to fall across political and sociological ideals. India has the key to the knowledge and conscious application of the ideal; what was dark to her before in its application, she can now, with a new light, illumine; what was wrong and wry in her old methods she can now rectify; the fences which she created to protect the outer growth of the spiritual ideal and which afterwards became barriers to its expansion and farther application, she can now break down and give her spirit a freer field and an ampler flight: she can, if she will, give a new and decisive turn to the problems over which all mankind is labouring and stumbling, for the clue to their solutions is there in her ancient knowledge. Whether she will rise or not to the height of her opportunity in the renaissance which is coming upon her, is the question of her destiny.

—The Foundations of Indian Culture

The Foundations of Indian Culture

Amid the global complex of man's cultural development India presents herself as a resplendent expression of the human in its higher spiritual reality. In geographical formation, in physical type, in linguistic variation, in cultural expression, in socioeconomic pattern, in intellectual acumen, spiritual discipline and religious experience, India contributes its full share to man's historical evolution. So vast and so diverse is the culture of India that to write of it is something to make the boldest and most competent of scholars, Indian or non-Indian, pause and reflect and set themselves severe limits in subject matter, period and mode of approach. It is small wonder then that so few comprehensive studies of India's cultural expression have ever been presented. Nor can we say that Aurobindo Ghose has himself fully succeeded in his own effort to respond to this challenge. What can be said is that he has, in these essays, made a significant statement on the culture of India: he has done this with literary style, with spiritual insight and on a comprehensive scale. These thirty-four essays reflect the mind of a person sufficiently intimate to share in India's deepest spiritual experience but sufficiently distant to see India as a whole—a feat rarely achieved in the writing of cultural history.

This vision of the whole is particularly difficult because India is such a forest of cultural developments that the writer from within India can hardly grasp its larger pattern, while writers from without can hardly encompass the particular details. Sri Aurobindo had the advantage of birth within India, education outside of India, then a return and mature experience of India from within, first by active participation in India's movement toward cultural and political liberation from Western dominance, then by long years of yogic meditation. In addition to this breadth of his experience and the encompassing character of his thinking, Aurobindo, just prior to composition of these essays on Indian culture, had written a series of essays on the larger human process, a series later published as *The Human Cycle*. Thus he had already dealt with the more universal issues of man's historical and cultural development just prior to writing specifically about India. During this same period, from 1914 to 1921, he had also written his larger spiritual synthesis entitled *The Life Divine*, his *The Synthesis of Yoga* and a long series of essays on the Bhagavad Gita. Thus when he came to consider the question

of Indian culture, its historical development and spiritual significance, he was coming to something much more specific than in
these works concerned with the universal destiny of mankind. These
other more detached works have a reflective calm that is absent from
this study on *The Foundations of Indian Culture.*

But if these other works gave expression to his insight concerning
the cultural development of man, they did not fully satisfy his wish
to write more directly about India and her cultural formation. The
occasion for this arose when a drama critic in England wrote a book
assigning Indian culture to a lower state of development and describing it as a less acceptable civilization than that of modern Western
society. While this book was hardly worthy of notice by a serious
thinker, it represented to Aurobindo, by the very force of its misund-
erstanding and even disdain of India, the instinctive attitude
adopted by Western man when faced with the distant regions of
south Asia. India appeared strange and mysterious, baffling, heathen,
superstitious, immoral, improverished; India seemed in need of
Western help not only economically and intellectually, but even
morally and spiritually. Such a presentation elicited from Sri Aurobindo an extreme reaction; it let loose the resentments he had long
held in check against this aspect of the Western intelligence, this
sense of superiority, this inability to understand even the most elementary facts about India, this crudeness and inhumanity of Western rationality, this feeling of superiority in the presence of a noble
culture and a people with some of the deepest spiritual insights ever
attained by human understanding.

Yet it was not only this feeling of resentment toward the West
that needed expression: there was also the feeling that the people of
India themselves were losing confidence in their own heritage despite the vast resources within their tradition, resources that might
for a while be neglected but which were by no means lost—they only
needed an opportune moment when they could again come forth in
a new period of expression in response to the needs of the new age.
The time for new development had now arrived. Sri Aurobindo
considered himself the herald of this new period, the one called to
remind the people of the danger they risked if the renewal of India's
cultural efforts were delayed any longer. In addition to his resentment against the West and his feeling that the time had come for
cultural renewal in India, a third need was experienced by Aurobindo: the need to recall the past glories of India and to pay tribute
to this achievement. This was a debt that he owed, an obligation he

recognized beyond any special function it might have in preserving or fostering the well-being of the society, even though he also recognized that this remembrance of past achievement was of primary importance in bringing about the renewal of India in its modern phase. Still a fourth motivation in writing these essays was the need to identify for the entire world the special role of India in the larger pattern of man's evolutionary development. For here there was a need of mankind to awaken from the self-induced trance of a secular scientific worldview that had led Western man to great accomplishment but which was also leading India and perhaps the entire human community into a cultural and human impasse. These, then, are the motivations that we find in these essays on the foundations of Indian culture.

No abstract considerations, these motivations were interior demands evoked by an impending crisis. Thus the feeling of a personal urgency, a national urgency and even an urgency for the global community of man. He identified with these urgencies much as the prophets identified with the Israel in the days of her trial, as Augustine identified with the Christian, Roman and human shock felt at the burning of Rome in 410 A.D., much as Mencius identified with the historical-political turmoil of his times, as Marx, in his *Manifesto*, identified with the self-alienation of man in the machine age. In all these cases we have the feeling of prophetic presence, of charismatic vision, a feeling of awe before a transformation process that goes deeply into the structure of human existence, not simply into some transient social or cultural issue.

As we do not expect Isaias or Jeremiah to give full justice to the empires assailing the country, as we do not expect Augustine to provide an academic history of Rome, as we expect none of these to provide a "balanced" view of their subject, so we cannot expect Aurobindo to give a "balanced" view of his subject. Like those in these other instances, he is communicating a message, not writing a history; he is guiding a transformation process, not adjusting to some institutional change. Yet if Aurobindo is creating a vision more than he is recording history or describing a culture, the one is integral to the other and it might be said that only in this way do we get to the "true" history, to the deeper reality of what is happening, or to the real depths of the cultural life of a people. This is the type of historical and cultural insight we find in Aurobindo. The "facts" he deals with are the obvious facts known to everyone with the slightest acquaintance with India's historical development, just as the temples of India are visible to every observer. But the question of the temple as well as the question of the historical records remains: what inner reality are they expressing, what is the cosmic-divine presence that is felt there, what governing role do they exercise over the historical process itself? This book of Aurobindo is an effort to answer these questions, an effort to go beyond, not only beyond the historical account itself, but even beyond the intellectual and rational understanding of these facts, back to the mystical meaning and divine presence behind these facts.

But if he was eminently successful in doing this with India, he was less successful in the comparison and observations that he makes with Western culture, whether in its ancient classical, medieval Christian or modern secularist phases. Since the modern West grew out of its medieval and ancient Mediterranean traditions, these prior phases of Western civilization must, in some manner, have prepared the way for the modern rationalism in knowledge, naturalism in culture and commercialism in economics. But here again the imbalance found in this work on Indian culture is extensively compensated for by the more just appraisal found elsewhere in his works, especially in *The Human Cycle.* It must be said that nowhere in his writings does Sri Aurobindo show any depth appreciation for the Christian mysteries, Christian spirituality or Christian culture. But if the earlier part of this study on Indian culture, particularly the first two parts, "Is India Civilized?" and "A Rationalistic Critic on Indian Culture," are overwritten in their aggressive attitude, they may well be indicating that a certain need does exist for examining once more whether there is not a certain truth in the proposition that Western man's approach to reality is pervaded so extensively by naturalism and rationalism that he tends to substitute technical perfection for spiritual depth and dogmatic faith for the transforming experience of the Divine. The extent to which this is done can hardly be recognized by Western man himself until the entire culture of the West is brought into contact with the spiritual achievements, with the unique sense of interiority found in India's culture. But here also there is need to compare the bright side of one culture with the bright side of the other rather than the bright side of one's own culture with the less bright or even the dark side of the other. This latter is precisely what Aurobindo does when he compares the naturalistic and sensuous aspects of Western renaissance art of Tintoretto with some of the more spiritual art of India; we wonder if he knew anything at all about Cimabue, Giotto, Fra Angelico or El

Greco, or if he ever really looked at any of the great religious art of an earlier period. The entire sequence of his studies on Indian culture is weakened considerably by constant derogatory references to the spiritual and religious aspects of Western culture.

This overstatement of the case against the West should not, however, lead to a downgrading of the high achievement of Sri Aurobindo in his presentation of Indian culture. With Aurobindo as with other such prophetic types, the message which so powerfully illumines some areas of reality leaves other areas in darkness. The essential message remains authentic; its perennial value and the vision that sustains it can, perhaps, find expression only within such limitations and even such distortions. The Christian world of the West has itself been victimized by its own failures in this regard throughout the centuries of its existence. So with Aurobindo: he is defending a cause, a cause that is imperiled by the West, which for the moment at least becomes the dragon to be slain. The greater visions seem always to rest on such fragile foundations and such inadequate judgment of what is outside the prophetic view at the moment. But even so, the experiences which such writers convey and the transformation processes they are interpreting remain valid; these fashion the pathways to the future for the cultures concerned and even, at times, for the larger human community.

The Night of India

While the main preoccupation for this work is the defense and exaltation of India's cultural heritage, the entire work comes out of Aurobindo's feeling for the "night of India." If he has a remarkable sensitivity for each of the great periods of India's culture he has a special feeling for the modern period, the period of tragic decline in the cultural life of India. In another work he describes the twentieth century in terms of the "shadow of a spirit that is yet unborn" but which is "preparing for its birth." He then notes: "This material world of ours, besides its fully embodied things of the present, is peopled by such powerful shadows, ghosts of things dead and the spirit of things yet unborn."[1] He understands with remarkable sensitivity this "womb" existence of the future in the present. Hardly

1. From *The Ideal of Human Unity*, in *Social and Political Thought*, BCL, 15:541.

anything is so central to his writing on historical and cultural topics. He constantly uses such transformation symbolism because he realizes that the past development of India, however glorious, belongs irretrievably to the past; to survive in any vital way it must undergo a death-rebirth transformation. His main effort is to keep the "ghosts of the past" from destroying the "spirit of things yet unborn." Everywhere we find reference to a moving toward, a rebirth, a renewal process, an emerging into something. These symbols of the dawn, of the blossoming, the incoming tide, the flowering, the awakening, the breaking and reshaping, the formation out of chaos, emergence of a new order dominate Aurobindo's thinking. The emergence metaphor is one of the strongest of all—an emergence out of the earth itself that corresponds to the descent of another force, a divine force that is coming down upon the earth. This is leading to fulfillment, to activation of human potentiality. As lightning in the darkness, the events in our times portend transformation, renewal, renaissance.

Yet all of this supposes the "night" of the present. An understanding of the creative function of the night is one of the more important aspects of Aurobindo's consideration of India. It is a night of remembrance for "our nights carry in them the secret of a greater dawn" (27). Thus the concern in Aurobindo's work with the past glories of India. He had written extensively on the decline of India when only "these philosophers who were at the same time Yogins" had kept "the soul of India alive through the gathering night of her decadence" (310). It was a night so dim that if someone from ancient India in the period of the Upanishads or from the days of high Buddhist spirituality, or even from the later classical age, were to appear in the present, he would experience "the sense of a national, a cultural debacle, a fall from the highest summits to discouragingly low levels" (29). But while this was truly a night, it was "a night filled at first with many and brilliant constellations and even at its thickest and worst it was the darkness of Kalidasa's . . . 'night preparing for dawn, with a few just decipherable stars' " (30). In all of this he refrains from placing the blame on any outside cause, not even on the imperial occupation of India by the British. It is a historical process emerging out of India herself. In the period after Shankara (eighth century A.D.) there was an extreme depreciation of life as somehow unreal, as hardly worth the living (71). "The hard binding of forms triumphed at last and there was a decline of the inspiring spirit, a stagnation of living force, a progressive decay of the outward structure" (110). At least some share of the blame rests on the teachings of the Buddhists and Shankara (181). Here, as in all of his writings, Aurobindo wishes to remedy in Indian culture any indifference to the physical elements of life, any neglect of the functioning of social institutions. He realizes that these are necessary. The healing of India's troubles must not be sought by some external adjustment or by some superficial change, but by an interior transformation, a higher manifestation of the spiritual. The new forms must emerge out of the spontaneities of inner vision, not simply in a crude conformation with Western institutions.

The Spiritual Quality of Indian Culture

To achieve this dawning of a new consciousness in India, a dawning adequate for the task of reshaping India's destinies in herself and in the world community, there is need for remembrance, a need for meditating on the heritage of the past. Only from this vantage point can the essential problems of the present be adequately seen and dealt with. Otherwise the identity of the Indian people will be lost; the tradition will remain enervated. Indian culture will be at the mercy of the winds of commercialism and secularism that blow so powerfully over the world in this century. Above all, Sri Aurobindo recognized the need to preserve the Indian mode of consciousness. More precisely, there is need to maintain that mode of interior awareness which brought forth the Vedic hymns, the Upanishadic intuitions, the heroic ethos of the epics, the new symbolism of the Puranas and Tantras as well as the intellectual achievements and devotional cults that have dominated the mind and emotions of India from the fifth century A. D. until the present. There is need to be faithful to this complex of traditions but also to be faithful to the aesthetic expression of these traditions, especially in the architecture and sculpture that give human shape to the landscape of India.

But before venturing into these realms in which the light of India shines with its own special brilliance, there is need to deal directly with the spiritual quality that has distinguished India from the beginning. In the first five chapters of the third part of *The Foundations of Indian Culture*, which deal with this spiritual quality, Aurobindo concerns himself with this ultimate source of India's life. This spiritual principle is more than the source of India's life and her greatness; it is the very thing that enables India to be at all. There is no question of cultural adornment or some special spiritual achievement; it is rather India's very existence psychically and emotionally, for man does not live, even physically, by economics alone, but primarily by the word, by vision, by the sustaining presence of the Divine. If this interior spiritual presence is less obvious at some periods in history, or if men in some societies seem to survive on the externals of life, neglectful of the spiritual, this is not true of India, for here, to a unique degree, the spiritual is the very substance of existence, as can be seen in Sri Aurobindo's characterization of India:

> The whole root of difference between Indian and European culture springs from the spiritual aim of Indian civilisation. It is the turn which this aim imposes on all the rich and luxuriant variety of its forms and rhythms that gives to it its unique character. For even what it has in common with other cultures gets from that turn a stamp of striking originality and solitary greatness. A spiritual aspiration was the governing force of this culture, its core of thought, its ruling passion. Not only did it make spirituality the highest aim of life, but it even tried, as far as that could be done in the past conditions of the human race, to turn the whole of life towards spirituality. (121)

This feeling of enormous energies contained in the furthermost regions of the human psyche, especially as these energies can be associated with the individual nations, and even with the general history of mankind, is everywhere evident in Aurobindo. To release these energies for the higher transformation of India and the nations of the world is the great task to which Sri Aurobindo set himself. The bonds of exteriorization and mechanization had shut up these energies. As its special duty, India has the mission of awakening man to the existence of these energies and teaching the methods whereby they can be activated. This mode of existence as a "spiritual culture" not only expressed itself with unique intensity in India, but "it was made consciously the grand uplifting idea of life, the core of all thinking, the foundation of all religion, the secret sense and declared ultimate aim of human existence" (127).

As the dominant form of the modern Western world is found in its concern for the vital natural forces of man and for the development of the rational principle of its being, so "the dominant note in the Indian mind, the temperament that has been at the foundation of all its culture and originated and supported the greater part of its creative action in philosophy, religion, art and life has been,

I have insisted, spiritual, intuitive and psychic," although "this fundamental tendency has not excluded but rather powerfully supported a strong and rich intellectual, practical and vital activity" (307). This spiritualizing of the totality of life "is the last vision of all that vast and unexampled seeking and experiment in a thousand ways of the soul's outermost and innermost experience which is the unique character of her past" and "in the end is the mission for which she was born and the meaning of her existence" (155). The "whole aim" of a great culture is "to lift man up to something which at first he is not." It is to transform his way of knowing, his way of living, his way of experiencing good and evil, beauty and ugliness. This is so important that if any civilization does not possess this aim, it can hardly be said to have a worthy human culture. Even when success is not achieved it would still remain true that "to have made this attempt is to have ennobled the life of the race; to have failed in it is better than if it had never at all been attempted; to have achieved even a partial success is a great contribution to the future possibilities of the human being" (173). Throughout this section on the spiritual dynamics of Indian civilization, Aurobindo challenges the assumption that body precedes spirit, that matter is prior to consciousness, that the higher emerges from the lower. Aurobindo's position is precisely the opposite of the Marxist position. He challenges the entire structure of the Western thought process in this period, although nineteenth-century rationalism was already being reformed by the increasing awareness of spirit throughout the twentieth century. Of this Aurobindo was aware, though he was also aware of a continuing dominance of the material and the pragmatic.

Reference to the "spiritual" in Aurobindo's work is so pervasive and so constantly designated as the solution to human problems that the question arises concerning the proper designation for the dominant trend in his work. How is Sri Aurobindo to be designated: Is he to be listed among the theosophists, or among the gnostics, or must some other way of describing him and his work be considered? Because of the emphasis that he gave to the physical and material life of man, it would be difficult to maintain that he supplanted the material with the spiritual or that he failed to distinguish the human from the divine. But there is an ultimate sense in which he did fail in establishing the clear and consistent distinctions that those committed to traditional thought and religious traditions find desirable. This is a continuing problem throughout much of India's intellectual history and no fully satisfactory way of dealing with this issue has yet been produced. Since Sri Aurobindo exhibits tendencies in both directions, it is not proper to categorize him absolutely in any of these ways. The best way of designating Aurobindo is to consider him as a "spiritual romanticist." He made extensive allowance for the material and the physical, but his emphasis on the spiritual seems to have in it something different from the ordinary religious emphasis on the presence and governing providence of the Spirit in earthly affairs.

Because of this spiritual emphasis Sri Aurobindo has become a cult figure to many of his followers. This is an unfortunate circumstance that has prevented many serious thinkers from giving to his teachings the attention they deserve. This lack of attention is also due, however, to the unwillingness of more objective, scholarly and analytical thinkers to deal adequately with the subjective, the intuitive and the more humanistic and cultural forces at work in the world. This is precisely the challenge that Sri Aurobindo is offering as he reflects upon the destinies of India and the destinies of man in the twentieth century when basic decisions must be made in India on whether to conform to the more objective and rational approach of the West or to maintain the spiritual approach of traditional India in order to sustain a more meaningful vision and to release the abundant psychic energies needed for building the future.

The Aesthetic Expression of Indian Culture

The second reflection to be undertaken in the night of India's decline concerns the cultural development of India as this is manifested in architecture, sculpture and painting. These subjects are covered in chapters six through nine of the third part of *The Foundations of Indian Culture*. Better than written scriptures, these visible monuments carried the impress of India's ancient mode of consciousness. With such realities before their eyes the people had less need of written scriptures or of reading skills to maintain their awareness of the divine presence throughout the cosmic-human order. So important did ancient India consider the expression of these spiritual ideas in all forms of art that the arts "were placed under the sanction of the Rishis and were made instruments of the spirit's culture" (169). There was above all in the art of India a powerful subjective, psychic element, an interior spiritual vision that was the immediate inspiration of the artist. Some of Aurobindo's finest observations concern these differences between Indian and Western artistic approaches. In his view Western art proceeds "on the basis of the forms already given us by physical Nature" whereas the Indian artist "begins from within, sees in his soul the things he wishes to express or interpret and tries to discover the right line, colour and design of his intuition which, when it appears on the physical ground, is not a just and reminding reproduction of the line, colour and design of physical nature, but much rather what seems to use as psychical transmutation of the natural figure" (247, 248). What he paints is less the physical form than the "forms of things as he has seen them in the psychical plane of experience"; it is these forms which the artist has "gone into himself to discover" (248). The classical Greek artist evolved a more symmetrical, more purely intellectual mode of expression while the Indian artist evolved a less intellectually pure but more spiritually free manner of expression. It is from this subjectivity, this freedom in relation to the pure idea that the "whole strangeness of the Indian use of line and mass, ornament and proportion and rhythm arises" (234). In an ultimate sense, the Western and the Indian artist are not looking at the same thing; they live in different worlds and "even where they meet in the object, see it from a different level or surrounded by a different atmosphere, and we know what power the point of view or the medium of vision has to transform the object" (234).

Presentation of the human body in the Indian tradition differs from its presentation in Western tradition. In the West there is an effort to express the contours of the body with a certain natural fidelity even when a religious ideal leads to modifications that heighten the spiritual impress of the figure. This fidelity to the physical contours is less pronounced in India, where the body is often presented with taut, almost swollen surfaces, as though expansion into the infinite could be achieved by the spirit's overcoming the resistance of body, matter and time and all that imposes limitation. There is also the opulence of much of India's art as though the enrichment of the total work with exaggerated splendor would compensate for the inherent poverty of the material involved. But whether in the form of the surface contours or the simplicity of a standing or seated figure, there is always the impression of a more than natural reality that breaks through or transforms the limited, controlled world of the human. Interpretation of this art is best done in the light of the ancient scriptures of India, for "the more ancient sculptural art of India embodies in visible form what the Upanishads threw out into inspired thought and the Mahabharata and Ramayana portrayed by the word in life. Indeed this sculpture like the architecture springs from spiritual realisation" (230). Everywhere Aurobindo insists on the deeper, transrational feeling, which is not the feeling of the merely imaginative side of the man but is the higher spiritual feeling, a type of experience that we might identify as "mystical" although in an Indian context the word has more cosmic implication than in a Western context, where the mystical is almost exclusively bound up with ideas of interpersonal communion with a divine reality.

Interpreting works of art that come down to us from the various civilizations brings us to the problem of cultural hermeneutics. Indeed, hermeneutics might be considered to be the principal concern of Aurobindo throughout this entire book on the foundations of Indian culture. This theme, which he repeats in every essay and almost in every sentence, states that the interpretation of Indian culture requires a grasp of the spiritual experience of India in its awesome depths. Otherwise the entire cultural process that has been at work in India from the beginning makes no real sense. This spiritual experience in the depths of India's consciousness has an enormous variety in its expression, but there is an ultimate unity of principle involved which has been understood in its true depth and significance by few scholars or critics in the modern period. By contrast, it seems to have been extensively understood in former periods, naïvely by the uneducated, with reflexive awareness by those of more cultivated appreciation, especially by those who were creating these great works of the past. The West was overcoming its former commitment to classical norms and developing a new, enlarged capacity for aesthetic understanding. This was evident from the interest being shown in the various arts of the Asian world. As Aurobindo notes, the sculpture and painting of ancient India "have recently been rehabilitated with a surprising suddenness in the eyes of a more cultivated European criticism in the course of that rapid opening of the western mind to the value of oriental thought and creation" (226).

The real difficulty was that of restoring to the Indian people themselves some awareness of the richness of their heritage. When Sri Aurobindo saw this new appreciation in the Western world he felt more than ever the plight of the Indian intelligentsia who had become alienated from their own traditions in favor of the earlier

Western classical and renaissance norms of aesthetic values. He is concerned "not only with the critical estimation of our art by Europe, but much more nearly with the evil effect of the earlier depreciation of the Indian mind which has been for a long time side-tracked off its true road by a foreign, an anglicised education and, as a result, vulgarised and falsified by the loss of its own true center" (226). This attitude, which led to an estimate of Indian sculpture and painting as "undeveloped inferior art" or as "a mass of monstrous and abortive miscreation," was in his own day changing for the better, but it still vitiated the artistic perception of a large numbers of Indian people. There still remained in India "a bluntness or absolute lacking of aesthetic taste" (226–227). So extreme was the general decline of artistic awareness that Aurobindo considered that the recovery of "a true and inward understanding of ourselves—our past and our present self and from that our future—is only in its commencement for the majority of our people" (227).

In the coming dawn of a new and more creative age in India the artist would contribute something quite special; at least this always remained the hope of Aurobindo. In the renewal of the artistic impulse in the Bengal region Aurobindo saw at least some signs of the awakening of a new consciousness and a new creative force, one that might easily spread to the other areas of the cultural life of India. This hope was not fully realized even though there have been new efforts throughout India to reassert in modern form something of the ancient genius. Outstanding ability to create in monumental sculpture remains a lost art. But if artistic power seems at present to be impoverished, there is a deepening awareness of the older traditions and of the inherent artistic power in the tradition. Just when this will break through into its full expression remains a hidden mystery of the future; but the very recollection of the past, the seeing of these ancient monuments with new appreciation, is already, as Aurobindo perceived, one of the ways into the freshness of a morning in which the "spirit yet unborn" may manifest itself.

The Literature of India

The third area of Sri Aurobindo's reflection in the midst of the Indian night concerns the literature of India, a subject covered in chapters ten through fourteen of the third part of the book. Here we find the direct expression of man's spiritual experiences in language and intellectual intuitions. This essay is divided into five sections: the Veda; Upanishads; Dharma Shastras and epics; the Classical Literature; the Puranas, Tantras, devotional literature and theologians. Appreciation of this full complex of India's literature is such a challenge that the author can be excused, at least in part, for giving only the slightest reference to Buddhist, Jain and Islamic writings, since the points he is making are sufficiently valid to serve as an overall view of the main types and periods of Hindu Indian literary production. To the more speculative writing the author brings intellectual insight, to the more poetic works he brings a sympathetic understanding of image, symbol, myth and imagination; to the epics he brings appreciation for the religious realism of the Mahabharata, and the spiritual idealism of the Ramayana; to the classical literature he brings a sensitivity to the refinements of this later period and the style and sublime content of Kalidasa; to the Puranas, Tantras and devotional hymns he brings a profound sense of the divine as experienced in these traditions. Although little consideration is given to the theologians from the post-Harsha to the modern period, he does indicate the importance of their work and the need for appreciating the manner in which these scholastic figures have given intellectual shape and substance to the Indian mind.

If Sri Aurobindo himself chose not to be a scholar of the past but a creator in the present of pathways to the future, he has followed in the sequence of India's creative personalities. For this purpose he has chosen as his own literary instrument the reflective essay as perfected by nineteenth-century English essayists. By this means he has not exactly recorded the past or given us a new analysis of the past, he has summed up the tradition, given it new shape and expression out of his own personal reflection. This selection of the most essential aspects of the past, this effort to identify inner meaning rather than engage in scholastic argumentation, requires a special talent. It also requires a highly developed personality in the writer, since what emerges is a personal statement. The validity of the statement rests upon the writer's ability to identify with the tradition so completely as to recreate the tradition in his own mind and express it within the new horizons of his own personality, his own vision, his own intellectual, imaginative and literary competence. This is something entirely different from the work of the academic scholar who seeks to comment on the past in some "objective" fashion. The efficacy of this essay style is its subjectivity. When this subjective identity is validly achieved, then the tradition itself speaks through a new voice, reveals itself in a new form, conveys an insight never before presented with such clarity. Above all the ancient is brought to fulfillment in the realities of a present. Those special aspects of the ancient tradition which speak to the live issues of the present, and upon which the future can be built, are brought forward, identified and renewed. In the essay form as developed in the English tradition Aurobindo found the perfect instrument for his interpretation of India's culture, in terms both of the values it brought to the present and of the guidance it offered for the future. By means of this profoundly humanistic instrument, he could give an overall summation of the literature and then dwell upon each of its major forms. For the essay is one of the best ways of enabling a literature to reflect upon itself. It is especially powerful in its capacity for description of the human situation, including the interior moods and thoughts and experiences of past masters who have handed down the insights and intuitions that were to guide Indian culture toward fulfillment of its historical mission.

Ideologically, Sri Aurobindo writes out of the Tantric yoga tradition. In and through this tradition, with its great emphasis on the interior spiritual modes of consciousness and the radiation of these modes of consciousness over the surrounding world, Aurobindo found his way back through the ages to the earlier founts of India's spiritual life. Unfortunately he never realized that India's spiritual development was rooted as much in the pre-Aryan soil and asceticism of India as in the Aryan peoples and their religious literature. Since discovery of these earlier sources of India's spiritual development did not take place until some time after his major writings were finished, Aurobindo never had the opportunity to indicate these more truly "Indian" origins of the culture about which he was writing. This deficiency is especially to be regretted since the Tantric tradition (including its concept of Shakti), which flourished so luxuriantly in North India, especially in the Bengal region, and which gave the most distinctive shape of his own personal spirituality, was derived more from these pre-Aryan and non-Aryan traditions than from the Aryan, Sanskrit tradition. In this manner Sri Aurobindo can be considered as one of the last and most forceful exponents in modern times of this native Indian tradition which has been modifying and transforming the incoming Aryan traditions, constituting what might be called the basic Indianization process. With uncanny instincts Aurobindo has allied himself and his entire interpretation of Indian culture with this primordial Tantric element of the tradition, with the spiritual and cultural dynamics that seem to emerge out of the earth itself. Aurobindo represents a further development, a purification, a strengthening and powerful adaptation of this Tantric tradition, in the present for creation of the future. One of the most effective descriptions in all his writings is his account of this inner force of the Shakti expressing itself in India's life and culture and so enabling India to rise up again gloriously in the sight of the nations.

> On the whole, what we see is a giant Shakti who, awakening into a new world, a new and alien environment, finds herself shackled in all her limbs by a multitude of gross or minute bonds, bonds self-woven by her past, bonds recently imposed from outside, and is struggling to be free from them, to arise and proclaim herself, to cast abroad her spirit and set her seal on the world. We hear on every side a sound of the slow fraying of bonds, here and there a sharp tearing and snapping; but freedom of movement has not yet been attained. The eyes are not yet clear, the bud of the soul has only partly opened. The Titaness has not yet arisen. (398).

One of the difficulties in writing about the literature of India is that hardly any of its literary forms corresponds to the basic intentionality, outer form or literary style of Western literature. Despite the fact that Western scholars have been studying India for centuries, little of the spiritual, intellectual and cultural experience contained in this literature has passed over to the West in any vital form; at least this has been true until recent years. In the last half of the twentieth century a more favorable situation has developed, although living communication remains minimal. Philosophers and theologians deliberately have kept themselves aloof from these traditions; they have refused to admit religious data from India within the horizons of their own thinking. In these past few years, however, those interested in spiritual and interior development have shown extensive interest in communicating with the religious and spiritual experience of India, particularly in learning Indian techniques of interiority. Yet the great danger is that this will be communicated in a shallow and ephemeral manner and the real depth of the experience indicated in this spiritual-religious literature of India may be lost. This was the concern of Aurobindo, especially at this time since the shallowness of Western interpretative studies was affecting many Indian scholars who had been educated according to Western norms of research scholarship.

In these essays Sri Aurobindo is not particularly interested in academic analysis or scholastic interpretation of Indian literature, but in the religious-spiritual meaning of this literature and the radiation of this meaning over the totality of Indian life. Specifically the work of Surendranath Das Gupta remains a far superior monument to scholarship in the thought literature of India to anything that Aurobindo would be capable of doing; but conversely, in his larger synthesis and interpretation of this literature Aurobindo is functioning on a plane of less interest to Das Gupta, for Aurobindo is an interpretative thinker in the larger spiritual and cultural dimensions of human affairs. He is more concerned to reinvigorate the tradition in the light of contemporary issues than to identify and list the vast and highly differentiated thought literature of the past. Both are needed. Aurobindo depended absolutely on such scholarship as that done by Das Gupta, but if the work of such research is to live in the present, it must enter into the basic life transformation processes of the present; it must assume responsibility for directing and activating this transformation, even as it is itself transformed and deepened by this new experience of the historical process. Similar consideration could be given to the other types of literature mentioned in these essays. Aurobindo is making an effort to identify the essential meaning of each type of literature and to make this available to contemporary man, for if India is to recover its creativity and if the world is to profit from the spiritual genius of India, this can only be done by vital contact with this ancient literature.

The Social-Political Context of Indian Life

After first reflecting on India's religious-spiritual experience, the aesthetic experience of India's past, and the expression of the culture in its language and literature, we come to "Indian Polity," the fourth and last of these remembrances made by Aurobindo in the night of India's decline. This subject appears at first to be a less rewarding and a less helpful series of remembrances, for it reveals the inadequacies of Indian economic, social and political life. In these three areas the achievement of India seems to be less impressive both now and in the past, although this is obviously a reading back into the past of the decline of the present. That there is some justice in this view can be granted, although it comes out of a Western society that is itself beginning to experience a disastrous sequence of changes in the structure and functioning of its own social and political forms.

Sri Aurobindo argues strongly that India cannot justly be looked upon as politically incompetent. Throughout the larger perspective of her history, India has produced sociopolitical structures as well as an economy that served the welfare and advancement of the people. These institutions, which flourished so effectively in an earlier period, achieved their high results mainly because of the highly religious and spiritual form of life which governed the total functioning of the society. India has from the beginning expressed in its social structures the same religious and spiritual values as were expressed in the architecture, sculpture and painting of the society and which were given detailed exposition through the literature. As the language was a sacred instrument of communication, as every work of art had its larger spiritual meaning, as the entire literature existed within this context, so too the social and political ideals. Every area of life was sensitive to the spiritual.

Here, precisely, is a most basic human issue: how can the economic, social and political areas of life be satisfactorily brought to express or at least to serve the higher, the more human, the more divine destiny of man. This has been the eternal question of man; it is the great challenge to the individual who often finds himself caught in a social, economic and political context in which the interior expansion of life is both aided and thwarted. This has become increasingly true of the Western world: the West has for the most part abandoned its effort to keep spiritual meaning in the social, political and economic orders of reality. These efforts are seen as idealistic, unreal, inherently frustrating to both the spiritual and the temporal aspects of life. Thus the decision to isolate these from each other, even to the point of educating its citizens in a context where the spiritual is excluded from human development. The religious and spiritual become, then, private matters, without social or political relevance. In actual fact neither those societies which have a religious and spiritual context for social existence nor those which have only a secular context for social existence have succeeded in producing a satisfactory human mode of being. Aurobindo observes:

> But the difficulty of making the social life an expression of man's true self and some highest realisation of the spirit within him is immensely greater than that which attends a spiritual self expression through the things of the mind, religion, thought, art, literature, and while in these India reached extraordinary heights and largenesses, she could not in the outward life go beyond certain very partial realisations and very imperfect tentatives,—a general spiritualising

symbolism, an infiltration of the greater aspiration, a certain cast given to the communal life, the creation of institutions favourable to the spiritual idea. (335)

Man can only look forward to the time when, in a third stage of the evolutionary process, he will finally discover and put into practice principles of a higher order in the functioning of human society. This will come about

> when man in the collectivity begins to live more deeply and to govern his collective life neither primarily by the needs, instincts, intuitions welling up out of the vital self, nor secondarily by the constructions of the reasoning mind, but first, foremost and always by the power of unity, sympathy, spontaneous liberty, supple and living order of his discovered greater self and a spirit in which the individual and the communal existence have their law of freedom, perfection and oneness. That is a rule that has not yet anywhere found its right conditions for even beginning its effort, for it can only come when man's attempt to reach and abide by the law of the spiritual existence is no longer an exceptional aim for individuals or else degraded in its more general aspiration to the form of a popular religion, but is recognised and followed out as the imperative need of his being and its true and right attainment the necessity of the next step in the evolution of the race. (338)

If the social and political life were outside this order, then the entire scheme of India's existence would collapse, for here as elsewhere it is to be remembered that "the whole basis of the Indian mind is its spiritual and inward turn, its propensity to seek the things of the spirit and the inner being first and foremost" (366). From this standpoint it sees "all else as secondary, dependent, to be handled and determined in the light of the higher knowledge and as an expression, a preliminary or field or aid or at least a pendent to the deeper spiritual aim" (366). Briefly stated, the pervading tendency of India is "to create whatever it had to create first on the inner plane and afterwards in its other aspects" (366). If this holds true in the other cultural areas of art and literature, it holds true even more forcefully in the vital order of human society, whether local, national or global.

This public and social, national and global structuring of human existence was Aurobindo's constant concern. He had himself engaged in revolutionary political activity for several years. In reaction to this experience he became increasingly aware that an interior change must be effected in humanity before a satisfactory human community could be established. Attraction to personal gain in economics, to prestige in the social order, to power in the political order—these were all too overwhelming to be resisted until motivations were sufficiently elevated. Aurobindo recognized that society was not soon to enter into a new mode of communal consciousness such that the setting aside of individual gain for the community on any of these levels would be looked upon as wisdom rather than folly, as commonsense rather than vain idealism, as the true source of power rather than of weakness for the individual, the nation and the human community.

Much more could be written on this point and the urgent manner in which Aurobindo experienced this night of India in its social functioning and its political institutions. If the night of India was so dark, it was largely because the structures of a former period had grown ineffective and sterile from within while from without India was feeling the modern compulsion to establish economic, social and political structures on the model of Western democratic and socialist states.

External Influences on Cultural Development

After these remembrances of past grandeur of India and the needed reassessment in the light of the present, there remained for discussion two issues of utmost concern in the practical order of establishing the new age for India. The first concerned the sources of renewal in India: was renewal to be solely out of the isolated heritage of India, or should outside influences, especially Western influences, be admitted? The second question concerned the final assessment of what the future held for India. Dealing first with Western influences on the renewal of Indian cultural activity, we should note that Aurobindo rejects the proposition that the renewal can come solely out of India. Whatever the situation of the past, India cannot live apart from the larger human community. The renewal must be "a powerful new creation in all fields." To preserve and nourish her own life India must confront "this raw, new, aggressive, powerful world with fresh diviner creations of her own spirit, cast in the mould of her own spiritual ideals" (385). Aurobindo is fully aware that in taking over cultural influences from without, India cannot take over merely the good things and leave out the bad things. If anything were taken over, "the good and the bad in it will

come in together pell-mell" (388). If India were to accept "that
terrible, monstrous and compelling thing, that giant Asuric creation,
European industrialism," then "we shall get too its social discords
and moral plagues and cruel problems." He did not see how, in that
event, the Indian people could avoid "becoming the slaves of the
economic aim in life and losing the spiritual principle of our culture"
(388). Aurobindo was not so naïve as to consider it possible to be
in touch with the basic trends of the Western world without being
confronted with the terrifying evils that accompany these trends.
But once such stupendous movements were introduced into the
human community, a confrontation with these forces had to be
made by each nation of the world. The one final support, the only
final support, was to establish such a strong cultural identity and such
an enduring core of spiritual vitality in the culture that it could
confront these enormous forces and grow stronger in the struggle,
assimilate the valuable aspects of things they offered while casting
off the deadly element they carried with them, much as a healthy
person who lives in the midst of contagion throws off the organisms
carrying the disease.

The human community is such that no nation can live in peaceful
isolation. This leads to a weakening of the organism from within
because of the lack of the challenge needed to evoke its inner forces.
External destructive forces must be transformed into envigorating
forces. This is the manner in which the future of India must be
shaped. All past history teaches the same basic truth: when different
cultural traditions meet, their most significant creativity is released
in the period of dissolution and reestablishment within the new
horizons that appear precisely at this moment when life and death
hang in the balance. The peril itself evokes the deeper resources of
the culture. This, in the case of modern India, is a terrifying experience, for of all major civilizations India seems to be the one least
prepared for such transformation. Yet Aurobindo claims that only
India, of all the Eurasian cultures, has the spiritual resources needed
to guide the ultimate transformation process needed to produce a
fully satisfactory future for man. If India is to be transformed by the
presence of the modern world, the modern world is also to be
transformed by the presence of India. The future world and the
future India must both emerge together out of the darkness in which
both presently exist. As he remarks concerning the people of India,
we cannot be ourselves alone in any "narrow formal sense, because
we must necessarily take account of the modern world around us and
get full knowledge of it, otherwise we cannot live" (393). Such a

transformation will require a type of courage and a type of intelligence which are more than human, more even than is contained within the Indian tradition itself. It will require a type of courage and a type of intelligence that can only be granted by that universal divine presence which is guiding the higher destinies of mankind at this time, and which surely will not abandon either India or the world at such a critical moment.

Renaissance of India

Throughout these essays Aurobindo concedes that India in modern times is in a period of transition, a period when the life process that accomplished so much in the past is no longer active in the ancient ways. He also states quite clearly the need for radical renewal, renewal in the deepest realms of man's being. This alone, he insists, could provide a satisfactory mode of existence for India either now or in the future. This renewal must be rooted in the ancient identity that India had established for itself in primordial times. India's heritage had within it an inexhaustible power for renewal if only it were properly understood and permitted to express itself in the new forms demanded in this new age. From the very beginning this series of essays has been concerned with establishing the identity of India in those most distinctive qualities that differentiate India as the unique culture and civilization that it is. Finally he has insisted that the fate of India is bound up with the fate of the world, while the fate of the world is in some ultimate sense bound up with the fate of India. He has expounded these basic propositions in many of his works, but perhaps nowhere so forcefully as in *The Human Cycle,* and particularly in the last of the essays collected in *The Foundations of Indian Culture,* "The Renaissance in India." The very word "renaissance" rings such a lengthy sequence of resonances across the historical expanse of the human community that hardly any word is more familiar to the culture historian. To "renew" is part of the daily cycle of nature as well as of man; it is as typical of a people as of an individual. But there are moments in the course of history when there occurs a transformation of such dimensions that not even this word "renaissance" seems to convey what is happening or the violence with which the transformation is taking place. These are the great historical convulsions. Aurobindo was trying to face this question of transformation in its most massive scale. It is this massiveness of his concern, the absoluteness of his vision and the comprehensiveness of his approach that overwhelm the reader—not only the ordinary educated reader, but even the scholar whose research has revealed to him only a portion of historical India and who, perhaps, has never thought seriously on the questions with which Aurobindo is concerned. Thus the scholar is hardly better prepared than the ordinary reader to understand the dimensions of Aurobindo's thought or to feel comfortable within his horizons.

Man's contemporary experience of a total human transformation through a convulsive process reminds a person of Augustine and his age and the manner in which he responded to the catastrophic events taking place throughout the Mediterranean world in his time, especially when Rome was burned in 410 A.D. Throughout these centuries of invasion by less civilized forces from eastern Europe and central Asia, the peoples of the western Roman empire considered that the world was threatened with a dissolution from which mankind might never recover. Augustine faced this issue and expressed a vision of hope in his work *The City of God*, a composition that sustained the whole of western Christendom throughout the intervening centuries until the rise of a strengthened and fully formed western Christian civilization in the twelfth and thirteenth centuries. So now with Aurobindo a threatening force was invading the realms of the human that formerly had been occupied by the spiritual insight, experience and divine presence which formerly gave meaning to the whole of existence. This raw destructive force rising out of the West and spreading over the world was imperiling the entire human venture. It is in response to this terror and in the hope of structuring a more worthy future that Aurobindo did his work. The only future adequate for the occasion was a divine future, a future in which the entire human community would participate in a higher experience that was soon to make itself felt out of the pervading darkness that was settling over the earth. Both Augustine and Sri Aurobindo were dominantly concerned with a positive response to the issue. There is no indication that Aurobindo will, in influence or insight, equal the significance of Augustine in the historical process, but the basic pattern has many similarities and insofar as it is possible to present some type of Augustinian figure arising in these times, we can say that Aurobindo represents at least one of the possibilities in Asia, as Teilhard de Chardin represents one of the possibilities in the West. In all three cases there is at least an awareness of the heroic dimensions of the human and the need to function on heroic scale. Thus Aurobindo recalls the days of heroic spiritual personalities capable of proclaiming a spiritual message in unspiritual times. Sri Aurobindo well expressed the need for courage on the heroic scale: "Without heroism man cannot grow into the Godhead."[2] In each of these instances there is an unwillingness to seek mere accommodation or to find a solution that will enable man simply to survive a critical period; rather, there is a throwing back of a challenge and the projection of a vast creative vision that is intended to guide mankind into a new historical period and which is to be realized by heroic human effort assisted by those divine forces that function in a special manner in such crucial moments.

The greatest theme in all the writings of Aurobindo is that of the Shakti principle. Here he aligns himself with the larger Indian tradition in a direct fashion, for this Shakti principle, which functions in the thought of India as the Tao in China or as the Holy Spirit in the Christian world, is the deepest organizing principle of things, the ultimate ruler of history and of human destinies, as well as the ultimate inspiration in those massive cultural creations that sustains humanity in his higher modes of being, both as individual and as a global human community. The cultural mission of India as seen within this ultimate horizon involves a forceful response to those modern influences which have both destructive and creative aspects:

> India must defend herself by reshaping her cultural forms to express more powerfully, intimately and perfectly her ancient ideal. Her aggression must lead the waves of the light thus liberated in triumphant self-expanding rounds all over the world which it once possessed or at least enlightened in far-off ages. An appearance of conflict must be admitted for a time, for as long as the attack of an opposite culture continues. But since it will be in effect an assistance to all the best that is emerging from the advanced thought of the Occident, it will culminate in the beginning of a concert on a higher plane and a preparation of oneness. (12)

Just how this "concert on a higher plane" will be experienced by mankind is beyond the power of Aurobindo to deal with, although he struggled with this subject in *Savitri*. Yet an intimation that such a concert must exist and somehow ultimately be realized seemed to him a necessary conviction to enable man to survive the historical realities of the present while bringing forth the energies needed for building the world of the future.

2. From *The Human Cycle*, ibid., p. 156.

THREE

The Vision of the Purushottama in

ESSAYS ON THE GITA

by Thomas J. Hopkins

I hold it therefore of small importance to extract from the Gita its exact metaphysical connotation as it was understood by the men of the time,—even if that were accurately possible. That it is not possible, is shown by the divergence of the original commentaries which have been and are still being written upon it; for they all agree in each disagreeing with all the others, each finds in the Gita its own system of metaphysics and trend of religious thought. Nor will even the most painstaking and disinterested scholarship and the most luminous theories of the historical development of Indian philosophy save us from inevitable error. But what we can do with profit is to seek in the Gita for the actual living truths it contains, apart from their metaphysical form, to extract from it what can help us or the world at large and to put it in the most natural and vital form and expression we can find that will be suitable to the mentality and helpful to the spiritual needs of our present-day humanity. No doubt, in this attempt we may mix a good deal of error born of our own individuality and of the ideas in which we live, as did greater men before us, but if we steep ourselves in the spirit of this great Scripture and, above all, if we have tried to live in that spirit, we may be sure of finding in it as much real truth as we are capable of receiving as well as the spiritual influence and actual help that, personally, we were intended to derive from it. And that is after all what Scriptures were written to give; the rest is academical disputation or theological dogma.

—Essays on the Gita

Introduction

The BHAGAVAD GITA is without question one of the world's great religious texts, and Sri Aurobindo one of the great religious teachers. *Essays on the Gita* is the interaction of the two, doubly rewarding as one of the most comprehensive commentaries on the Gita and one of the clearest and most revealing of Sri Aurobindo's writings. The combination does, however, present certain problems for the reader.

Sri Aurobindo assumes that the reader knows or has before him the text of the Gita as he reads the *Essays,* that he is familiar with the epic background of the Gita, and that he has some knowledge of other interpretations of the Gita's teachings. The *Essays* is, moreover, not only a commentary on the Gita but an integral part of Sri Aurobindo's intellectual and spiritual biography. Biographical analysis is beyond the scope of this introduction, but the influence of personal experiences can be inferred from a summary of events leading up to publication of the *Essays* in 1916–1920. As they did for Aurobindo himself, these events serve as a bridge between Aurobindo's life and the teachings of the Gita.

THE BIOGRAPHICAL CONTEXT OF *ESSAYS ON THE GITA*

Sri Aurobindo, born in India (1872) but educated in England (1879–1893), was a proponent of Indian independence even before he returned to India in 1893. He promoted the cause of Indian nationalism actively beginning in 1893, first in writing but increasingly through direct political involvement. His strong statements in support of complete independence and his association with revolutionaries led to his arrest in 1908 on a charge of conspiracy. He was kept in solitary confinement for a year in the Alipore jail in Calcutta while British officials carried out a prolonged investigation and trial of Aurobindo and his accused co-conspirators. Much of his time during this year of enforced retirement was spent reading and rereading the Gita, learning its inner meaning and deriving from it new levels of spiritual practice.

Sri Aurobindo had started yoga practice on his own as early as

1904, but in January of 1908 he received formal instruction for several days from Vishnu Bhasker Lele, a Maharashtrian yogi. Lele taught him the technique of quieting the mind and removing all extraneous thoughts, leading to the experience of oneness with the ineffable unchanging Brahman. A few months later Aurobindo was in Alipore jail with all the time he needed to perfect his yoga. Practicing his yogic disciplines and reading the Gita, Aurobindo began to have intense religious experiences in which he perceived in all his surroundings the presence of the Lord as Narayana, Vasudeva or Krishna. From the experience of impersonal Being he had moved to a new stage of awareness of the personal Lord in all things and all persons, confirming on an experiential level the teachings of the Gita.

The conspiracy trial ended in 1909 with Aurobindo's acquittal. He could then have returned to work in the nationalist cause, but his experiences in Alipore jail had given him a new spiritual awareness. Soon after his release he began a new journal, *Karmayogin*, dedicated to "the growth of national life and the development of the soul of the nation." Its early issues reflected Aurobindo's new orientation and included his translations of the Isha, Kena and Katha Upanishads in addition to essays on education, art and politics.

The new journal was short-lived, however, for less than a year later, when Sri Aurobindo was again threatened by arrest, he decided to leave Calcutta. After a month and a half in hiding he left for what was to be his permanent home, the French territory of Pondicherry south of Madras. There he spent his first four years in relative isolation and silence, exploring the realities revealed in his increasingly intense yoga practice. The silence was finally broken in 1914 with the launching of yet another journal, *Arya*, in which the mature results of his discoveries were set forth in monthly installments.

The first issue of *Arya* was published on August 15, 1914, Sri Aurobindo's forty-second birthday. Three major works were started simultaneously in this issue: *The Life Divine, The Synthesis of Yoga* and *The Secret of the Veda*. Successive chapters of *The Life Divine* and *The Synthesis of Yoga* appeared monthly until *Arya* ceased publication in 1921. A fourth major series was started in the second issue with Aurobindo's commentary on the Isha Upanishad and was continued with a commentary on the Kena Upanishad in 1915–16. This series was completed in the July issue of 1916 along with *The Secret of the Veda;* in the following issue Aurobindo began his *Essays on the Gita*.

The series of essays on the Gita appeared originally in forty-eight successive issues of *Arya*, from August 1916 until July 1920. They benefited greatly from Aurobindo's previous work on the Vedic hymns and Upanishads and the two years he had already spent on *The Life Divine* and *The Synthesis of Yoga*. The completed *Essays* is in every sense a mature work, drawing not only on Aurobindo's earlier studies and writings but also on his political activity, his experiences with yoga, and his growing vision of human potential. The Gita had sustained Aurobindo through his year in Alipore jail; more than reading and thinking about it, he had lived by it and learned where it could lead him. All of this experience, refined by years of spiritual development, he poured into his commentary on the Gita.

The Gita and its message had far more than personal significance for Sri Aurobindo. The "guns of August" were booming and England was at war when the first issue of *Arya* was published. By the time the *Essays on the Gita* appeared, the war had become a world war and Indian troops were in the field to support the British cause. By the time the series ended in 1920, Gandhi was leading the Indian National Congress in a policy of noncooperation with British rule. The nationalist movement had split into rival factions on a variety of political and social issues, with frequent appeal to the authority of the Gita in support of quite different programs and policies.

Sri Aurobindo was keenly aware of the contemporary issues. The opening sections of the *Essays*, especially Chapters Five and Six, "Kurukshetra" and "Man and the Battle of Life," are a brilliant discourse on the realities of strife and conflict in human affairs, applicable alike to the problems of war and the struggle for national independence. Though he had retired from active politics, Aurobindo did not denounce worldly activity or even the destruction of warfare; rather, like the Gita itself, he sought to place them—and those involved in them—in the proper perspective. *Essays on the Gita* is an answer to the problems and confusions of the time, drawing on the timeless wisdom of Gita. The relevance of this answer is clear when we look at the background of the Gita and the problem of human decision it sets forth.

THE NARRATIVE SETTING OF THE GITA

The Gita first appeared in the Indian tradition as part of a great encyclopedic epic poem, the Mahabharata.[1] The present text of the Mahabharata is the product of centuries of gradual addition of new material to an original core. The dates of both the original epic and its supplements are a matter of controversy, but it seems clear that the Gita is relatively late and was probably inserted into the existing text somewhere between 200 B.C. and 100 A.D.[2]

The main story line of the Mahabharata traces the rivalry between two groups of cousins for control of the family kingdom of Hastinapura. The protagonists are descendants of the original ruler of Hastinapura, King Bharata, from whom the family name, Bharata, and the title of the Maha ("Great") Bharata epic are derived. The story centers on a time when the kingdom had passed down to two brothers, Dhritarashtra and Pandu. The normal succession of kingship was confused because Dhritarashtra, the elder brother, was blind and could not legally rule. Pandu thus ruled in his place, and it was expected that the kingship would pass from him to his five sons, the Pandavas: Yudhishthira, Bhima, Arjuna, Nakula and Sahadeva.

Succession was further confused, however, when Pandu died before his eldest son, Yudhishthira, was old enough to take the throne. The Pandavas became wards of their uncle, Dhritarashtra, who raised them at court with his own eldest son, Duryodhana, and Duryodhana's ninety-nine younger brothers. Bitter rivalry developed between the Pandavas and Dhritarashtra's sons during their years of training in the strategems of warfare and the martial arts. Duryodhana, hoping to win the throne for himself, played on his father's conflict between love for his son and duty to his dead brother.

1. The Mahabharata contains over 70,000 verses in eighteen books or Parvans. The 700 verses of the Gita make up chapters 23–40 of the sixth of these books, the Bhisma Parvan.

2. Most scholars agree that the oldest positions of the epic date from at least as early as 400 B.C. and that most of the later portions were added before the first or second century A.D. The major portion of the Mahabharata can thus be placed after the early Upanishads (800–500 B.C.) and before the formulation of the classical philosophical *sutras* (aphoristic teachings) that marked the rise of specific schools of technical philosophy from the first century A.D. onward. This chronology places the later portions of the Mahabharata in the period during which Buddhists and Jains were developing their monastic orders and advocating retirement from active involvement in worldly life, a fact of some significance in understanding the thrust of the Gita's teachings.

Various attempts to remove the Pandavas completely were unsuccessful, but Dhritarashtra was persuaded to divide the kingdom in half and give the better portion to his son. Even with this disadvantage, however, the Pandava kingdom flourished. Yudhishthira became the greatest of the world's rulers, and Duryodhana was even further consumed by jealousy.

Determined to win by any means, Duryodhana challenged Yudhishthira to a gambling match with their respective kingdoms as stakes. Yudhishthira, giving in to his major weakness, gambled and lost. The Pandavas were forced into exile for thirteen years but with the promise that, if they met certain conditions during that period, they would receive back their half of the kingdom. The conditions were met, but Duryodhana refused to keep the promise even under the threat of war.

All efforts to negotiate failed. The rival sides each gathered together an enormous army of allies for a final showdown pitting Dhritarashtra's sons and their teachers Bhishma and Drona against the Pandavas and their friend Krishna, a king of the Yadavas who agreed to serve as Arjuna's charioteer. The armies assembled in two mighty opposing lines on the field of Kurukshetra, poised and eager for battle. Conches, drums, horns and the roars of the warriors signaled their impatience to begin. At this critical moment Arjuna, greatest of the Pandava warriors, rides to the forefront of the battle-line with his charioteer Krishna and begins the discourse known as the Bhagavad Gita.

> "Faced with this battle," he asks, "what is my duty?
> Should I fight or not fight?"

THE RELIGIOUS BACKGROUND OF THE GITA

Insertion of the Gita into the epic narrative at this point is dramatically effective, but it is not a part of the original account. Throughout the rest of the Mahabharata, both before and after the Gita, Krishna is a human figure: a prince and ruler of the Yadava tribe, a friend and counsel to the Pandavas, and the brother of Subhadra, one of Arjuna's several wives. In the Gita he is transformed into a divine teacher who reveals himself to Arjuna as the

Lord of the Universe. He is Brahman, the cosmic Absolute; he is Vishnu, the creator and preserver of the world; he is world-destroying Time who consumes all creatures. This is neither the language nor the concepts of the older epic, but an assertion of the new theism that informs so much of the teaching material added to the Mahabharata in its later stages.

We can roughly trace the process by which the Mahabharata was shaped into its final form. The earliest additions to the epic were mainly priestly homilies inserted into the structure of the story to elaborate points of moral and religious duty and reinforce priestly authority. The epic was ideal for this purpose. Since it was not a Vedic text, it was accessible to those who had not been initiated into Vedic study and were excluded from Vedic knowledge. The popular appeal of the epic gave the added material widespread circulation and served as a primary means of educating the masses and, since doctrines associated with the gods and heroes of the epic had greater authority than those from more mundane sources, the teachings presented in this way were not only more widely distributed but more readily accepted than they otherwise might have been.

The same reasons applied with even greater force to the teachings of the new theistic sects that arose from the second century B.C. Their deities were not the great Vedic gods, but popular deities such as Siva, Vishnu and Vasudeva-Krishna. Their doctrines and practices were substantially different from those of the Vedic tradition, and they had no preexisting body of authoritative texts to support their position. The Mahabharata, with its established authority and eclectic character, was ready-made for their use. Use it they did. Others had already added large quantities of material to the early epic, but the theistic sects did more than add new material: they appropriated the Mahabharata as their own. Existing portions were revised to conform to their teachings, and hundreds of chapters of sectarian teachings were inserted into the narrative. In the final stages of this process the Mahabharata became primarily a didactic vehicle for the worshipers of Vishnu in his various forms. One of these forms was Krishna, in whose behalf the Gita was first set down.

The Gita stands at the dramatic center of the epic, between the years of developing conflict and the carnage of the Pandavas' final bloodstained victory, providing a moment of clarity in which Krishna gives Arjuna a new understanding of his life and a new commitment to action in the impending battle. The authority of the Gita is in no way compromised by recognizing that it is a later addition to the narrative, that it arises out of a particular set of historical circumstances and that its purpose is to synthesize a variety of existing religious and philosophical positions into a new vision of the truth. Its authority rests rather on the truth of its vision, the adequacy of its synthesis and its capacity to illumine those who turn to it for guidance. In the time and place in which it first appeared it met the needs of those who sought a higher truth, but those who set it down believed also that it contained truth for all men in all times and places. How far this belief was justified can be seen only when we look at the Gita's teachings: the problems it poses, the answers it provides and the truths that later commentators found in it.

The Teachings of the Gita

The Gita is a deceptively complex text. The basic format is simple: a conversation between Arjuna and his charioteer, Krishna, on the problem of Arjuna's duty as a warrior. It begins and ends with Krishna's insistence that Arjuna's duty is to fight, that he must enter the impending battle with full confidence in the rightness of his action. Between the first and last statements of this position, however, the full range of Indian religion and metaphysics has been brought into the discussion, Krishna is revealed as the Lord of the Universe and Arjuna is not so much persuaded as transformed by a vision of the truth far beyond anything he imagined at the outset. The problem of understanding the Gita is thus initially a problem of recognizing the issues, following the developing stages of the discussion and noting the changes that occur as the conversation moves from one level of understanding to the next.

THE STRUCTURE AND APPROACH OF THE GITA

The basic questions posed in the Gita derive from its place in the Mahabharata narrative. The Gita, as Sri Aurobindo notes in the *Essays*, must be seen as "an episode in an epic history of nations and their wars and men and their deeds"; it "arises out of a critical moment in the soul of one of its leading personages face to face with the crowning action of his life, a work terrible, violent and sanguinary, at the point when he must either recoil from it altogether or carry it through to its inexorable completion" (9). The ethical and philosophical arguments in the Gita are not presented abstractly, but arise directly from the epic setting. The moral crisis which begins the discourse is brought on by the battle of Kurukshetra, and this context is seldom lost sight of:

> The author has not only taken pains to interweave his work inextricably into the vaste web of the larger poem, but is careful again and again to remind us of the situation from which the teaching has arisen; he returns to it prominently, not only at the end, but in the middle of his profoundest philosophical disquisitions. We must accept the insistence of the author and give its full importance to this recurrent preoccupation of the Teacher and the disciple. The teaching of the Gita must therefore be regarded not merely in the light of a general spiritual philosophy or ethical doctrine, but as bearing upon a practical crisis in the application of ethics and spirituality to human life. (9)

The questions and problems dealt with do not remain the same throughout, however. Arjuna's perception changes as Krishna leads him to new levels of awareness. Arjuna has little initial understanding of the issues he has raised. Seeing only the surface of the problem, he seeks a practical answer to what he perceives as a question of social duty. To see more than this, to gain the knowledge that will free him from his dilemma, he must become aware of the greater reality within which he and his problem exist as only passing phenomena. Krishna leads him to this awareness by progressive stages of instruction, moving from basic principles to a final vision of the truth that will release Arjuna to act in freedom.

Krishna's teachings contain a number of interwoven elements and themes. The progressive *revelation* to Arjuna begins with basic distinctions and gradually moves toward an overwhelming vision of Krishna as the highest reality of the universe, the Purushottama— the Supreme Self or Supreme Person—beyond the personal Lord and the impersonal Absolute, underlying all phenomena and pervading all creatures with his essence. Paralleling this is a progressive *synthesis* of existing religious and philosophical systems into an all-encompassing world view centered on the Purushottama, a synthesis that reinterprets and absorbs the Vedic sacrificial tradition, Upanishadic speculation about the Self and Brahman, priestly principles of social and ritual duty, asceticism and popular theistic beliefs and practices.

Running through both these progressive developments is what is often seen as the main thematic structure of the Gita, a description of the three yogas or disciplines—action, knowledge and devotion —by means of which the final goal of salvation can be obtained. All of these strands intersect, combine and are further refined in the course of the Gita's expositions, making the final text extremely rich and exceptionally open to multiple interpretation. Almost all of the major concepts in the Gita are multifaceted, emerging with altered meaning and significance at each new stage of the teaching; each is the nexus of a complex set of relationships that involves all the rest. To understand the Gita and follow its development we must be aware of this built-in multivalence and note the shifting patterns as Krishna's teaching unfolds.

An effort will be made in the sections that follow to identify some of the major issues and indicate the progressive stages of the Gita's development of these issues. The discussion will focus on the text of the Gita itself, with no attempt for the moment to bring in Aurobindo's position. These sections will serve as a guide to the issues Aurobindo discusses, and references will be made to the relevant portions of the *Essays*, but as far as possible the summary presented here will be neutral with regard to the various existing commentaries. Only in the final section will we look at the major alternative explanations of the Gita's teachings and deal directly with Aurobindo's interpretation.

ARJUNA'S DILEMMA

The Bhagavad Gita, "The Song of the Lord," begins with Arjuna's dilemma: to fight or not to fight. Arjuna is no novice to warfare at this point in the epic. He is the foremost of the Pandavas in military skills, renowned as a great archer and fierce fighter. His problem is neither inexperience nor lack of courage, but the special circumstances of the battle of Kurukshetra. Arrayed before him in the opposing army are numerous relatives and friends and his former teachers Bhishma and Drona. If he goes into battle and kills them, he can acquire only sin as a result. Slaying one's kinsmen destroys both the family and its dharma; lawlessness then prevails, and the end result is social and moral chaos. Would it not be better to let himself be killed than to kill even his wicked cousins for the sake of a mere kingdom?

Krishna's initial reply to Arjuna is on the same level, the level of social convention and family duty. If Arjuna is so concerned about dharma, he says, he should look to the proper performance of his own dharma, the duties of a warrior born to a family of warriors and kings. Arjuna's dejection in the face of battle, his disgraceful unmanliness and faintheartedness, are themselves a lawless rejection of the duty that is his.

But, Arjuna replies, Bhishma and Drona also are in the opposing army. If I should slay them, my victor's spoils would be soaked in the blood of these revered teachers. Would it not be better to withdraw from the struggle entirely and live as a world-renouncing mendicant, free of the results of such an action? Are wealth and worldly power worth such a price? I don't know whether it would be better for us to conquer them or them to conquer us. "My own nature overpowered by weakness of spirit, my mind confused about dharma, I beg you: tell me for certain what is best" (11.7).[3]

Arjuna adds to this plea the formal statement and request of one who chooses a preceptor: "I am your disciple; teach me, who am seeking refuge in you" (11.7). Without waiting for a response, however, he reaffirms his paralysis of will: "I do not see anything that will remove the sorrow that dries up my powers. . . . I will not fight" (11.8–9). He poses to Krishna the problem of how to bring his weakly committed student to the level of understanding he must have to act with wisdom. He poses also another problem lightly touched on here but repeated throughout the Gita: why must one act at all? In a world in which performance of social duties often has bad or at best ambiguous results, is it not better to retire from the world and avoid the consequences of action altogether?[4]

3. Translations from the Gita are mine unless otherwise indicated. Translations consulted include S. Radhakrishnan, *The Bhagavadgita* (London: George Allen and Unwin, 1967); Eliot Deutsch, *The Bhagavad Gita* (New York: Holt, Rinehart and Winston, 1968); Swami Vireswarananda, *Srimad-Bhagavad-Gita with the Gloss of Sridhara Swami* (Madras: Sri Ramakrishna Math, 1964); and Franklin Edgerton, *The Bhagavad Gita* (Cambridge: Harvard University Press, 1944). The Sanskrit text is in the Radhakrishnan and Edgerton editions in transliterated form and in the Vireswaranada edition in Devanagari script.
4. Aurobindo deals with the implications of this teacher-disciple relationship in Chapters Two and Three of the First Series of the *Essays* ("The Divine Teacher" and "The Human Disciple"). Chapters Five and Six ("Kurukshetra" and "Man and the Battle of Life") are a discourse on war and destruction in human affairs as a setting for Arjuna's dilemma in the face of battle. Chapter Seven ("The Creed of the Aryan Fighter"), pp. 52–55, deals with Arjuna's argument against fighting and Krishna's initial response.

THE WISDOM OF SANKHYA

Krishna does not respond directly to Arjuna's arguments at this point. Instead, once Arjuna has accepted him as his teacher, he shifts the discussion immediately to a new level. Arjuna's failure of will has been brought on by concern over those whom he might kill. This anxiety, Krishna says, is misplaced; he "mourns for those who should not be mourned." "There was never a time when I did not exist, nor you, nor these rulers of men; nor will there ever be a time when we shall cease to exist. As the embodied [soul] passes through childhood, youth and old age in this body, so [when this body dies] it passes to *another* body. The sage is not confused by this. . . . He who thinks that this [embodied soul] is a slayer, and he who thinks it is slain, both fail to understand; it neither slays nor is slain. It is not born, nor does it die, nor, having come to be, does it cease to be; unborn, eternal, and permanent, this primeval embodied one is *not* slain when the body is slain. . . . It is called unmanifest, unthinkable and unchangeable; knowing it as such, you should not mourn" (11.-11–12, 19–20, 24).

This, Krishna says, is the wisdom of Sankhya. As used here and elsewhere in the Gita, the term "Sankhya" refers primarily to intellectual or analytic discrimination, especially discrimination between the eternal nonmaterial soul on the one hand and the body and the rest of the material world on the other. This distinction is for the Gita the prime form of Jnana, "knowledge," so much so that the terms Sankhya and Jnana are often used interchangeably. Sankhya implies more than just this basic distinction, however, for the distinction itself is based on a comprehensive world view which separates reality into two fundamental principles, called Purusha ("soul" or "consciousness") and Prakriti ("matter" or "unconscious energy"). The Gita does not accept these dualistic principles as the ultimate realities of the universe, as does the later philosophical school known as Sankhya. It does, however, presuppose the polarity of Purusha and Prakriti in its assertion of the absolute distinction between the soul and the body, and it assumes throughout the Sankhya description of the phenomenal world as an evolute of Prakriti.

Purusha, the male principle of pure consciousness in the Sankhya world view, is eternally undifferentiated, is not subject to change or alteration and does not participate in any action. This principle is sometimes referred to in the Gita as the Purusha, sometimes as "the embodied" or "the self" (Atman), always in clear distinction from the body and the material world. The body, the material world, all the phenomena that constitute the nonself: these belong to Prakriti. Prakriti, the dynamic feminine principle, is primordial Nature, the creative energy source from which the entire world of changing phenomena has evolved. Purusha is eternally immutable, but Prakriti is capable of infinite differentiation and manifestation. The agents and substance of this manifestation are the three *gunas* ("strands" or "qualities") which constitute her inner nature: *sattva*, *rajas*, and *tamas*. Activated by Prakriti's creative impulse, the gunas differentiate themselves. They evolve out of the unformed primal energy of Prakriti, combining with each other in varying ways to produce the diversity of natural phenomena.

The gunas represent a spectrum of qualities that can be variously defined in physical, psychological or moral terms. Sattva is purity, whiteness, equilibrium, intelligence, goodness; rajas is turbulence, redness, dynamism, emotion, passion; tamas is inertia, darkness, lethargy, ignorance, dullness. All of the phenomena of nature, from the most subtle levels of the intellect to the grossest forms of matter, are made up of special combinations of these three factors. In the evolution from Prakriti the finest products are the first to evolve. The highest evolute is the Buddhi, "intellect," "will," "intelligent will," from which evolves the *ahamkara*, the "I-factor," the principle of egoism. Next comes *manas*, the "thought organ" or "mind," which mediates between the higher principles and the lower sense organs and organs of action that follow. Last to be formed are the subtle and gross elements of matter. It is important to note in this structure that the mental or intellectual faculties—the mind, the ego, the intellect and will—are among the products of the three gunas that have evolved from Prakriti; they are indeed the most refined of these products, but nevertheless belong entirely to the material world. This is essential to an understanding of the next portion of Krishna's teaching when he turns from "the wisdom of Sankhya" to a discussion of the problem of human action.

KARMA YOGA

The "wisdom of Sankhya" is characterized by intellectual awareness or knowledge, specifically knowledge of the total distinction
between self and nonself. It is this position which the Gita later
refers to as jnana yoga, "the yoga of knowledge for men of discrimination [Sankhyas, 'those who follow the Sankhya method of intellectual discrimination']" (111.3). This is the first of the Gita's three
ways to salvation, but the yoga of knowledge as initially defined
seems to imply withdrawal from activity in the world. The Gita
therefore sets alongside it a second yoga, karma yoga, "the yoga of
works [Karma] for men of action [yogins, 'those who follow the yoga
method of disciplined action']" (111.3). This yoga of works, which
Krishna first describes in 11.39–72, assumes the Sankhya distinction
between the self and the nonself and with it the Sankhya view of
evolution from Prakriti. The emphasis, however, is on the implications of this for human action. The goal of Sankhya is knowledge,
but the goal of "the wisdom of yoga" is release from the bondage
of action (11.39).[6]

It is not action itself which Krishna wants to eliminate, but the
bondage of action that leads to continuing rebirth. Bondage and
rebirth are not caused by actions per se but by attachment to the
fruits of action, attachment to the enjoyment, power and wealth that
may be gained or lost by actions. The attempt to abstain from action
and works is not the solution to bondage, for they are not its cause;
the solution is a purified Buddhi ("intelligent will") that eliminates
the attachment that brings rebirth. "You have a right to action
alone, not to its fruits," Krishna says.

"There should be no motivation for the fruits of action, nor should
there be attachment to inaction. Abiding in yoga, abandoning attachment, do your work with an even mind in success and failure alike,
for evenness of mind is called yoga. Action is far inferior to Buddhi
yoga, the yoga of the intelligent will, so seek refuge in the Buddhi;
those whose motive is fruits are pitiful. One who has disciplined his
Buddhi leaves behind in this world both good and evil deeds; strive

6. Sankhya and yoga are discussed at length in Chapters Eight and Nine ("Sankhya
and Yoga" and "Sankhya, Yoga and Vedanta"), a diversion "into the arid tracts
of metaphysical dogma," as Aurobindo puts it, as a necessary background for the
Gita's discussion of yoga that begins with 11.39. Chapter Ten ("The Yoga of the
Intelligent Will") then deals with 11.39–72.

therefore for yoga, for yoga is skill in works. Abandoning the fruits born of action, the wise, having disciplined their Buddhis, are freed from the bondage of birth and reach the state that is free from sorrow" (11.47–51).

Arjuna is overwhelmed by the subtleties involved in Krishna's analysis of his dilemma. He is still not sure what he should do, and Krishna's description of yoga creates new uncertainties. His puzzlement is focused on an apparent inconsistency in what Krishna has said. The "wisdom of Sankhya" is characterized by knowledge of the distinction between self and nonself. Yoga also depends upon this distinction, for Krishna has told him to be "free from the three gunas and from duality, abiding always in purity, not caring for possessions but possessed of his self [Atman]" (11.45). Since Krishna has said that the means to this perfected state is a Buddhi disciplined and free from desire, and has stated explicitly that "action is far inferior to the discipline of the Buddhi" (11.49), why then does he insist on action and urge Arjuna on to the most terrible works of all in the impending battle? (111.1).

Krishna's reply is a comprehensive discussion of karma yoga, "the yoga of action" appropriate for men of action. Although Krishna distinguishes this yoga from "the yoga of knowledge for men of discrimination," he immediately makes clear that there is in fact no alternative to action in the world; complete inaction is not a real possibility.

"A person does not attain freedom from [the bondage of] action by not undertaking works, nor does he attain perfection even by renouncing them, for no one can remain a non-actor even for a moment; everyone is made to act helplessly by the gunas born of Prakriti. A deluded person who sits restraining his organs of action while he reminisces on the objects of the senses—he is called a hypocrite. But he who engages his organs of action in the yoga of action, controlling his senses with his mind and remaining unattached—he excels. Do the work prescribed for you, for action is better than inaction; even the maintenance of your body is not possible without action" (111.4–8).[7]

To live in the world is to be engaged in action, for without action there is no existence. One might argue that cessation of existence through inaction is a valid means to the goal of release, but Krishna

7. See *Essays*, pp. 98–103, for a discussion of these verses.

warns against those deluded people who try to gain freedom or
perfection merely by rejecting or renouncing action, thinking that
inaction involves nothing more than controlling the organs of action.
He has stated earlier (11.51) that those who attain freedom from
sorrow and rebirth are those wise persons who have disciplined their
Buddhis and abandoned the fruit born of their actions. He now
reaffirms this by contrasting the deluded with those who excel, those
who, unattached, engage in action while controlling their senses
with their minds.

Bondage is not caused by the organs of action but by attachment
to the fruits of their works, and this is a matter not of the organs
of action themselves but of the mind and the Buddhi, the intelligent
will. If the mind and Buddhi are properly disciplined there is no
attachment to fruits and thus no bondage even if the organs of
actions are engaged in work—provided this work is one's allotted
work (111.8), work in accordance with the yoga of action (111.7).
The wise person, the one who excels, does not act at random; though
unaffected by the results of his actions, he does what he ought to
do. The Gita thus comes back again to Arjuna's initial question:
what *is* my duty, my dharma, the action that I ought to do?

ACTION, KNOWLEDGE AND SACRIFICE

Krishna answers this postponed question with an extended discussion of action as sacrifice. "This world," he says, "is in bondage to
action other than that done for the purpose of sacrifice; therefore,
free from attachment, perform action for that purpose" (111.9).
Sacrifice *(yajna)* was created so that humanity might nourish the
gods, and the gods in turn nourish the earth and its creatures. One
who only takes the benefits of the world without giving back sacrifice
in return is a thief (111.12); one who does not help here to turn the
wheel thus set in motion is evil and sensual and lives in vain (111.16).
"But the man who would have delight in the Self (Atman) alone,
be pleased with the Self, and be satisfied only in the Self—for him
there is no work that *must* be done, there is no personal motive in
what *has* been done or in what *has not* been done, nor is he
dependent on all these creatures for any purpose; therefore always
without attachment do the work that must be done, for a person
attains to the highest doing work without attachment. King Janaka

and others attained perfection by means of action alone; so should you also act, having in view only the maintenance of the world" (III.17–21).[8]

This statement provides the essential rationale for the yoga of action and serves also as a basic link with other parts of the Gita's teaching. The earlier Vedic tradition viewed the fire sacrifice as the source of creative power by which the universe was brought forth and maintained. The sacrificial plot and the ritual fires of the sacrifice were a microcosmic model of the universe, a parallel ritual universe by means of which man could establish contact with the powers of the macrocosm. The sacrifice was made effective by a combination of knowledge and action: the knowledge contained in the structure and hymns of the ritual established the essential links between the sacrifice and the cosmos; ritual action, karma, properly performed in accordance with prescribed duties, brought about the desired results.

The Vedic concern for both knowledge and action in the sacrificial ritual gave rise to two parallel lines of development. Speculation about the underlying reality of the sacrifice led to speculation about the nature of the universe and finally to the problem of man's place in the universe. This development culminated in the final group of Vedic texts, the Upanishads, in which the dominant interest is the search for right knowledge. The need to define right action in the sacrifice led to a parallel elaboration of the concept of karma. As the search for knowledge moved from the sacrifice to the problem of man in the cosmos, so concern for proper action was expanded to include the problem of man in society. New texts called Dharma Shastras were produced to provide guidance in the performance of domestic and social duties as well as ritual duties *per se*, extending the concept of proper action, or dharma, to all aspects of life.

The two developments were to some extent in conflict. The Upanishads emphasized the identity of the inner self of man, his Atman, with the Reality that underlies the cosmos. This Reality, Brahman, is universal Being, undifferentiated consciousness; the Atman, identical with Brahman, is thus in its own true nature other

8. The concept of action performed as sacrifice for the maintenance of the world is extremely important in Aurobindo's understanding of the Gita. Chapters Eleven, Twelve and Thirteen all deal with this concept and its implications: "Works and Sacrifice," on III.1–9; "The Significance of Sacrifice," on III.10–20 and IV. 22–35; and "The Lord of the Sacrifice," a summary statement on the Gita's doctrine of sacrifice.

than and independent of the phenomena of the manifest world. Though the Atman resides in the body, it is in essence free of the body. Embodiment is brought about by ignorance of the true nature of the self and a resulting desire for individual phenomenal existence, which leads in turn to actions that perpetuate the embodied condition in an endless round of rebirths. Release from ignorance and desire and thus from rebirth can come only through knowledge of the self and its identity with Brahman. Since it is knowledge alone that brings release, the wise should direct their attention to the attainment of knowledge. Action belongs to the body and the phenomenal world; it is of interest only to the extent that one must know how to free one's self from the bondage of action. Ultimately the one who has Jnana, true knowledge, becomes free of the effects of actions. Knowledge and action thus stand in final opposition; one is the goal and the other the barrier to the goal.

The Dharma Shastras agreed with the Upanishadic view that the final goal of life was to attain knowledge of Brahman and the self, and thus achieve release from the bondage of rebirth. Their perspective was quite different, however, for their main concern was the maintenance of society and their emphasis was thus on karma and dharma: the actions that man ought to perform in carrying out their respective social duties. Their approach was to divide society into classes *(varnas)* and human lives into stages *(ashramas)*, and to assign duties appropriate to each. Thus the Brahmins, the priestly class, had the basic duties of teaching Vedic knowledge and performing rituals for the rest of society; Kshatriyas, the warriors and rulers, had the duty of protecting society by bearing arms and fighting; Vaishyas were assigned the duties of trade, cultivation of the land, and raising cattle; Shudras, the lowest of the four classes, had the basic duty of serving the other three classes. Only if all classes carried out their duties could the welfare and order of society be preserved.

As a reflection of this concern, the most important stages of life for the Dharma Shastras were studentship and life as a householder. Members of the three upper classes were initiated into Vedic study and spent the early portion of their lives studying Vedic texts and rituals. They were then expected to marry and become householders, raise a family and fulfill their obligations to society. Householdership especially was seen as the foundation of the social order. Only after this essential stage in life was completed could a person retire from life in the world and become a "forest dweller" or *sannyāsin* (a "renounced person"), abandoning all social and family ties to concentrate on the attainment of desirelessness and knowledge. Thus, though the Dharma Shastras recognized the Upanishadic ideal of renunciation as an acceptable goal, they placed renunciation or sannyasinhood at the end of one's career when all social duties had been completed.

The conflicts between knowledge and action, renunciation and duty, lie in the background of the Gita's discussion of alternatives. Arjuna's concern over his proper dharma arises from a conflict of principles: would it not be better to renounce actions than to act and incur the consequence of bad karma? The emphasis on Jnana in the Sankhya doctrines and in the yoga of knowledge implies a goal of renunciation and inactivity once the distinction between self and nonself is realized. Krishna on the other hand urges Arjuna to fight regardless of the outcome, to fulfill his duties as a warrior. We must recognize the existence of these issues if we are to appreciate Krishna's elaboration of the concept of sacrifice as a way to reconcile apparently conflicting views.

SACRIFICE, DUTY AND RENUNCIATION OF THE FRUITS OF ACTION

The earlier Vedic tradition had viewed the sacrifice (yajna) as a model of the universe, a ritually defined space where cosmic realities and powers were manifested on earth. The performance of yajna was the duty of trained priests whose specialized knowledge and correct actions channeled these powers and made the sacrifice effective. Even after society as a whole was ritualized in the Dharma Shastras, the offering of sacrifices was still seen as a separate ritual activity, one among the many duties to be performed by members of the three upper classes. Krishna's teaching is a further and final step in the expansion of the ritual principle to society, but one which at the same time transforms the Vedic meaning of sacrifice and ritual action. The whole cosmos, he says, is a sacrifice, and all actions are ritual actions. There is one all-inclusive structure of reality, one encompassing cosmic sacrifice, in which all beings are ritual participants. Participation is not a matter of special privilege or special obligation; all beings by the fact of their existence are involved in the ongoing universal sacrifice that constitutes and maintains the manifested world. The question is not *whether* one participates, but *why* and *how* he performs the duties he is given.

The only valid reason for action, Krishna says, is the maintenance of the world. If one performs actions in hope of personal gain, then one is bound by attachment to the fruits of these actions. To be free of this bondage one must act not for oneself and not for the rewards that action may bring; he must act for the sake of the world, without attachment, offering his actions as a sacrifice. "Even I," Krishna continues, "for whom there is nothing whatsoever in the three worlds that *must* be done, nor anything to be gained that must be gained—even I am engaged in work. For if ever I were not un-wearied in action, men would follow my path. If I were not to perform work, these worlds would perish and I would be the cause of confusion; I would ruin these people. As the ignorant engage in action with attachment, so the wise, wishing to maintain the world order, should act without attachment. A person with knowledge should not bring about confusion in the minds of those without knowledge who are attached to work; disciplined and performing work himself, he should make all work attractive. Actions are per-formed entirely by the gunas of Prakriti, but he who is deluded by eogism thinks, 'I am the doer.' Now he who knows the truth of the separation from both actions and the gunas, knowing that the gunas act only on the gunas, he is not attached. But he who knows the whole should not unsettle those slow-witted ones who know only a part—those who, deluded by the gunas of Prakriti, are attached to the actions of the gunas" (111.22–29).

The knowledge that frees one from bondage is the knowledge that the self is totally separate from the gunas and that action involves the gunas only. One whose intellect and will have been transformed by this knowledge has nothing to gain by action, for he knows that both action and its fruits belong to Prakriti. And yet even the Lord himself works in the world; is the enlightened person to reject such a model? And if he acts on this example, if he accepts the call to work for the welfare of the world, what is he to do? How is he to act? Krishna now turns to this question, reconciling in his answer the concepts of duty, sacrifice and renunciation.

Krishna has told Arjuna earlier that he should act while renounc-ing the fruits of his actions and that he should perform his actions as a sacrifice. He now moves the teaching to a higher stage by revealing himself as the one to whom renunciation and sacrifice should be given. "Renouncing [*sannyāsa*] all actions to me, with your consciousness fixed on the highest Self, free from desire and egoism, your affliction gone—fight! . . . Even one who has knowledge acts in accordance with his own nature [Prakriti]. Beings follow nature. What can restraint accomplish? Attraction and repulsion with regard to sense objects are both established in the senses; one should not come under their control, for they are his enemies. One's own dharma, though imperfect, is better than another's dharma well performed. Better death in one's own dharma; the dharma of someone else is dangerous" (111.30, 33–35).

The enlightened person, Krishna says in these verses, does not hunt for a course of action. His past actions have brought him to his present birth and given him his present nature; his own duty, his swadharma, is in conformity to that nature. If he tries to follow someone else's dharma he must go against his own nature, motivated by attraction and repulsion of the senses. Seeking another set of duties is no solution, for it involves him in yet another bondage to action. He should instead free himself from Prakriti by renouncing his actions to the Lord. Free from egoistic desire and anger, he should surrender the performance of his swadharma to the gunas of Prakriti. What ought to be done will be done in accord with the tendencies of his own nature when once his Buddhi is fixed on the higher Self instead of being led astray by the ego, mind and senses.

We can see here a major step in the Gita's solution to the conflict between karma and jnana in the earlier Upanishadic and Dharma Shastra traditions. These do not for the Gita present contradictory demands that must be resolved by an either/or choice or by an emphasis first on performance of duties and then on pursuit of knowledge as a sannyasin who has renounced all worldly dharma. Properly understood, karma and jnana are not only compatible but complementary. The solution is found first in the Sankhya distinction between the self and Prakriti. The yogin disciplined by the yoga of action realizes the freedom of the self by purifying his Buddhi through meditation. Controlling the ego, mind and senses with his Buddhi, with his self centered on the immutable cosmic Self, he attains the state of equanimity and union with the Self that is the goal of knowledge. Attainment of this goal does not, however, require cessation of works or renunciation of one's dharma. True renunciation, true sannyasa, is the renunciation of the fruits of action while acting in accord with one's dharma; it is works performed as a sacrifice and not to satisfy desire; it is, in the ultimate view, renouncing all actions to the Lord, renouncing all claim to personal agency of actions in the knowledge that all actions are performed by the gunas of Prakriti.

BHAKTI YOGA

The Gita's synthesis of knowledge and action in sacrifice, the first solution to Arjuna's dilemma, is substantially completed by the end of Chapter III. The third major component of the final synthesis, devotion to the Lord, is so far suggested only in Krishna's references to his work for the preservation of the world (111.22–24) and his instruction to Arjuna to renounce all actions to him (111.30). A new level of teaching begins in Chapter IV with Krishna's revelation of himself as a divine Avatar, "The Lord of all beings" born into the world "for the protection of the good, the destruction of the wicked, and the establishment of dharma" (IV.6–8).[9] From this point on, the highest sacrifice is seen to be sacrifice to the Lord in devotion, uniting knowledge and action with elements of popular theistic religion in an increasingly more comprehensive teaching.

The Gita's teaching about the Lord and devotion proceeds by a series of steps in which, as in the first three chapters, the synthesis is expanded and elaborated to include more and more elements. These steps are arranged—no doubt quite consciously—in blocks of three chapters each, beginning with Krishna's revelation of himself as a divine Avatar in Chapter IV. The balance of Chapter IV and Chapters V and VI are a more detailed reworking of issues developed in the first three chapters, with emphasis on the problems of action and inaction,[10] knowledge and the renunciation of the fruits of action,[11] and yoga.[12] The role of the Lord is developed most fully in the last of these chapters, in a discussion of who is the best yogin.[13]

"That person is both a *sannyāsin* and a yogin," Krishna says, "who does the work that should be done without concern for the fruits of

9. Sri Aurobindo devotes chapters Fourteen through Eighteen to a discussion of Avatarhood and the principle of divine action: "The Principle of Divine Works," on 111.20–26; "The Possibility and Purpose of Avatarhood," on IV.5–15; two summary chapters on "The Process of Avatarhood" and "The Divine Birth and Divine Works," and "The Divine Worker" on IV.15–22, V.3–13 and V.21. The attention given to these issues is a measure of their importance for his interpretation of the Gita.

10. See *Essays*, Chapter Nineteen, "Equality."

11. See *Essays*, Chapters Twenty through Twenty-two, "Equality and Knowledge," "The Determinism of Nature" and "Beyond the Modes of Nature."

12. See *Essays*, Chapters Twenty-three and Twenty-four, "Nirvana and Works in the World" and "The Gist of the Karmayoga."

13. See *Essays*, Chapter Twenty-three, "Nirvana and Works in the World," on V.21–29 and VI.1–47.

action, not he who gives up his sacred fire and performs no rituals. Know, O Arjuna, that what they call 'renunciation' is yoga, for no one who has not renounced personal desire becomes a yogin" (VI.1–2). How then does one become a yogin, what does he do? Krishna stresses the need to conquer the self by the Self, and describes the process of meditation which should be followed. The process is the one made familiar in the classical yoga system, but the end result is one which reflects again the Gita's synthetic purpose. "With the self calmed, free from fear and firm in the vow of celibacy, let him sit controlling his mind with his thoughts on me, absorbed in me. Thus disciplining himself at all times, the yogin of subdued mind attains to peace, the supreme Nirvana that abides in me" (VI.14–15). Such a yogin "sees me everywhere and sees all in me, . . . worships me abiding in all things, exists in me" (VI.30–31).

The goal of yoga practice is thus the perpetual consciousness of the Lord, and the greatest yogin the one who has this consciousness. Of all the paths and all the yogas, the highest is the one that leads to devotion. "The yogin is greater than those who practice austerities [*tapas*], he is considered greater even than those who have knowledge and those who perform ritual actions; therefore, be a yogin. And of all yogins, the one full of faith who is devoted to me, with his inner self abiding in me, he is considered by me to be the most disciplined" (VI.46–47).

Having now brought together renunciation, yoga, knowledge and devotion, Krishna turns in the next three chapters to the world order and the metaphysical principles of Sankhya and the Upanishadic Brahman.[14] In Chapter VII he describes his twofold nature consisting of Prakriti and "the life-soul by which this world is supported," declaring himself to be both the origin and dissolution of the world. The whole universe, he says, is strung on him like jewels on a string, and all beings are from him alone, although—deluded by the gunas

14. Sri Aurobindo's commentary on VII.1–14, "The Two Natures," is Chapter One of *Essays on the Gita, Second Series*, originally published as a separate volume but now bound together with the First Series in the standard edition. The twenty-four chapters of the Second Series are divided into two sections: Part One (Chapters One through Twelve), "The Synthesis of Works, Love and Knowledge," which covers Chapters VII through XII of the Gita; and Part Two (Chapters Thirteen through Twenty-four), "The Supreme Secret," on the Gita XIII through XVIII. In contrast to the First Series, the verses covered in each chapter are identified in footnotes to help the reader orient himself to the commentary.

of Prakriti—they do not recognize him as being higher than the gunas and imperishable. His divine creative power (Māyā) consisting of the gunas is hard to pass beyond, but "those who resort to me alone, they cross beyond it." The foolish think of him only in terms of the manifest, not knowing his higher nature, which is unmanifest, immutable, unborn and imperishable; but those who are free of the delusion caused by desire and hatred worship him alone as the highest goal.

The Sankhya principles are then related to various Upanishadic principles in Chapter VIII, where Krishna identifies his unmanifest and imperishable nature with Brahman, "what the knowers of the Veda speak of as the Imperishable [Akshara]" (VIII.11). Those who attain this highest state are not reborn. This highest state alone is free from the cycle of rebirth and the even greater cycle of creation and dissolution of the universe. All manifestations, the whole multitude of beings, come forth from the unmanifest (i.e., Prakriti) at the time of creation and are again destroyed at the end of the world cycle. But beyond this unmanifest that is the source of creation and dissolution is a higher reality, the Akshara. "This Akshara they speak of as the highest goal, having attained which they do not return. That is my supreme abode. This is the Supreme Spirit [Purusha], in whom all beings abide and by whom all this is pervaded; it is attainable by unswerving devotion" (VIII. 21–22).

The discussion developed in these two chapters is completed in Chapter IX. Krishna here declares himself to be the supervisor of Prakriti who, taking hold of Prakriti, sends forth again and again this multitude of beings. His Self, however, while bringing forth and supporting all beings, is free of the effects of this activity: "These actions do not bind me; I am seated as one who is indifferent, unattached to these actions" (IX.9). This, he says, is his divine yoga. The foolish see only the outward forms of his manifestation; those who know him as the imperishable source of all beings worship him with undeviating mind, honoring him with devotion. Devotion is here unambiguously stated as the means by which even those excluded from Vedic knowledge can reach the highest goal; it is the means for all, whether women, Shudras, Brahmins or kings. The final instruction is clear: "Fix your mind on me, be devoted to me, perform sacrifice to me, honor me; thus having disciplined thyself and having me as your goal, you shall come to me" (IX.34).

THE VISION OF THE PURUSHOTTAMA

The Lord has so far been identified as Brahman, to whom all knowledge and sacrifices are directed, and as the Supreme Spirit, the Akshara, master of creative Māyā and supervisor of Prakriti, who has brought forth all of creation by his Yogic powers. The next section, Chapters X–XII, describes the manifestations of the Lord and his revelation to Arjuna of his Universal Form, concluding with a long description in Chapter XII of the yoga of devotion. The final stage in the Gita's metaphysics, however, comes in Chapter XV in what Krishna calls "the most secret doctrine," the doctrine of the Purushottama, or Supreme Spirit.

"There are," Krishna says, "two spirits in this world, the Perishable [Kshara] and the Imperishable [Atshara]. The Perishable is all beings [i.e., Prakriti], and what is unchanging [i.e., Brahman, the Self, the Purusha] is called Imperishable. But there is another, the Highest Spirit [Purushottama] called the Supreme Self [Param-atma], who enters the three worlds and sustains them as the immutable Lord [Ishwara]. Since I transcend the Perishable and am higher even than the Imperishable, I am celebrated in the world and in the Veda as the Purushottama. He who, undeluded, knows me thus as the Purushottama—he is the knower of all and is devoted to me with all his being. Thus has this most secret doctrine been spoken by me; realizing this doctrine, one will become enlightened and will have done all his work" (XV.16–20).

The Purushottama revealed in this passage is the highest reality in the Gita's metaphysics, the final all-encompassing principle that holds together the various strands of the Gita's synthesis; it is the full revelation of the Lord as the ultimate goal of knowledge, action and devotion. And when Krishna makes the final summary of his instruction to Arjuna in Chapter XVIII, it is the Purushottama that stands behind his teaching. Having reviewed his earlier teaching, Krishna in this conclusion of his discourse tells Arjuna to "hear again my supreme word, the most secret of all. You are greatly beloved by me, therefore I will speak for your good. Fix your mind on me, be devoted to me, sacrifice to me, honor me, and you will come to me; I promise you truly, for you are dear to me. Abandoning all dharmas, come to me alone for shelter; I will release you from all sins, so be not grieved" (XVIII. 64–66).

If the Gita is read as a progressive teaching which moves from partial answers to a final comprehensive doctrine, then this "supreme word," "the most secret of all," must be taken at face value as the essential core of the Gita's position. Putting the passages in XV and XVIII together, the Gita thus says that one who knows the Lord as the Purushottama and comes to him alone for shelter attains enlightenment, completion of all his works and release from all sins: the goals of the paths of jnana, karma and bhakti respectively. There are not in the end three goals, but only one, the knowledge or vision of the Purushottama; not one path only, but all three together, lead to this result.

This is in essence the position taken by Sri Aurobindo in his *Essays*, where he argues at length for both the progressive teaching and the primacy of the Purushottama in the Gita's doctrinal scheme.[15] This is not, however, the only possible reading of the Gita. The progressive teaching is ignored or denied by many interpreters, while some opt for one or another exclusive path to a less inclusive goal. It is a tribute to the authority of the Gita that all the major interpreters accept its synthesis of paths and goals. The problem, as Aurobindo sees it, is the effort by most interpreters to limit the force of this synthesis by emphasizing one or another strand as more important or more basic than the others. This is to deny the revolutionary import of the Gita's teaching.

In Aurobindo's view, the Gita subsumes all existing goals under the final goal of the vision of the Purushottama. This is the goal of all paths together and cannot be realized until each of the paths merges with the others and knowledge, devotion and sacrifice are one. Aurobindo's argument for this view, and his responses to the major alternative interpretations, will be considered in the final section below.

Sri Aurobindo and the Gita's Interpreters

Sri Aurobindo stands in a long line of commentators on the Gita stretching back to the first known commentary more than a thousand years earlier. The Gita served a variety of needs and was drafted into service for many causes during these centuries. Since the Gita

15. See especially Chapter Twenty-four of the First Series ("The Gist of the Karmayoga"), and in the Second Series Chapter Three ("The Supreme Divine"), Chapters Seven and Eight ("The Supreme Word of the Gita" and "God in Power of Becoming") and Chapters Twenty-two through Twenty-four ("The Supreme Secret," "The Core of the Gita's Meaning," and "The Message of the Gita").

encompassed a wide range of different doctrines in its synthesis, it provided openings for many different readings that emphasized one or another of its strands as the central theme. It became as a result an authoritative text for more different schools of thought than any other Hindu scripture, with each school interpreting its teachings to support special doctrines or concerns. Any new commentator, Aurobindo no less than others, thus must indicate how his reading differs from previous interpretations. In practice this means taking into account the major commentaries which have emerged as authoritative texts in their own right.

SHANKARA'S ADVAITA INTERPRETATION

The earliest surviving commentary on the Gita is the *Gita-Bhashya* ("Gita Exposition"), written around 800 A.D. by the great monistic philosopher Shankara. The Gita by Shankara's time was already treated as a separate text independent of the Mahabharata. It had acquired an authoritative status second only to the Vedas and was too important to be ignored by anyone who wanted to establish the legitimacy of his own position. Thus, although Shankara's main purpose was to confirm the truth of the monistic philosophy of the Upanishads, he had to show that the teachings of the Gita were compatible with the larger scheme set forth in his commentaries on the major Upanishads and in his masterwork, the *Brahma-sūtra-bhāshya*, in which he presented a consistent Advaita (nondualistic) interpretation of Upanishadic teachings.

Shankara's towering status as a philosopher and religious leader gave his commentary on the Gita a unique authority that made all previous commentaries obsolete. His interpretation of the Gita, however, was heavily biased by his insistence that final release was possible only through knowledge of the pure unqualified Brahman which is the one unchanging Reality of the universe. Jnana-yoga, interpreted as union with Brahman through knowledge, was thus for Shankara the Gita's highest teaching, consistent with the teaching of the Vedic Upanishads; karma-yoga and bhakti-yoga are the Gita's lower teaching, intended for those who are not yet ready for jnana and require further purification by means of works and devotion. Bondage for Shankara was the result of ignorance and could be removed only by knowledge. Devotion is directed to a Lord with qualities, and so is incompatible with the final knowledge of the qualityless Brahman; and, since the world is the product of the illusory power of Māyā, action in the world will fall away when knowledge destroys illusion. Thus, says Shankara, though Krishna in the Gita at times teaches both devotion and action, he does so only out of compassion for those who are still enmeshed in the qualities of Māyā and require a means within their ability to guide them on the path to knowledge.

Shankara's great authority gave widespread acceptance to this interpretation of the Gita, and it has remained one of the dominant interpretations down to modern times. Aurobindo, however, is unalterably opposed to this position and criticizes it throughout the *Essays* as a limited reading of the Gita.[16] The Gita asserts to the very end, he says, that action is not only a preparation but itself the means of liberation (79). Shankara's view of Māyā as illusion is not the position of the Gita (78–79), nor does the Gita teach, as do Shankara and the Māyāvadins, that "Māyā ceases for the soul by its return to its true and eternal status as the one Self, the Brahman, and the cosmic action disappears" (79). The Gita does not teach the impersonal Godhead or Brahman as the final goal, nor does it teach that there is no object in works and no reason for sacrifice once the final goal is reached. Aurobindo well summarizes his objection to Shankara's view in the following lengthy text:

> If this were so, the Gita would lose all its meaning; for its first and central object would be defeated. But the Gita insists that the nature of the action does matter and that there is a positive sanction for continuance in works, not only that one quite negative and mechanical reason, the objectless compulsion of Nature. There is still, after the ego has been conquered, a divine Lord and enjoyer of the sacrifice, *bhoktāram yajñatapasām*, and there is still an object in the sacrifice. The impersonal Brahman is not the very last word, not the utterly highest secret of our being; for impersonal and personal, finite and infinite turn out to be only two opposite, yet concomitant aspects of a divine Being unlimited by these distinctions who is both these things at once. God is an ever unmanifest Infinite ever self-impelled to manifest himself in the finite; he is the great impersonal Person of whom all personalities are partial appearances; he is the Divine who reveals himself in the human being, the Lord seated in the heart

16. Aurobindo's objections to Shankara and Advaita philosophy appear in many of his writings. See especially *The Synthesis of Yoga* and *The Life Divine* and the essays on these works in this volume.

of man. Knowledge teaches us to see all beings in the one impersonal self, for so we are liberated from the separative ego-sense, and then through this delivering impersonality to see them in this God, *ātmani atho mayi*, "in the Self and then in Me." Our ego, our limiting personalities stand in the way of our recognizing the Divine who is in all and in whom all have their being; for, subject to personality, we see only such fragmentary aspects of Him as the finite appearances of things suffer us to seize. We have to arrive at him not through our lower personality, but through the high, infinite and impersonal part of our being, and that we find by becoming this self one in all in whose existence the whole world is comprised. This infinite containing, not excluding all finite appearances, this impersonal admitting, not rejecting all individualities and personalities, this immobile sustaining, pervading, containing, not standing apart from all the movement of Nature, is the clear mirror in which the Divine will reveal His being. Therefore, it is to the Impersonal that we have first to attain; through the cosmic deities, through the aspects of the finite alone the perfect knowledge of God cannot be totally obtained. But neither is the silent immobility of the impersonal Self, conceived as shut into itself and divorced from all that it sustains, contains and pervades, the whole all-revealing all-satisfying truth of the Divine. To see that we have to look through its silence to the Purushottama, and he in his divine greatness possesses both the Akshara and the Kshara; he is seated in the immobility, but he manifests himself in the movement and in all the action of cosmic Nature; to him even after liberation the sacrifice of works in Nature continues to be offered.

The real goal of the Yoga is then a living and self-completing union with the divine Purushottama and is not merely a self-extinguishing immergence in the impersonal Being. (124–125)

RAMANUJA'S VAISHNAVA BHAKTI INTERPRETATION

Sri Aurobindo shows somewhat more agreement with the second major classical commentary on the Gita, the *Gītā-bhāshya* written by the Vaishnava philosopher-theologian Ramanuja some 300 years after Shankara. Ramanuja, though later in time, was much closer than Shankara to the position of the worshipers of Krishna and Vishnu who produced the Gita. He was himself an ardent devotee of Vishnu and, as a leader of the South Indian Vaishnava community, was one of a long line of teachers inspired by the devotion of the great Tamil poet-saints known as the Alvars. He was, like Shankara, a Vedanta philosopher in the sense that he derived the authority for his teachings from the Upanishads, but he vehemently disagreed with the interpretation given to these texts by Shankara and his Advaita followers.

In opposition to Shankara, Ramanuja argued in his commentary on the Gita and elsewhere that the phenomenal world is real, not illusory; that individual selves are real and eternal; that the bondage of these selves is not illusory but the result of ignorance and the effects of karma; and that release comes not through knowledge of the impersonal unqualified Brahman but through knowledge of the Lord endowed with all auspicious qualitites, knowledge that has the nature of devout meditation. Bhakti-yoga is not a "lower teaching" that must give way eventually to the jnana of the Advaitins; it is the ultimate means of release. Devout meditation stemming from devotion leads to a perpetual blissful knowledge of the Lord which is both the means and the goal of release. This goal and the religious practice it entails are consistent with the metaphysical principles of the Upanishads and are the goal and means taught by Krishna throughout the Bhagavad Gita.

Sri Aurobindo's objection to this position is more moderate than his criticism of Shankara's Advaita doctrines, but he is unwilling to accept the sectarian form of Ramanuja's arguments and the insistence on bhakti yoga as the one true teaching of the Gita. The aim of the Gita, he says, "is precisely the opposite to that of the polemicist commentators who found this Scripture established as one of the three highest Vedantic authorities and attempted to turn it into a weapon of offence and defence against other schools and systems" (6).

Ramanuja and other sectarian proponents of devotion "speak of the Gita as if the doctrine of devotion were its whole teaching and put in the background its monistic elements and the high place it gives to quietistic immergence in the one self of all" (27). To do so is to ignore the great strength of the Gita's synthesis as a "harmony of the three great means and powers, Love, Knowledge and Works, through which the soul of man can directly approach and cast itself into the Eternal" (7).

> Undoubtedly its emphasis on devotion, its insistence on the aspect of the Divine as Lord and Purusha and its doctrine of the Purushottama, the Supreme Being who is superior both to the mutable Being and to the Immutable and who is what in His relation to the world we know as God, are the most striking and among the most vital elements of the Gita. Still, this Lord is the Self in whom all knowledge culminates and the Master of sacrifice to whom all works lead as well as the Lord of Love into whose being the heart of devotion

enters, and the Gita preserves a perfectly equal balance, emphasising now knowledge, now works, now devotion, but for the purposes of the immediate trend of the thought, not with any absolute separate preference of one over the others. He in whom all three meet and become one, He is the Supreme Being, the Purushottama (27).

THE GITA AS A "GOSPEL OF DUTY"

Alongside the monistic interpretation of Shankara and the sectarian devotional emphasis of Ramanuja is the more modern view of the Gita as a "Gospel of Duty." Aurobindo mentions Bankim Chandra Chatterji as the one "who first gave to the Gita this new sense" (32). The position was adopted by many advocates of political and social reform within the Indian nationalist movement to give sanction to their secular activities, and in more traditional ways both B.G. Tilak and M.K. Gandhi stressed the primary importance of karma yoga in the Gita's teaching.

The main impact of Tilak's and Gandhi's views came during and after publication of the *Essays,* so Sri Aurobindo has nothing to say directly about their interpretations.[17] His main criticism is in any case directed at those who removed the Gita's teaching on dharma from its religious and spiritual context and thus isolated karma yoga from jnana and bhakti yoga. Those who interpret the Gita in this way as a Gospel of Duty alone "have laid an almost exclusive stress on the idea of equality, on the expression *kartavyam karma,* the work that is to be done, . . . and on the phrase 'Thou hast a right to action, but none to the fruits of action' [II.47] which is now popularly quoted as the great word, *mahāvākya,* of the Gita" (32). This read-

17. B.G. Tilak's commentary on the Gita, *Bhagavadgitā-Rahasya,* or *Karma-Yoga-Śāstra,* was first published in Marathi in 1915, in Hindi in 1917, and in English in 1936. Gandhi did not publish a full-scale commentary on the Gita, but his interpretations are found throughout his published works and have been collected in a number of books on Gandhi and the Gita edited by various of his disciples: *Discourses on the Gita* (V.G. Desai), *Teachings of the Gita* (A.T. Hingorani), *Gita and Gandhiji* (R.S. Betai), and *The Gita According to Gandhi* (Mahadev Desai). Both Tilak and Gandhi view karma yoga as the central theme of the Gita in much the same way as Shankara and Ramanuja view jnana and bhakti yoga, respectively, but both preserve the entire range of the Gita's teaching. An even more balanced karma yoga position is found in Vinoba Bhave's *Talks on the Gita,* a series of chapter-by-chapter discourses to his fellow political prisoners by a disciple of Gandhi who drew also on the tradition of Jnanesvara's *Jñānésvari,* a thirteenth-century Marathi commentary on the Gita by the great Maharashtrian saint who was both an Advaitin and a devotee of Vishnu.

ing of the Gita ignores the progressive teaching and locates the primary message in the first three or four chapters, a position that Aurobindo firmly rejects:

> The rest of the eighteen chapters with their high philosophy are given a secondary importance, except indeed the great vision in the eleventh. This is natural enough for the modern mind which is, or has been till yesterday, inclined to be impatient of metaphysical subtleties and far-off spiritual seekings, eager to get to work and, like Arjuna himself, mainly concerned for a workable law of works, a *dharma.* But it is the wrong way to handle this Scripture (32).

> The tendency is to subordinate its elements of knowledge and devotion, to take advantage of its continual insistence on action and to find in it a scripture of the Karmayoga, a Light leading us on the path of action, a Gospel of Works. Undoubtedly, the Gita is a Gospel of Works, but of works which culminate in knowledge, that is, in spiritual realisation and quietude, and of works motivated by devotion, that is, a conscious surrender of one's whole self first into the hands and then into the being of the Supreme, and not at all of works as they are understood by the modern mind, not at all an action dictated by egoistic and altruistic, by personal, social, humanitarian motives, principles, ideals. Yet this is what present-day interpretations seek to make of the Gita. We are told continually by many authoritative voices that the Gita, opposing in this the ordinary ascetic and quietistic tendency of Indian thought and spirituality, proclaims with no uncertain sound the gospel of human action, the ideal of disinterested performance of social duties, nay, even, it would seem, the quite modern ideal of social service. To all this I can only reply that very patently and even on the very surface of it the Gita does nothing of the kind and that this is a modern misreading, a reading of the modern mind into an ancient book, of the present-day European or Europeanised intellect into a thoroughly antique, a thoroughly Oriental and Indian teaching. That which the Gita teaches is not a human, but a divine action, not the performance of social duties, but the abandonment of all other standards of duty or conduct for a selfless performance of the divine will working throughout nature; not social service, but the action of the Best, the God-possessed, the Master-men done impersonally for the sake of the world and as a sacrifice to Him who stands behind man and Nature. (27–28)

THE INTEGRAL VISION OF THE GITA

Sri Aurobindo clearly opposes any effort to restrict the Gita's teaching to the confines of any sectarian or dogmatic system. The

Gita's synthesis must be taken seriously as a genuine blending of previously separate strands into a final integral vision of the truth. More accurately and more literally it is the report of a vision that can lead others to realize the vision for themselves. The danger and temptation is to stop short at some prior point or become satisfied with a partial truth. This tendency must be firmly resisted; the plateaus of the teaching must not be mistaken for the peak, and the reader must move on with Arjuna to the point at which all paths merge. This point is found in Krishna's final discourse where the previous paths are reviewed and the final great word is spoken:

> What the great, the supreme word of the Gita is, its *mahāvākya*, we have not to seek; for the Gita itself declares it in its last utterance, the crowning note of the great diapason. "With the Lord in thy heart take refuge with all thy being; by His grace thou shalt attain to the supreme peace and the eternal status. So have I expounded to thee a knowledge more secret than that which is hidden. Further hear the most secret, the supreme word that I shall speak to thee. Become my-minded, devoted to Me, to Me do sacrifice and adoration; infallibly, thou shalt come to Me, for dear to Me art thou. Abandoning all laws of conduct seek refuge in Me alone. I will release thee from all sin; do not grieve." (XVIII.62–66)
>
> The argument of the Gita resolves itself into three great steps by which action rises out of the human into the divine plane leaving the bondage of the lower for the liberty of a higher law. First, by the renunciation of desire and a perfect equality works have to be done as a sacrifice by man as the doer, a sacrifice to a deity who is the supreme and only Self though by him not yet realised in his own being. This is the initial step. Secondly, not only the desire of the fruit, but the claim to be the doer of works has to be renounced in the realisation of the Self as the equal, the inactive, the immutable principle and of all works as simply the operation of universal Force, of the Nature-Soul, Prakriti, the unequal, active, mutable power. Lastly, the supreme Self has to be seen as the supreme Purusha governing this Prakriti, of whom the soul in Nature is a partial manifestation, by whom all works are directed, in a perfect transcendence, through Nature. To Him love and adoration and the sacrifice of works have to be offered; the whole being has to be surrendered to Him and the whole consciousness raised up to dwell in this divine consciousness so that the human soul may share in His divine transcendence of Nature and of His works and act in a perfect spiritual liberty.
>
> The first step is Karmayoga, the selfless sacrifice of works, and here the Gita's insistence is on action. The second is Jnanayoga, the self-realisation and knowledge of the true nature of the self and the world, and here the insistence is on knowledge; but the sacrifice of works continues and the path of Works becomes one with but does

not disappear into the path of Knowledge. The last step is Bhaktiyoga, adoration and seeking of the supreme Self as the Divine Being, and here the insistence is on devotion; but the knowledge is not subordinated, only raised, vitalised and fulfilled, and still the sacrifice of works continues; the double path becomes the triune way of knowledge, works and devotion. And the fruit of the sacrifice, the one fruit still placed before the seeker, is attained, union with the divine Being and oneness with the supreme divine Nature (34–35).

In this passage Aurobindo views the Gita in terms of the paths by which humanity moves toward God, each path merging with the next in a series of steps until all merge together in union with the divine nature. The emphasis is on human action: sacrifice of works, self-realization, adoration and seeking of the supreme Being. In his final summary, however, Aurobindo reverses this perspective and describes the Gita instead in terms of divine revelation. In the language of the Gita, this revelation is in the form of a series of secrets revealed to Arjuna to guide him on his way.

The first secret (guhyam) is described in IX.1 and XI.1 as "the secret of wisdom combined with knowledge," "the supreme secret concerning the Self." This secret, Aurobindo says, is the secret "that all spiritual knowledge reveals to us, mirrored in various teachings and justified in the soul's experience, . . . the secret of the spiritual self hidden within us of which mind and external Nature are only manifestations" (538). It is this truth that is revealed in the early chapters of the Gita, that Vedanta, Sankhya and Yoga all teach in many ways, and toward which all the different ways of yoga turn our minds and lives.

The first secret might be defined as ordinary spiritual knowledge, the knowledge of Purusha and Prakriti that leads to self-realization and renunciation of the fruits of action. The more secret thing (guhyataram), first revealed in the fifteenth chapter of the Gita, is "the profound reconciling truth of the divine Purushottama, at once self and Purusha, supreme Brahman and a sole, intimate, mysterious, ineffable Godhead" (538). This more profound knowledge "escapes from the elementary distinction of spiritual experience between the Beyond and what is here. For the Transcendent beyond the worlds is at the same time Vasudeva who is all things in all worlds; he is the Lord standing in the heart of every creature and the self of all existences and the origin and supernal meaning of everything that he has put forth in Prakriti" (538). This Lord is both the Lover and Beloved of the soul and the Master of all works and sacrifice, the object of that devotion which merges all paths and all yogas. "An inmost opening to this deeper, truer, more secret mystery" is, for Aurobindo, the essential condition for "the Gita's Yoga of integral knowledge, integral works and integral Bhakti. It is the simultaneous experience of spiritual universality and a free and perfected spiritual individuality, of an entire union with God and an entire dwelling in him as at once the frame of the world's immortality and the support and power of our liberated action in the world and the body" (539).

Yet even this is not the highest truth. The most secret thing of all *(guhyatamam)* is revealed in Krishna's final discourse in XVIII. 64–66, the "supreme word . . . that the Spirit and Godhead is an Infinite free from all Dharmas" (539). This Infinite rules the world according to fixed laws and leads man through all his dharmas: "Yet the Spirit and Godhead transcends all these things, and if we too can cast away all dependence on Dharmas, surrender ourselves to this free and eternal spirit and taking care only to keep ourselves absolutely and exclusively open to him, trust to the light and power and delight of the Divine in us, and, unafraid and ungrieving, accept only his guidance, then that is the truest, the greatest release and that brings the absolute and inevitable perfection of ourselves and nature" (539).

This is the final goal for both the Gita and Sri Aurobindo. It is a goal and a way offered only to those in whom the Lord "takes the greatest delight because they are nearest to him and most capable of oneness and of being even as he" (539). The final realization is thus a mutual effort by God and man: man moves along the paths to God, and God reveals the secrets that guide him by revealing Himself to man as Avatar and Teacher. Man must eventually go beyond the manifested Lord to the vision of the Purushottama as Infinite Being, but Being is not passive and impersonal; Being enters the world to reveal its greatest secret. Man's means of ascent is through the descent of Being as the Avatar: "the manifestation from above of that which we have to develop from below; . . . the descent of God into that divine birth of the human being into which we mortal creatures must climb; . . . the attracting divine example given by God to man in the very type and form and perfected model of our human existence" (148).

FOUR

A New Yoga for a New Age:

A Critical Introduction to

THE SYNTHESIS OF YOGA

by J. Bruce Long

All life is a secret Yoga, an obscure growth of Nature towards the discovery and fulfillment of the divine principle hidden in her which becomes progressively less obscure, more self-cons-cient and luminous, more self-possessed in the human being by the opening of all his instruments of knowledge, will, action, life to the Spirit within him and in the world.

To conquer the lures of egoistic existence in this world is our first victory over ourselves; to conquer the lure of individual happiness in heavens beyond is our second victory; to conquer the highest lure of escape from life and a self-absorbed bliss in the impersonal infinite is the last and greatest victory.

—The Synthesis of Yoga

Introduction

One of the more remarkable features of the thought of Sri Aurobindo is his conviction that the most effective way for a traditional
culture, such as India, to achieve modernity is not by divesting itself
of its rich past and adopting new forms of belief and practice willy-
nilly, but by synthesizing and "modernizing" as many of the essential elements of its ancient tradition as possible. He joins the company of such seminal figures in contemporary thought as Gandhi and
Vivekananda in India, Heidegger and Teilhard in Europe, Tillich
and Eliade in America in positing the "modernity of tradition,"[1] as
the indispensible first principle of contemporary thought. In Sri
Aurobindo's case, this paradoxical view of the relationship between
past and present is the natural expression, speaking in historical and
cultural terms, of his spiritual vision of the essential uniformity (i.e.,
nonduality) of reality at all levels.

Sri Aurobindo envisions the contemporary world as:

> a huge cauldron of Medea in which all things are being cast,
> shredded into pieces, experimented on, combined and recombined
> either to perish and provide the scattered materials of new forms or
> to emerge rejuvenated and changed for a fresh term of existence. (1)[2]

Sri Aurobindo's commitment to work toward the synthesis of yoga
worldwide rests upon a dramatically apocalyptic vision of the modern world. He is convinced that during the twentieth and twenty-
first century mankind will cross the threshold into a new world, a
creative era in the drama of cosmic evolution, the likes of which has
occurred only once before—i.e., during the period marked by the
transition from lower animal to *Homo sapiens*. The description of
his apocalyptic vision of the emerging world age is sufficiently
provocative to merit quoting in detail:

> The whole trend of modern thought and modern endeavor reveals
> itself to the observant eye as a large conscious effort of Nature in man

1. *The Modernity of Tradition* is the title of a provocative book (Chicago: University
of Chicago Press, 1967) which brings into focus the rich bulk of religious and
cultural resources which the ancient Brahminical tradition has to contribute to the
modernization of India.
2. Subsequently the page numbers appearing in parentheses within the body of the
paper are references to Sri Aurobindo's *The Synthesis of Yoga*, BCL, 20 and 21.
All citations of other works by Sri Aurobindo and other authors appear in the notes.

to prepare a sufficient basis in man's physical being and vital energies and in his material environment for his full mental possibilities. By the spread of education, by the advance of the backward races, by the elevation of depressed classes, by the multiplication of labour-saving appliances, by the movement towards ideal social and economic conditions, by the labour of Science towards an improved health, longevity and sound physique in civilised humanity, the sense and drift of this vast movement translates itself in easily intelligible signs. The right or at least the ultimate means may not always be employed, but their aim is the right preliminary aim,—a sound individual and social body and the satisfaction of the legitimate needs and demands of the material mind, sufficient ease, leisure, equal opportunity, so that the whole of mankind and no longer only the favoured race, class or individual may be free to develop the emotional and intellectual being to its full capacity. At present the material and economic aim may predominate, but always, behind, there works or there waits in reserve the higher and major impulse.(10–11)

Sri Aurobindo asserts with a characteristic boldness that traditional Indian Yoga is one of the "dynamic elements" to be employed in bringing the new world into being. But, he adds, that under existing circumstances, it is unlikely that Indian yoga in any of its existing forms can be used effectively to promote the advent of this new order. For yoga to be effective, its true power and aim must be rediscovered and reappropriated in keeping with a world view in which ancient and modern, Eastern and Western views and values can be fully integrated.

A New Yoga for a New Age

In attempting to define more precisely the novel elements in his own yoga, Aurobindo observes, "I have never said that my yoga was something brand new in all its elements. I have called it the integral yoga and that means that it takes up the essence and many processes of the old yogas—its newness is in its aim, standpoint and the totality of its method."[3] He then proceeds to present three novel elements which he believes distinguish his Yoga from previous yogas in some crucial manner. In contradistinction to the yogas of the Upanishads, Shankara and Patanjali, Aurobindo's integral yoga aims "not at a departure out of the world and life into Heaven or Nirvana, but a change of life and existence. . . . Here the object is the divine

3. *Letters on Yoga*, BCL, 28:99.

fulfillment of life;" not at "an individual achievement of divine realisation for the sake of the individual, but something to be gained for the earth-consciousness here, a cosmic, not solely a supra-cosmic achievement"; and not at a partial method of lifting man out of his involvement in the world of matter and mundane consciousness but at a "purpose which is as total and integrated as the aim set before it, viz., the total and integrated change of the consciousness and Nature." He concludes by observing that, had he found these elements embodied by already existing disciplines, he would not have expended the time and energy required to search for a newer and more adequate path to self-realization. He challenges his readers with this proclamation: "Our yoga is not a retreading of old walks but a spiritual adventure."[4]

Sri Aurobindo charges modern man in light of the pressures and potentialities of the present age to recover the ancient power and goals of yoga for two reasons. First, to recover the powers of yoga as described in ancient scripture in order to gain effective mastery over one's own self *(swarāj)* and over the social and natural realms *(samrāj)*. Secondly, to foster the discovery of a universal system of beliefs and values which will provide a context of meaning for all men, regardless of the religious and cultural conditions under which they exist. Modern man, Aurobindo asserts, faces the challenge of bringing "to the surface the profoundest reason of its [yoga's] being in that general truth and that unceasing aim of Nature which it represents and finds by virtue of this new self-knowledge and self-appreciation its own recovered and larger synthesis" (1–2).

This "larger synthesis" of thought and belief will materialize only as men find a means to overcome the dilemma which has haunted traditional Yoga in past centuries. That dilemma, succinctly stated, is: if a man searches for God, he loses life; if he seeks to conquer life, he loses God. Aurobindo offers a way of escape from this dilemma along a path which "reunite[s] God and Nature in a liberated and perfected human life or, in its method, not only permit[s] but favour[s] the harmony of our inner and outer activities and experiences in the divine consummation of both" (4). What is required, then, is nothing less than a complete and uncompromising synthesis of all yogas toward the final aim of realizing a single, all-encompassing discipline of life and thought.

4. *Ibid.*, p. 101.

Sri Aurobindo's Interpretation of Traditional Yogas

One feature of Sri Aurobindo's writings which must strike the attention of any thoughtful reader is the thoroughly Indian outlook which they manifest. Despite the unmistakably universal scope of his message, it seems to this writer, when reading Aurobindo's writings, that he is eavesdropping on a multivolume monologue which a most sophisticated and articulate contemporary Hindu is addressing to his fellow Hindus.

Keeping in mind, therefore, the thoroughly Hindu nature of Aurobindo's world view, idiom and styles of expression, we turn now to a brief consideration of his views of traditional Hindu yogas. We will adopt this approach to his thought as an heuristic device for defining more precisely his conception of Integral Yoga as it is related to these traditional psychophysiological disciplines. We will review in rapid succession the following yogas: hatha, raja, karma, jnana and bhakti.

HATHA YOGA

The aim of hatha yoga is the complete mastery of the physical and psychic powers in man. This aim is accomplished by expanding and rendering more flexible the powers of the physical and vital modes of life in order that the practitioner may accommodate a greater "inpouring" of vital, psychic, intellectual and spiritual energies from the realm of the overmind (583). Purification of the intellect and the elevation of the mind into the sphere of intuitive knowledge must be preceded by a purification and a tempering of the physical frame and the sensual instruments. By the performance of various standardized postures *(āsanas)*, the nervous restlessness of mind, body and senses is stabilized and tranquilized; the channels which conduct the energies from the "Ocean of Life" are cleared of all pollutants and weaknesses and all systems are readied for proper respiration. The exercise of *prāṇāyāma*, or control of the breath, performs a twofold task: First, it completes the conditioning of the body by purifying the mind-body organism of all physical and psychical contaminants. Second, it quickens to life the so-called serpent-power, the "pranic dynamism in the vital sheath" opening the entire being of the practitioner to dimensions of experience and activity denied to persons existing in a "normal," undisciplined condition. The psychical and physical powers lying in state of dormancy at the deepest reaches of a person's being, gradually will be provoked into moving through higher and higher centers *(cakras)* of mind and body and, in turn, will awaken "the forces of each successive nodus of our being, the nervous life, the heart of emotion and ordinary mentality, the speech, sight, will, the higher knowledge, till through and above the brain it meets with and it becomes one with the divine consciousness" (583).

The immediate and short-range result of these practices is an increase in the vitality, health and ebullience of the physical and sensual instruments and an intensification of the enjoyment of life in the physical dimension. The limitations of this yoga, if pursued as an end in itself, is that in the long-term a person will expend these newly acquired powers of health, vigor and longevity on the satisfaction of self-indulgent physical pleasures. If such powers are not directed toward a higher level of mental and spiritual development, they will ultimately dry up and dissipate from lack of support by a deeper and broader realm of spirituality.[5]

RAJA YOGA

Raja yoga utilizes the stabilized, pacified and strengthened faculties of the body and the senses for the purpose of perfecting the mental *(citta)* and ultimately the spiritual *(ātmika)* faculties. The primary instrument in raja yoga is the mind in the form of our ordinary faculty of thought. The energies of the intensely vitalized physical forms are brought to a peak of preparedness for the purpose of ordering and stabilizing the mind and heart (583–584). Operating from within this newly stabilized and purified state of body, mind and heart, all the varied powers of a person's being are concentrated

---

5. Elsewhere Aurobindo says, "The physical body is therefore a basis of action, *pratiṣṭhā*, which cannot be despised, neglected or excluded from the spiritual evolution: a perfection of the body as the outer instrument of a complete divine living on earth will necessarily be a part of the gnostic conversion" (668). Cf. "Perfection of the Body," in Sri Aurobindo, *The Mind of Light*, ed. Robert A. McDermott (New York: E. P. Dutton & Co., 1971), pp. 34–51.

on the concrete realization of higher and purer states of consciousness. The senses are gradually directed by the conscious mind to give
less and less attention to objects in the inner and outer worlds. In
due course, all the human faculties are routed toward a higher sphere
of awareness where one frees himself from the concerns and attachments which bind the soul *(jīva)* to the world of ignorance and
death. The ultimate goal of raja yoga, stated in traditional Indian
terms, is, on the one hand, Swarajya, self-rule or sovereignty over the
inner realm of mind and spirit where the powers of Life flow through
a limited, personalized channel, and, on the other, Samrajya, world-
mastery, "the control by the subjective consciousness of its outer
activities and environment" (32). While the goal of hatha yoga, in
part, is the realization of a state of equilibrium and stability between
the inner and outer realms of experience, the aim of raja yoga is the
complete concentration of all one's powers within. To achieve this
state, the yogin must gradually isolate himself (or rather, his *Self,* as
Absolute Spirit or Purusha) from everything that hinders the realization of Absolute psychophysiological stillness, quietude and solitude.

According to Patanjali's teachings in the *Yogasūtras*[6] "*yoga is
concentration (samādhi)*", a conscious and deliberate isolation of the
conscious mind *(citta)* or the thinking-substance *(buddhi)* from all
contacts and entanglements with objects of physical and mental
sensation and the multiplication of the bonds of karma resulting
therefrom. By the stabilization of the mind-stuff, the restriction
of all fluctuations *(vṛtti)*, by means of the removal of all hindrances
(kleśa), the mind becomes more and more centrally concentrated
(samādhi), one-pointed *(ekagraha)* and clarified *(śobhana)* of all
pollutants *(tamas)*, with the ultimate result that partial and errone-
ous knowledge *(avidyā)* gives way to true, real and changeless knowledge *(vidyā)* of the Eternal unity *(puruṣa)*. In a word, "yoga is the
stabilization of the movements of the mental-substance."

According to Aurobindo, the imperfections of this traditional
system of yoga lie in its tendency completely to isolate *(viyukta)* the
self from the world of concrete objects and ordinary experiences and
to remain aloof from the world of ordinary discourse in an ethereal
realm of blissful consciousness or complete spiritual isolation. The
two disciplines (represented by Aurobindo as forming only one facet

6. English translation: James Haughton Woods, *The Yoga-System of Patanjali, or
the Ancient Hindu Doctrine of Concentration of Mind,* Harvard Oriental Series,
(vol. 17 (Cambridge, Mass.: Harvard University Press, 1914; reprinted, Delhi:
Motilal Banarasidass, 1966), I.2.

of the total complex of integral yoga) suffer from two additional limitations. Hatha yoga makes an excessive, if not an exclusive, claim upon the person to develop the powers of the body and "lower" mind at the expense of the rest of the person. Because of the limitations of the instrument utilized in this discipline (i.e., physical and psychic qualities), if practiced as an end in itself, hatha yoga will manifest itself as being deficient in those instruments and energies necessary for higher advancement. Raja yoga suffers from an exaggerated attachment to the mind and its offspring. If the practitioner is to attain a larger, more enduring and more completely satisfying state of spiritual perfection, he must undertake the triple disciplines of works, knowledge and devotion.[7]

KARMA YOGA

The Way of Works demands that a person become a submissive instrument for the operation of the powers of the Divine Will. The karmayogin prepares himself for a life of obedience by purifying himself of all egoistic attachments to ideas of "I" and "mine." He must divest himself of the notion that he is the initiator of his deeds and the enjoyer of their fruits *(karmaphala)*. Having done so, he will be freed from the karmic effects which bind his soul to the cycle of redeath and rebirth. In due course, he becomes fully accomplished in all his actions by realizing that all his faculties—body, mind, heart and will—are nothing but a receptacle of divine powers and a medium through which Absolute Spirit works to bring the world to a state of fulfillment. Through selfless action, with both action and its fruits directed by the Eternal Absolute, the karmayogin will come to perceive "the divine in all energies, in all happenings, in all activities" and will arrive at an "unegoistic participation of the soul in the cosmic action" (35).

Even during his formative years as a young law student at Cam-

---

7. While every system of Vedanta uses the three "departures"—i.e., Upanishads, Bhagavad Gita and Brahmasutras—each Vedantin finds his interpretation of Vedanta expressed most clearly in one or another of these texts. Shankara found the basis for his "nondualistic Absolutism" in the early Upanishads and the Brahmasutras. Ramanuja seems to have had a preference for the "pantheistic theism" of the Gita, while Madhava singled out the dualistic portions of the Upanishads and the Gita as definitive. For Sri Aurobindo, the essence of integralism seems to be consumately embodied in the Gita, which itself is the kind of grand synthesis which he believes is most representative of the Eternal Truth.

bridge University, later as a teacher of English at Baroda College (1893–1905) and finally as a political prisoner in the Alipore jail in Calcutta, Aurobindo manifested in all his actions a deep commitment to a life of effective action. He discovered the ethical and spiritual basis for such a commitment in the threefold discipline of the Bhagavad Gita.[8] In one of the most moving statements in all his writings, he tells of his discovery of the principle of effective spiritual activity in the Gita:

> His strength entered into me and I was able to do the *sādhana* of the Gita. I was not only to understand intellectually but to realize what Sri Krishna demanded of Arjuna and what He demands of those who aspire to do His work, to be free from repulsion and desire, to do work for Him without the demand for fruit, to renounce self-will and become a passive and faithful instrument in His hands, to have an equal heart for high and low, friend and opponent, success and failure, yet not to do His work negligently.[9]

In strict adherence to his quest for a principle on the basis of which all spheres of reality and all the powers of the human person could be fully and naturally synthesized to form a single "ethic," Aurobindo rejected the life-negating and action-renouncing injunctions of the Vedanta of the Upanishads. Instead, he embraced the necessity to "remain in action but without attachment to the fruits of action." Throughout his writings, he reiterates the charge of Lord Krishna to Arjuna, the hero of the Pandava armies, "not by abandoning actions utterly is one freed from [bondage to] actions, nor by renunciation alone does one achieve perfection."[10] For, in the final analysis, there is no way man can avoid altogether the performance of deeds because of the fact that every phase of his bodily existence is determined by the constitutive strands *(trigunas)* born of material nature *(prākṛti)*.[11] Given man's inescapable involvement in the

---

8. Sri Aurobindo concurs with the message of the Gita that the survival of the universe and the maintenance of a harmonious operation of its instruments depends upon the perpetuation of salutary action—human and divine. In keeping with his "realistic" view of life and the world, he rejects the Vedantin and Sankhyan views that action of any nature is self-defeating. He asserts that all forms of behavior (the evil as well as the good) are forms of divine self-manifestation. In the words of another contemporary spokesman for Vedanta, "God cannot be known or experienced except through his own act" (S. Radhakrishnan, *The Principle Upanishads* [London: George Allen & Unwin, 1953], p. 53).
9. Uttarpara Speech," in *Karmayogin*, II, p. 3. Quoted in Robert A. McDermott (ed.), *The Essential Aurobindo* (New York: Schocken Books, 1973), p. 8.
10. Bhagavad Gita, III.4. The translation is mine.
11. *Ibid.*, III.5.

realm of action, it is far better that he willingly engage in life of action than that he evade action altogether. By trying to escape from the necessity *(vidhi)* to engage in action for the welfare of the world, one will contribute to the decay of his own mind and body.[12] The universe itself is established upon and maintained by means of the deeds of all human beings who are freed from attachment to their fruits. Action only, then, is man's proper task,[13] and "yoga is skill in actions."[14] All actions are proper actions (i.e., arising from ethical motivations, being executed by pure means and tending toward a worthy goal) which are performed as a sacrifice.[15] In the spirit of the "integral ethic" of the Gita, Sri Aurobindo makes a clear distinction between *kāma-karmya* (i.e. actions performed from selfish motivation), *akarman* (i.e., inaction, actionlessness) and *naiṣkarmya* (i.e., actions performed in freedom from attachment to their fruits). It is the latter ethic which resides in the region midway between self-aggrandizing action and actionlessness that Aurobindo enjoins the seeker after total integrality to follow.

BHAKTI YOGA

The Way of Devotion is the path which leads from love of self and those things which affirm and support it; to concern for other selves as they exist in organic relationship to one's self; to a wider and more enduring appreciation for all selves in the world and a deep affection for the entire created order; and finally, to a selfless devotion to God. The bhaktiyogin is a person for whom life is coeval with love and for whom a loss of love leaves in its wake a loss of the will to live. The final goal on which he expends all his energies of body, mind and heart is the achievement of a total, uncompromising devotion to God. Every available form of affective experience may be employed to foster the expansion and enrichment of his capacity for love. Even those feelings and activities which under normal circumstances are considered uncultured, if not immoral, may play a vital role in his quest for self-mastery through divine service. The bhaktiyogin aims at nothing less than the transformation of the

---

12. *Ibid.*, III.8.
13. *Ibid.*, II.47.
14. *Ibid.*, II.50.
15. *Ibid.*, III.10–16.

whole of life into a perpetual sacrifice of self for the sake of others and God. If one perseveres in his determination to identify self with God, he will gradually learn to love and obey the inner and outer dictates of the One Eternal Spirit "without being diminished or abrogated by their [differences among things] present limitations and apparent dissonances" (158).

In summary, Sri Aurobindo articulates a comprehensive and synthetic view of reality based upon Krishna's teaching in the Bhagavad Gita that the paths of works, knowledge and love are not three distinct ways but one multivalent path leading to a single goal. Perfect knowledge of God will quite naturally be expressed in complete love of and dedication to him. Pure love of God inevitably gives rise to perfect knowledge and God-centered action. And finally, unswerving surrender to the dictates of the Divine Will will spring from a deep knowledge of God's nature and law and a perfect love of his person. "It is in this triple path that we come most readily to the absolute knowledge, love and service of the One in all beings and in Its entire manifestation" (35).

In order to bring into sharper relief Aurobindo's estimation of traditional Indian yogas and the uses to which he dedicates them in defining his own yoga, we pause to make two additional observations. First, like Gautama the Buddha, he rejects the paths of radical asceticism and unlimited self-indulgence, together with the compromise between the two. The first two methods he believes offer incomplete answers to the problems of existence and produce a distorted view of Reality. The third is only a partial and ineffective antidote to the diseases of egoism, ignorance and self-deception. The first method destroys the natural evolutionary forces of life;[16] the second binds man even more irretrievably in the chains of Imperfection, and the third isolates him between heaven and earth without providing him a definite place on which to stand (616, 631). Secondly, given the fact that integral yoga views the means and the goal of man's spiritual quest within a wider perspective than that of the previous yogas, it follows quite naturally that these yogas, taken singly, can play no more than a secondary role in preparing the

---

16. He rejects the path of Spiritualism or Idealistic Monism on the basis of his conviction that "all that presents itself here in our outward nature in perverse or imperfect forms has a significance and utility which come out when we get back to the greater truth of divine being" (77; cf. 108–109, 228–229, 559–560).

disciple for the larger yoga still before him. Or, as Aurobindo remarks elsewhere, "the silence of the Ineffable is a truth of divine
being but the Word which proceeds from that silence is also a truth,
and it is this word which has to be given a body in the conscious form
of the nature" (680).

The ultimate *raison d'être* of integral yoga was previewed by both
Vedanta and Tantric yoga as "a full perfection and enjoyment of the
spiritual power, light and joy in the human existence, and . . . a
supreme experience in which liberation and cosmic action and enjoyment are unified in a final overcoming of all oppositions and dissonances" (587). Once again, however, the serious limitations of these
traditional yogas, as they developed historically, is their failure to
invest both the finite and infinite worlds with equal reality and value.
The sacred texts of both Vedanta and Tantrism posit the transcen-
dence of oppositions and union with the quintessential One as the
goal of the life process. But, in Aurobindo's judgment, these yogas,
in the end, failed to actualize the program of self-perfection which
they had proposed because of either certain imperfections in the
conceptions of these systems or failings by the practitioners to ad-
here faithfully to the dictates and goals of these other yogas. He is
confident that integral yoga will compensate for both types of
inadequacies in other disciplines by defining mankind from the
perspective of a higher truth, a wider perspective and a deeper
experience than the others. In specific terms, integral yoga views
man as

> a spirit in mind much more than a spirit in body and assumes in him
> the capacity to begin on that level, to spiritualize his being by the
> power of the mind, opening itself directly to a higher spiritual force
> and being and to perfect by that higher force so possessed and
> brought into action the whole of his nature. . . . To arrive by the
> shortest way at the largest development of spiritual power and being
> and divinise by it a liberated nature in the whole range of human
> living is our inspiring motive. (586)

As the sadhaka achieves a purer and more effective mastery of the
disciplines of mind, will, heart and body, he experiences within
himself a gradual merging of the various paths of self-cultivation in
the formation of a single, all-embracing sadhana.

> The individual Yoga then turns from its separateness and becomes
> part of a collective Yoga of the divine nature in the human race. The
> liberated individual being, united with the Divine in self and spirit,

becomes in his natural being a self-perfecting   the
perfect outflowering of the Divine in humanit

THE YOGA OF SELF-PERFEC1

According to the terms of the philosopł
world of phenomenal existence is to be regarc
tion of the devil or a self-delusion of the soul, ł
of the Divine." The realm of "names-and-i
though marred by a fault of imperfection at ᴅᵥ
(when viewed through the eye of wisdom), is found to ᴀ
forms and content through which the Divine Spirit (Purushᴀ-ᴄᴠ
Brahman) is springing into greater and greater reaches of seⁱⁱ
manifestation. The "fully realized being" *(jīvanmukta)* realizes in
the depths of his being that all psychosomatic phenomena are but
signatures of the World Spirit and, conversely, that the World Spirit
plays itself into manifold being through the various modes of psycho-
materiality (411,853).

Integralism conceives of ultimate Reality as being a composite
manifestation of Absolute Spirit by means of various simultaneous
postures. That is, the Eternal Self reveals itself, and thereby fulfills
itself, at various levels of being and activity: as transcosmic Being and
absolute freedom, outside the realm of relativity; as Infinite Consciousness pervading and supporting the sphere of relativity; and as
a multiplicity of individual beings functioning as channels of manifestation of the Absolute Spirit.

One interpreter of Sri Aurobindo's teachings has stated the kernel
of integralism as follows:

> We can afford neither to suppress material nature nor blindly to
> follow her promptings. Similarly, we can hardly afford either to ignore
> the demands of the Spirit or to be carried off by them in utter
> disregard of the elemental forces of material nature. . . . Integralism
> stresses the concept of balanced harmony between the material and
> the spiritual.[17]

---

17. H. Chaudhuri, "The Integral Philosophy of Sri Aurobindo," in H. Chaudhuri
and F. Spiegelberg (eds.), *The Integral Philosophy of Sri Aurobindo* (London:
George Allen & Unwin, 1960), pp. 29–30.

The Nature of Integral Perfection

Sri Aurobindo defines integral yoga in the most succinct terms as "the turning of one or of all powers of our human existence into a means of reaching the divine Being" (583). He criticizes all traditional forms of yoga for limiting themselves to the utilization of "one main power of being or one group of its powers," and proclaims that in integral yoga "all powers will be combined and included in the transmuting instrumentation" (583).

"A Divine perfection of the human being" and the complete spiritualization of the universe is the goal of integral yoga. The integration of each of the several powers and capacities of man (physical, vital, psychic, mental, supramental and spiritual) within himself and the unification of all the human faculties with the powers of the cosmos and ultimately with the World Spirit which energizes and supports the world, is the fundamental precondition for the mastering of this yoga.

As a means of achieving the goal of spiritual unity and with it a complete possession and enjoyment of the whole divine nature, the integral yogin will draw upon the disciplinary resources provided in piecemeal by the various traditional systems of yoga. But he will make use of the ideas and practices of each of the other disciplines in such a way that he will forge them together to form a single discipline of mind and body and thereby will avoid the limitations which attach to each of them when employed separately. After having completed the initial purification of body and mind ordinarily achieved through the practice of bodily postures *(āsanas)*, breath control *(prāṇāyāma)* and mental concentration *(samādhi)*, the sadhaka will strive to perfect his cognitive, volitional and emotional faculties by following the triple way of knowledge *(vijñāna)*, action *(karman)* and devotion *(bhakti)*. Although each discipline is cultivated by use of its own proper instrument (e.g., hatha yoga works through psychophysical faculties, raja yoga through the mental-psychic, the way of knowledge through cognitive and spiritual, etc.), in essence all the various ways are but one way and "all power is in the end one, all power is soul power."

Sri Aurobindo discovered in Indian Tantrism a system of beliefs and a method of self-cultivation which previewed and forecasted, though in imperfect and limited forms, the central ideal of integral yoga. We will follow him in appealing to Tantric yoga as a historical model of integral yoga. Tantric yoga arises out of a capacious vision

of the universe as constituted of two interrelated primal entities—
Purusha and Prakriti, Brahman and Shakti, with Spirit manifesting
itself by means of material reality or rather presenting itself in the
guise of material power. This comprehensive system of physical and
mental cultivation utilizes both hatha and raja yoga as instruments
of preparation. It employs hatha yoga for the purpose of enlarging
and strengthening the physical and neurological systems by the
opening up of the centers of power in the mind-body organism. It
pursues the path of raja yoga with its purification and expansion of
human consciousness through meditation and concentration, along
with the assistance of the tools of knowledge, action and love—as
a multifaceted means of arriving at a yoga in which all powers,
instruments, faculties and goals are fully synthesized.

But, while drawing upon the earlier yogas, Integral Yoga goes
beyond the various specific yogas by aiming for two higher goals: (1)
to assemble, concentrate and discipline all the qualities, capacities
and motive forces in man and to elevate them to a "diviner spiritual
level," and (2) to move beyond the liberation of the soul into a
wholly transcendent realm of isolated unity, to "a cosmic enjoyment
(bhukti) of the power of the Spirit."

Starting as it does from the method of Vedanta to arrive at the
goal of Tantra, integral yoga conceives of man not so much as a mind
in a body but as a spirit inhabiting and utilizing mind. Its ultimate
aim is to effect the complete spiritualization of the human being by
the power of soul in mind. The initial indication that such a stage
has been reached is the liberation of the soul from ignorance and the
limitations of its natural finite existence and the experience of a
union with the Divine Self. Tantric yoga expands the conceptions,
techniques and goals of each of the other yogas in service to a
spiritual liberation of a fuller perfection which does not develop at
the expense of the integrity of the individual being. It reports man's
spiritual quest as a progressive actualization of the power of Eternal
Divine Spirit within the here and now.

The nature of the final object of integral yoga might be clarified
by analyzing it according to its three essential objects: first, the
liberation of the individual soul and achievement of perfect union
with the Divine; second, the supreme enjoyment of the perfect
union between individual soul and the Eternal Self; third, the transmutation of the fruits of this divine union into a natural cooperative
activity with the Divine Spirit in promoting the work of the spirituality throughout the human world. What had originally taken shape

as an individual private discipline of body, mind, will and spirit, in due course, "becomes a part of the collective Yoga of the divine Nature in the human race" (587).

The human self, therefore, will progressively expand into the larger, purer and loftier realms of spiritual unity by combining the two yogas and the three instruments to form a single, multifaceted method. As the individual self (*jīva*) achieves a more complete enduring mastery of the self in its bodily vital, mental, moral and spiritual aspects, concentrated personal effort will give way gradually to the creative and salutary urgings of the Divine Spirit. As Sri Aurobindo says,

> All life is a secret Yoga, an obscure growth of Nature towards the discovery and fulfilment of the divine principle hidden in her which becomes progressively less obscure, more self-conscient and luminous, more self-possessed in the human being by the opening of all his instruments of knowledge, will, action, life to the Spirit within him and in the world. (591)

The initial gropings of the human spirit after wholeness, stability and luminosity can come to full maturity only after all faculties have been opened up to something beyond them. This is an unescapable necessity for two reasons: first, because man's total being is larger, deeper and higher than the sum of his human parts; and secondly, because only that higher and larger spiritual reality, within whose essence man himself is established, can provide the breadth of vision and the depth of perseverance necessary for the arrival at the state of full self-realization.

> To grow into the truth and power of the Spirit and by the direct action of that power to be made a fit channel of its self-expression, —a living of man in the Divine and a divine living of the Spirit in humanity—will therefore be the principle and the whole object of an integral Yoga of self-perfection. (592)

Integral Perfection as Complete Equanimity

This state of self-perfection which has just been mentioned is defined in the terms of integral yoga as complete and undisturbed equality (*samatā*). This state of equality comes into being when all signs of conflict among the various levels of human life (physical, vital, mental, etc.) between individual human beings, and between mankind and the Divine Spirit, have been dissolved.

The state of equality is defined by Aurobindo as the unambiguous sign of spiritual liberation (675). The achievement of this state of absolute stability and purity is dependent upon the experience of spiritual liberation, which in turn is dependent upon the "opening out of mortal limitation into the illimitable immortality of the Spirit" (647). The sadhaka gradually achieves a unity with Brahman by realizing the presence, power and activity of Brahman in all parts of human nature and within all spheres of the universe. By identifying one's own self with the Self in all things, one will break the chains of egotism and the delusive action of the three gunas and ultimately arrive at a state of perfect tranquility. To be equal-minded is to be equal and one with all things in spirit, mind, heart and natural consciousness.

The answer to the question as to why the achievement of an effective control over one's self (swarajya) and over the world (samrajya) is dependent upon the realization of equality is quite simply that the supreme divine nature itself which both constitutes and supports the human world, is itself established on equality.

Equality, from the viewpoint of God, is "a detachment, the calm of an equal regard, a superiority to reactions which trouble . . ." (671). From the perspective of an integrated self, equality is described as the "self-possessed and luminous works of a free spirit governing its nature and in tune with the universal being" (672–673). It is "a wise impersonality, a quiescent equality, a universality which sees all things as the manifestation of the Divine" (673). This state is expressed in the form of a willing and submissive, but not a wholly passive, instrument working toward a universal harmony. This state of perfect harmony will remain beyond man's grasp until he has perfected the initial purification of all facets of his being (bodily, vital, emotional, mental). All polluting and befuddling elements which arise from ignorance and self-delusion must be rooted out and the self must be liberated from all the ties that bind. Equality must be achieved within the vital being by unifying the body and nervous system of all powers of conflict and disturbance. Equality of the heart is accomplished by casting away all impulses of pleasure and pain, all motives of attraction and repulsion. Equality of mind is derived by transcending in the mental faculty all self-aggrandizing attachment "to intellectual preferences, judgments, opinions, imaginations," etc. which we appeal to in attempting to defend our private ideological kingdom from outside attack.

The journey of the soul to the state of equality leads along a twofold path of passive restraint and active cultivation (681). The negative or passive movement involves (1) the steeling of the *will* against all attacks of phenomenal Nature upon the body, mind and heart, so as to avoid the dual temptation of either striking back in anger or recoiling into the shell of our inner self in despair or apathetic resignation; (2) promoting an indifference of *mind* by rejecting the attraction and repulsion of all phenomena in a spirit of "disassociation and disuetude" (684); and (3) submitting the *heart* to a willing affirmation of all things and events within the phenomenal world as manifestations of the Divine Will. Simultaneous with and complementary to this movement into passive quietude, the affirmative cultivation of divine self-realization must be pursued. This movement demands a unifying knowledge that all things exist with oneself and one's self within all things, all things in God and God in all things (686–687).

The properties of the person existing in a state of perfect equality are (1) *samatā*—a freedom from all personal preferences arising out of an acceptance of the goodness of all things as expressive of the Divine Nature, (2) *śānti*—an enduring tranquility which submits to no disturbing forces whatsoever; (3) *sukham*—a spontaneous inner delight which nothing can deplete; and (4) *ānanda-līlā*—an energetic but free playfulness of the self in its affirmation of the whole of life.

As a result of the purification of the self in body, heart and mind and the liberation of all its faculties, capacities, qualities and motives from the binding forces of self-centered consciousness, the sadhaka realizes a number of benefits which will assist him in rising to yet higher levels of self-perfection. He experiences an increased capacity to accept in the spirit of love and joy all events which occur in the finite realm. In addition, he comes to possess an augmented sympathetic understanding of all people without preferential regard for their views, values or style of life. Finally, he achieves a nondiscriminatory appreciation for all states of being and consciousness, of all persons and events and of all the challenges and opportunities for spiritual growth (687).

Nature and Role of Shakti in Integral Perfection

Given the mental, moral and spiritual infirmities which remain after the sadhaka has attained the higher levels of self-cultivation, the human soul cannot transcend its present imperfect state without support and guidance from some external strength.

> To divinise the perfected nature we have to call in the divine Power of Shakti to replace our limited human energy so that this may be shaped into the image of and filled with the force of a greater infinite energy, *daivi prākṛti, bhagavatī śakti.* (666)

The Divine Shakti, the World Mother or the Consort of Absolute Spirit, is the tireless and ever-industrious energy, which pervades, undergirds and invigorates the entire cosmos. It is she whose presence and activity within the human soul becomes supremely evident once that self has become sensitized to the reality of Absolute Spirit. She provokes and directs all the yearnings, thoughts and endeavors of the finite self toward the full actualization of perfect spirituality.

Shakti is Nature (Prakriti) ensouled by Spirit (Purusha), acting by will of the Lord (Ishwara) which is her own will and whose presence in her movement she always carries with her (cf. fn., 205). Prakriti or Nature-Force standing in front and Shakti or Conscious-Force standing behind her—these inner and outer forces of the Universal Mother give rise to all activity in the universe (203–204).

In a word, the Divine Shakti at the higher and purer levels of perfection "reveals itself as the presence or potentiality of the infinite existence, consciousness, will, delight" (735). Once the way has been opened to her, she assists the self in diminishing the disruptive and misleading activity of the three gunas (rajas, tamas, sattva), stills the mind and directs it to focus its vision upon the possibilities of complete spiritual realization and ever after instills the self with the moral and spiritual energies necessary to arrive at its goal. By placing undivided faith *(śraddhā)* in the power of Shakti to liberate man from the forces of the lower nature and to bring him into fuller actualization of his higher nature, Shakti will transport the human soul into full consciousness of the Ishwara and finally, prepare the sadhaka for the purifying and elevating work of the supermind.

The Nature of the Supermind

The preliminary purification and liberation of the lower self and elevation of the entire being to the level of higher self is accomplished by two somewhat distinct but complementary processes: (1) by a purification of physical, vital and mental levels of one's nature, by stilling the mind, heart and will within a "large and luminous static equality" (755) and (2) by replacing the lower nature with the enlightened activity of the universal divine Shakti under the control of Ishwara. But unless man willingly opens himself up to the presence and guidance of an Intelligence that is "infinitely greater, more extended in knowledge, compelling in self-power, larger both in the delight of its self-existence and the delight of its active being" (757), he will be unable to rise above the state of "imperfect perfection" to which he has arrived. In order to proceed to the goal of absolute perfection, a person must make room within the mental level of his being for the entry of a supramental power.

In attempting to sketch Sri Aurobindo's conception of this supramental power, which alone possesses the capacity to transport man beyond his present level of existence, we could do no better than present a selection of his statements on the nature of supermind:

> Supermind has . . . a positive and direct and living experience of the supreme Infinite. The Absolute is beyond personality and beyond impersonality, and yet it is both the Impersonal and the supreme Person and all persons. (283)

> It [supermind] reveals Sachchidananda. It reveals the Truth behind the scattered and ill-combined suggestions of our mentality and makes each to fall into its place in the unity of the Truth behind; thus it can transform the half-light of our minds into a certain totality of light.(405)

> The supermind sees directly the spirit and essence, the face and body, the result and action, the principles and dependences of the truth as one indivisible whole and therefore can work out the circumstantial results in the power of the essential knowledge, the variations of the spirit in the light of its identities, its apparent divisions in the truth of its oneness. (761)

> The intellectual thought refines and sublimates to a rarefied abstractness; the supramental thought as it rises in its height increases to a greater spiritual concreteness. (805)

> The supramental thought . . . presents always the idea as a luminous substance of being, luminous stuff of consciousness taking significative thought form and it therefore creates no such sense of a gulf between the idea and the real as we are liable to feel in the mind, but is itself a reality, it is real-idea and the body of a reality. . . . *It is an intensely sensible vibration of being, consciousness and Ananda* [emphasis added]. (805)

The supermind manifests itself to the sadhaka who has prepared himself to receive it, according to three attributes: (1) unmediated self-knowledge by the Self in all things, a knowledge by identity and unity which grasps every object of knowledge "as itself and in itself, and not as a thing other than or divided from it . . ." (757); (2) total knowledge springing from an all-encompassing vision which sees the universality of a particular and the particularistic appearances of the universal, the Absolute in the relative and all relatives within the Absolute; and (3) direct truth-consciousness which possesses immediate, luminous and holistic knowledge of the entire universe not by "depending on indications and logical or other steps from the known to the unknown," but by direct apprehension of all things in their ontological essences.

When the supermind is summoned into action by a human soul which has prepared itself sufficiently for the final stages of the "spiritualization of all zones of being," it elevates the mental consciousness, creates a transitional intuitive mentality ("insufficient in itself but greater in power than the logical intelligence") and then elevates and transforms the intuition into "true supramental action." In this ultimate state of elevation, enlargement and purification, the lower mind and the upper mind have been merged, such that self sees the Self in all things and all things in the Self. Furthermore, "its observation must therefore be subjectively objective and much nearer to, though not the same as, the observation of our own internal movements regarded as an object of knowledge" (825). The consciousness of the supermind is cosmic in its scope and is within the Self of the Universe, which is now seen to be identical with the individual self, that all the objects of knowledge are presented as essentially constitutive of everything but conditioned by nothing.

Supramental Transformation

It might be profitable to glance once again at a succinct statement of the aims and means of integral yoga.

> All the works of the mind and intellect must be heightened and widened, then illumined, lifted into the domain of a higher Intelligence, afterwards translated into workings of a greater nonmental Intuition, then again transformed into the dynamic outpourings of the Overmind radiance, and these transfigured into the full light and sovereignty of the supramental Gnosis. (139)

In preparing a road map to guide the footsteps of the uncertain traveler, Aurobindo describes the elevation of the human intellect as occuring in four stages: (1) a steadying and calming of the mind for the achievement of quietude and spiritual freedom; (2) an opening of the mind and heart to the impulsions and initiatives of the Divine; (3) an elevation of the thoughts of the physical mind into the mind in the subtle body and, at the same time, embracing the transformative power of the Divine Essence, which descends from the realm beyond the temporal sphere; and (4) a transformation and fulfilment of the mind by first cultivating and extending the intuitive mind and then integrating it with the full range of supramental energy (771–777).

The power of intuition acts in the person whose powers of knowledge peak at the level of intellect, in a secret and covert manner. The results of intuition are often mistakenly interpreted as products of bare perception or pure ratiocination. But, in fact, intuitive experiences, though they may come in fits and starts, are reflectors of the surrounding and supporting supramental presence which exceeds the intellect in power of knowledge by far greater degree than the intellect transcends the senses.

But intuition in its various forms should not be confused with liberative or supramental knowledge *(vijñāna, prajñā)*. That absolute form of knowledge arises only after a person has transcended even the upper levels of intuitive insight and ascended to the realm of Sachchidananda (pure Being, Consciousness and Bliss). The development of the various faculties of intuition, therefore, occurs in the area between the intellectual mind and the true supramental nature (778). As Aurobindo states the matter:

> The subsequent transformation of the intellect is possible because all action of the intellect derives secretly from the supermind. . . . The transformation can be brought about by the removal of the limitation and the elimination of the distorting or perverting element . . . [but] an intervention of the supramental energy is needed that can light up and get rid of its deficiences of thought and will and feeling. (776)

The transition from the level of intellectual to intuitive knowledge of the self and the world depends upon "an intervention of the supramental energy" which has the power to "light up and get rid of [the mind's] deficiencies of thought and will and feeling" (776). At this point in the process, "the higher comes down and largely takes the place of the lower, but also the lower changes, transforms itself into material of the action and becomes part of the substance of the higher being" (781). Clues of the active presence of the supermind should be looked for in the mental or intellectual mind, for it is there that man exists in closest proximity to the Supermind.

The transformation of the intellect progresses as mental ideas (i.e., products of a mental process of fabricating "abstract notions" out of scattered fragments of sense data and memories) are replaced by *intuitive insights*. Although the product of intuition is still a mere representation, it is nonetheless "a living representation, and not an ideative symbol, a reflection that is lit up with something of the truth's real substance" (785). As intuition is of the nature of a memory, "a luminous remembering of the self-existent truth, so the inspiration is of the nature of truth hearing: it is an immediate reception of the very voice of truth, . . . of the nature of direct sight, *pratyakṣa-dṛṣṭi*" (785). As such, this knowledge is self-referential and self-validating, requiring for its confirmation no additional proof from the realm of sense experience or intellection.

Again, Aurobindo refines the conception of the development of intuitive knowledge (785 ff.) by presenting it as progressing through four distinct but interrelated stages of supramentality: (1) *Intuitive Discrimination*, analytical insight which produces critical judgments without benefit of new information; (2) *Suggestive Intuition*, synthetic insights which yield novel views and novel facts without critical judgment, (3) *Revelation of Reality* in its essential form as an "immediate presentational form," but lacking the power to broadcast this knowledge to all of its members—Form without Power of conviction and action, and (4) *Inspirational Insight*, which "delivers the fire and dynamism of the experience of the Truth, but withholds a clear, well-ordered and unambiguous vision of Reality in its unified complexity and complicated uniformity." Each of the items within each of the two pairs of levels of knowledge cooperate in providing "Clarity of Form" (nos. 1 and 3) and "Power of Expression" (nos. 2 and 4) by way of promoting the final movement from the mental into the supramental level of knowledge and being.[18]

The supermind, which is penultimate to Absolute Brahman (Sachchidananda) reverses the whole order of the thinking process (813). As a result of this movement upward and outward from the mental into the supramental sphere, two alterations of consciousness occur: first, there is a reversal of the status and function of the physical, vital and intellectual minds with that of the intuitive mind,

18. For further elaboration of the conception of the nature and function of the intuitive mind in the persual of integral perfection, consult Sri Aurobindo's *The Life Divine*, BCL, 18, and 19:919 ff.

such that the intuitive mind and supermind, which previously played
only a minor role in the formation of consciousness, now assume a
formative and pervasive role. Second, the formation of thought and
will now occurs entirely on a supramental level, producing a self-
illuminating knowledge and a self-validating volition (787–788).
From here on, the person experiences a decrease of analytical knowledge, combined with a unification of the supramental intuition,
inspiration and revelation into a single, self-referential activity pervaded and supported by an unbroken light of wisdom and a highly
concentrated store of the power of action. The human mind, which
is beginning to merge with the supermind, now begins to operate
from a different vantage point:

> It deals with life and action and knowledge like the mental will and
> reason, but not starting from matter, life and sense and their data and
> relating to them through the idea of truth of higher things. It starts
> on the contrary from the truth of self and spirit and relates to that
> through a direct spiritual experience assuming all other experiences
> as its forms and instruments the things of mind and soul and life and
> sense and matter. (791)

All sensation, thought, volition and action become pure Ananda. No
sign of a residue of sensual distortion, intellectual ignorance, volitional arrogance or behavioral immorality will remain. All human
faculties which previously were stilled and subordinated to the direc-
tives of Shakti, Purusha and the supermind now experience a total
supramentalization and spiritual transformation. This supramental
transformation alters the entire range of man's being and consciousness; it brings the total human being into a limitless reservoir of
sense, vitality, feeling, consciousness and life, which, in turn, con-
victs all the normal modes of knowledge and action of being minus-
cule and impotent by comparison.

Having destroyed all nescience arising out of the inconscience of
Nature such that everything is a unity of the "cosmic consciousness
which will be its own, the unity of being of the infinite which will
be its own being" (852), the resultant creature of supramental consciousness being and will, will recognize that the "timeless Infinite"
and "the Infinite deploying in itself and organising all things in
time" (853) are one and the same. The limitations and distortions
of mechanical causalistic reason, together with undisciplined and
unpredictable intuitive intelligence, will have been left behind. As
a result, all segments of temporality (past, present and future), all

segments of the causal process (antecedent and immediate causes
and the product) and all actualities, possibilities and imperatives
(868 ff.) will be grasped in direct and instantaneous knowledge-event
and the proper course of action will be undertaken without any
lingering element of doubt, hesitation or ineffectuality (869).

Conclusion.

In conclusion, we will pass in rapid review Sri Aurobindo's interpretation of the other yogic systems, and some of the additions and
subtractions which he feels are necessary to promote a way of life
which will be at once universally adequate and locally applicable. We
will terminate the discussion of *The Synthesis of Yoga* by presenting
what appear to be both affirmative contributions and negative weaknesses in Aurobindo's integral yoga.

Sri Aurobindo never claims that integral yoga is an absolutely
novel system of thought and practice but only that its "aim, standpoint and totality of method" are significant innovations over previous traditional disciplines. The intellectual standpoint and practical
method by which this enterprise of the total spiritualization of the
universe is to be pursued is that of unqualified Integralism. That is,
the progressive actualization within the realm of matter and Spirit
of a perfect harmony between the outer and inner spheres of life,
united in a state of wholeness and transformed by the integration
with a Power or a Being which exists both beyond and within the
human soul.

The discipline and method of integral yoga is deeper, broader and
more fully integrative than more strictly worldly enterprises such as
modern science, technology, medicine and social revolution. The
latter enterprises seek to resolve personal and collective conflicts by
altering the structures of society and all forms of interpersonal behavior as an avenue to greater justice for all individuals and vested
interest groups. Furthermore, the aims of Integral Yoga are both
more universal and more concrete in nature than those of the traditional religions, in that the latter aim for the realization of sainthood,
life after death in a perfect celestial realm or a kingdom of heaven
on earth. The aim of Integral Yoga is to stimulate and bring to the
surface of human life "a secret Yoga, an obscure growth of Nature
towards the discovery and fulfillment of the divine principle hidden
in her" (591), resulting from man's opening of his total being to the

Divine Spirit which undergirds and pervades his self and the total world. Integral yoga seeks to bring to full self-realization the omnipresent reality of spiritual being, not by leaping from this world into another, transcendent realm nor by means of self-annihilation, but by development from our present half-lighted uncertain and confused state of being, a consciousness of the universal pervasiveness of spiritual essence, which is, in fact, the essence of our human selves (595).

The goal of integral yoga is achieved not by closing down the senses and the mind and isolating the individual consciousness from all contact and involvement with the world of matter but by opening up the human being at all levels of consciousness (from vital through supramental) to the limitless universe of pure spirituality which finds its life in the material (651). The goal of integral yoga is not self-annihilation in another world but spiritual transformation within this world, divine realization not only in the immobility of the world soul but also in the movement of Nature. This yoga seeks to realize its goal by assembling the various traditional Indian disciplines and concentrations, harmonizing and, if possibly, fusing them by a grand synthesis which rids each of them of its particular parochialism.

In *The Synthesis of Yoga*, spirit or soul is all-important as an instrument in the taking up of Shakti. Unlike Tantrism, which begins at the lowest level where the physical dimension holds sway and emphasizes the action of awakened Shakti on the nervous system and the body, integral yoga will begin at the level of spirit with the assumption that the preliminary preparation has been carried forward.

While earlier, more traditional yogas placed major importance upon the individual's role in realizing salvation within himself and unto himself in isolation from society and the world and defined the means to salvation in radically individualistic terms, integral yoga is to be a "collective yoga of the divine nature in the human race" (587). The powers of body, mind and spirit which are cultivated, purified and elevated within each individual, will serve as an instrument of perfection for the unhindered movement of the Power of Divinity in the world of humanity. This yoga aims at the ultimate source of all but not to the exclusion of that which it transcends, rather as "the source of an established experience and supreme state of the soul which shall transform all other states and remould our consciousness of the world into the form of its secret truth" (305–306).

In formulating the structure of his thought and expressing it in terms which are comprehensible to an audience conversant with Indian thought, Sri Aurobindo has combined the monistic pantheism of Advaita Vedanta and the practical spiritualistic monism of Sankhya with the practical disciplines of the yoga of Patanjali along with a small but significant element of scientific realism from the West. This rich and heady amalgamation of strands of philosophical ideology and practical disciplines is unified by the threefold way of the Bhagavad Gita and the basic structure of the entire enterprise provided by Tantrism.

It must be said, however, that despite the universal scope of his vision of world transformation, his philosophy suffers from a rather serious parochialism. For the tangible boundaries of his philosophy are established within the historical and ideological limits of Hindu thought only. Sri Aurobindo does not seem to be cognizant of the crucial formative roles which Buddhism, Islam and Jainism have played in the development of Indian culture. In the mind of Sri Aurobindo, integralism seems to take its life and direction from Hindu philosophical thought, with but a small dependence upon Indian sectarianism (e.g., Vaishnavism, Shaivism, etc.) and almost no debt to the non-Hindu traditions in India.

However, he has performed a task of Herculean dimensions in opening up and enlarging the confines of traditional Hindu thought and demonstrating in a most convincing way in his own works the possibility of absorbing and renewing foreign elements within his own symbol system.

Furthermore, he has pointed the way toward a larger, deeper and richer amalgamation of ideologies, axiologies and theologies between East and West than heretofore has been accomplished. The highly ingenious way in which he fuses a vision of human development in concert with world evolution through great expanses of time with the well-nigh limitless possibilities for human perfection within this finite realm, has given many of his disciples and readers a buoyant optimism that, despite present difficulties and discouragements, mankind possesses enormous potential for intellectual, moral, spiritual and cultural development which may yet be brought to concrete realization. Most impressive is his unflagging optimism which asserts that even in man's falterings and fallings there is subtle but fruitful movement toward the realization of a wider, deeper, wiser and more effective human maturity.

On the other hand, there remain for the reflective Western reader, even after careful and thoughtful reading of *The Synthesis of Yoga*, a host of perplexing questions which await a more adequate treatment than they have received in Aurobindo's works. We will conclude discussion, therefore, with the presentation of a few of these issues which we believe raise some doubt concerning either the integrated wholeness or the applicability of Sri Aurobindo's integral yoga.

1. Sri Aurobindo clearly rejects the Vedantin doctrine of the illusoriness of the finite world together with the implication that this limited realm must be understood to be either unreal (Māyā) or only relatively real. But the twofold question remains with regard to his relationship to Adwaita Vedanta: *(a)* has he succeeded in avoiding the claim that the temporal-spatial realm is illusory and hence lacking in real value (some of his statements concerning the relationship between the Supermind and Sachchidananda, on the one hand, and the realm of Purusha-Prakriti, on the other, seem to indicate that he has not been successful in this regard); *(b)* has he demonstrated that, from the perspective of Integralism and by means of the practice of integral yoga, a person can embrace both the finite and Infinite realms and thereby achieve a "total and integrated change of the consciousness and nature"? In a word, does Integral Yoga as it is spelled out in *The Synthesis of Yoga* provide mankind as a whole and for all time with a means of winning both God and the world, without losing his soul to either? While the logic of his arguments seems invulnerable, the applicability of its techniques and the realizability of its aims worldwide remain open questions.

2. From the point of view of Westerners for whom the reality of evil and sin has played a central role in formulating a definition of man, God and the world, Aurobindo would appear to have given insufficient credence to the reality of evil in his world view. To many Westerners, all Hindu thinkers tend to treat the problem of evil too cavalierly and nonchalantly. The Hindu nondualistic perspective and the concomitant belief that good and evil (together with all the other sets of polar oppositions) are nothing but complementary facets of a single reality, must appear to those who have been nursed by the milk of Moses and the Hebrew prophets, of Jesus, Augustine and Aquinas, to meld the polarities together and to pass over the dilemma posed by their contrariety without actually confronting the problem of conflict seriously. Sri Aurobindo, no doubt, would respond to this contention with the observation that Westerners are too preoccupied with the problems of sin and evil and that, were they to view the world through the spectacles of nondualistic Truth,

they would perceive that good and evil are but two sides of the same reality, are nothing but chimeras in the passing scene of life, and therefore do not deserve the excessive dotage which Western thinkers have bestowed upon the topic.

3. Sri Aurobindo asserts on numerous occasions in this and other writings that Integral Yoga will enlarge, enrich and ultimately transcend the modes of life and thought which are embodied in the various religious traditions to which past human history has given life. The question remains, however, whether Sri Aurobindo has provided mankind with a way to overcome and pass beyond the limited visions of traditional religions and, therein, a way to bring into concrete reality a universal community of man, or whether he has merely left behind a system of thought and values and a way of life which will become nothing more than one more religio-philosophical system, competing for the intellectual, moral and financial support of great numbers of adherents alongside all the currently existing cults—perhaps more expansive in scope and richer in texture than many other traditions but still a religiously oriented cult. There are signs, even at this early period, of the spread of Aurobindoism, that this indeed may be the case.

4. The question which must arise inevitably when confronting a highly eclectic and synthetic system of thought is this: despite the obvious gains in incorporating a great diversity of ideas and perspectives within a single philosophical orientation, does one not face a far greater danger than sterile scholasticism and intellectual parochialism? Namely, does one not run the risk of identifying entities which are clearly distinct and arise from quite different existential bases and thereby bypass or ignore intellectual distinctions which are crucial in defining one's intellectual position and style of life? From the viewpoint of religious theism, nothing is more devoid of religious meaning than a pallid universalism, just as in the eyes of a historicist, nothing is more destructive of the integrity of historical facts than a philosophical Idealism.

In a word, the questions to which we must submit Sri Aurobindo's philosophy of Integralism in the end are these: Is it fully integrative of all the philosophical perspectives, religious ideologies and patterns of existence which he wishes to accommodate? Does his philosophy possess sufficient intellectual rigor to rescue man from all forms of vapid spiritualism and idealistic utopianism? And does it have sufficient spiritual depth to ward off the temptation of intellectual arrogance and religious shortsightedness?

Without attempting to answer these and other questions in this paper, we conclude by simply pausing to listen once again to the words of Sri Aurobindo in all their rich and multivalent meanings:

All life, spiritual, mental or material, is the play of the soul with the possibilities of its nature; for without this play there can be no self-expression and no relative self-experience. Even then, in our realisation of all as our larger self and in our oneness with God and other beings, this play can and must persist, unless we desire to cease from all self-expression and all but a tranced and absorbed self-experience. But then it is in the individual being that this trance or this liberated play is realised; the trance is this mental being's immersion in the sole experience of unity, the liberated play is the taking up of his mind into the spiritual being for the free realisation and delight of oneness. (419)

Topical Index to *The Synthesis of Yoga*

A Pragmatic Approach to

THE HUMAN CYCLE

by Eugene Fontinell

Therefore the individuals who will most help the future of humanity in the new age will be those who will recognise a spiritual evolution as the destiny and therefore the great need of the human being. . . . They will be comparatively indifferent to particular belief and form and leave men to resort to the beliefs and forms to which they are naturally drawn. They will only hold as essential the faith in this spiritual conversion, the attempt to live it out and whatever knowledge—the form of opinion into which it is thrown does not so much matter—can be converted into this living. They will especially not make the mistake of thinking that this change can be effected by machinery and outward institutions; they will know and never forget that it has to be lived out by each man inwardly or it can never be made a reality for the kind. They will adopt in its heart of meaning the inward view of the East which bids man seek the secret of his destiny and salvation within; but also they will accept, though with a different turn given to it, the importance which the West rightly attaches to life and to the making the best we know and can attain the general rule of all life.

—*The Human Cycle*

DESPITE THE FORMIDABLE difficulties which accompany an attempt to understand a philosophical or cultural perspective different from one's own, we are now profoundly aware of the necessity for such an effort. Only by trying to see reality through other philosophical or cultural eyes can we avoid identifying our glimpse of truth with "The Truth." Even if our understanding of another philosophy or culture remains quite limited, the dialogical experience may still serve to enrich and deepen our own ideas, our horizons, and increase our possibilities for thought and experience. Of course, the long-range purpose of such dialogue cannot be simply to achieve a better understanding of permanently irreconcilable traditions or world views. The hope must be that eventually there will emerge a synthesis in which the different viewpoints, insights and experiences are transformed without being obliterated. But so monumental a synthesis will not be accomplished easily or through any single effort. There will have to be numerous dialogues of a more limited nature which prepare the way for a more conscious and direct synthesis. As a minimum, such preparatory dialogues should fulfill two requirements. First, they should liberate the living insights of the thinkers involved in the dialogue from the abstract categories in which these insights have become enclosed. Secondly, such dialogues should surface the "touchings" or "resonances" or "convergences" between the traditions, particularly in those aspects in which they appear most disparate if not fundamentally opposed.

These introductory observations are by way of indicating the scope and intent of this essay. In considering Sri Aurobindo's *The Human Cycle* from a pragmatic perspective, there is no pretense of effecting or even attempting a synthesis of Aurobindoism and pragmatism. The aim is much more modest—it is to initiate a dialogue between these traditions by comparing several of the central themes of this work with similar themes in pragmatism.[1] The emphasis will be upon the convergences between Aurobindo and pragmatism

---

1. By simply referring to "pragmatism" I do not wish to give the impression that there is a hard and fast philosophical system which corresponds to this label. I agree with Amelie Rorty, who states: "Pragmatism, like most philosophic 'isms,' is best thought of as a label for a range of views bearing a general family resemblance." *Pragmatic Philosophy* (New York: Doubleday & Co., Anchor Books, 1966), p.v. Some of the chief characteristics of my version of pragmatism will emerge in the comparative section of this essay; I would simple note here that James and Dewey are the primary sources for this version. For a fuller treatment of my view of pragmatism, see *Toward a Reconstruction of Religion* (New York: Doubleday, 1970).

rather than upon their differences. Such an emphasis is, I believe, quite faithful to the spirit of Aurobindo. Though he never minimized or sentimentalized what he believed to be important differences between Eastern and Western viewpoints, he unequivocally affirmed the indispensability of both for the fruitful development of humanity.

I am aware of the dangers involved in an irenic approach, the chief danger being that attention will be focused on superficial similarities which mask profound differences. There is no denying that a fuller treatment of both Aurobindo and pragmatism would bring forth the distinctive richness of the respective traditions as well as important divergences. Nevertheless, I firmly believe that only after we see that these traditions are not totally and diametrically opposed can we then employ their very real differences in moving to a more encompassing perspective. What is important, therefore, is not whether there are more differences than similarities between these traditions, but whether their respective ideas, categories and formulations are the bearers of insights which demand ever new modes of expression in order that they be of continuing service to humanity. On this point there is fundamental agreement between Sri Aurobindo and pragmatism. It is well known that the pragmatic tradition maintains that ideas or categories are instrumental; that is, they are not ends in themselves but are for the sake of the development of human life. Sri Aurobindo is equally firm in his refusal to attribute absolute definitiveness and finality to any idea or system of ideas. Such freezing of our categories is a formidable obstacle to the emergence of a higher mode of consciousness. This consciousness cannot come

> if we chain the Spirit to some fixed mental idea or system of religious cult, intellectual truth, aesthetic norm, ethical rule, practical action, way of vital and physical life, to a particular arrangement of forms and actions and declare all departure from that a peril and a disturbance or a deviation from spiritual living.[2]

In the section of his essay entitled "Pragmatic Convergences," the following themes will be considered: evolution, life, experience,

---

2. Sri Aurobindo, *The Human Cycle*, BCL, 15: 229. Page references to this work will hereafter appear in parentheses at the end of the citation. Cf., S.K. Maitra, *The Meeting of East and West in Sri Aurobindo's Philosophy* (1968), p. 259: "But from Sri Aurobindo's point of view, any conception of the world from the standpoint of any of the principles that have so far emerged, cannot be anything else than that of a block universe, for it shuts the door upon new world-views that will emerge with the emergence of principles which we only very dimly understand at present."

the future and hope. In each instance the intent will be to indicate the possibilities for a fruitful dialogue between Aurobindo and pragmatism with respect to the theme under consideration. Even such a brief comparative analysis should make clear that Aurobindo is not a sentimental idealist and that the pragmatism of William James and John Dewey is not a crude practicalism. Aurobindo's idealism is inseparably bound up with practical life. In *Ideals and Progress* he states: "Man approaches nearer his perfection when he combines in himself the idealist and the pragmatist, the originative soul and the executive power."[3] Needless to say, a pragmatist would not find acceptable an interpretation of pragmatism which restricts it to "executive power." Aurobindo, however, is calling for a synthesis, a more intimate and organic relation between "originative soul and executive power" and whether the result is labeled "Pragmatic Idealism" or "Idealistic Pragmatism" is of no importance whatever.

If Sri Aurobindo's stressing the role of ideals does not involve a rejection of the practical, neither does pragmatism's emphasis upon the practical exclude the need for ideals. While highly critical of ideas or ideals which are unrelated to concrete life, James and Dewey both reject any "capricious pragmatism based on exaltation of personal desire."[4] Dewey explicitly rejected the narrow and pejorative meaning assigned to the term "practical" by many philosophers.

> Instead of being extended to cover all forms of action by means of which all the values of life are extended and rendered more secure, including the diffusion of the fine arts and cultivation of taste, the processes of education and all activities which are concerned with rendering human relationships more significant and worthy, the meaning of "practical" is limited to matters of ease, comfort, riches, bodily security and police order, possibly health, etc., things which in their isolation from other goods can only lay claim to restricted and narrow value.[5]

Sri Aurobindo argued that "the most vital issue of the age is whether the future progress of humanity is to be governed by the modern economic and materialistic mind of the West or by a nobler pragmatism guided, uplifted and enlightened by spiritual culture and knowledge."[6] Perhaps the most significant feature of *The Hu-*

3. Sri Aurobindo, *Ideals and Progress*, BCL, 16: 305–306.
4. John Dewey, *Experience and Nature* (New York: Dover, 1958), p. 242.
5. John Dewey, *The Quest for Certainty* (New York: Minton, Balch & Co., 1929), p. 32.
6. Sri Aurobindo, *Ideals and Progress*, BCL, 16: 326.

man Cycle is that it presents us with a vision of just such a "nobler pragmatism." Since ours is an age in which the richest metaphors are so quickly emptied of meaning, I refer to Aurobindo's vision with some hesitation. But it is precisely because the term "vision" has been so cheapened by indiscriminate use that its depth must be restored. One step in the direction of such restoration is to maintain that a "person of vision" is not a visionary. Aurobino is a case in point. "A man's vision," James tells us, "is the great fact about him,"[7] and this would be true of Aurobindo even if he had given us no work other than *The Human Cycle*. But Aurobindo is no visionary in the superficial sense of the term, for he does not present us with airy speculations spun out of fanciful and whimsical desires. His vision is rooted in and permeates even the most basic and primitive modes of experience but this vision is such that it enables us to see the living possibilities in these experiences.

Sri Aurobindo is a person of vision because he illuminates the past and the present by casting a beam of light into the darkness which lies before us. Dewey perceptively observes that "it is not sheer revolt against things as they are which stirs human endeavors to its depths, but vision of what might be and is not."[8] This text could well stand as the headnote for *The Human Cycle*. At the present time we are engulfed by a wave of criticism which borders on a hatred of the present condition of man while wallowing in a nostalgia for a primitive past. In *The Human Cycle* there is a senstive appreciation of the values and achievements of earlier ages as well as perceptive and incisive critiques of the contemporary world. But Sri Aurobindo avoids both nostalgia and bitterness because he sees the past and the present as organically related to what we are becoming.

It is this sense of balance which is so strikingly present throughout *The Human Cycle:* not a mechanical balance which statically juxtaposes opposing views, but an organic, integrating balance in which conflicting ideas, movements and perspectives are transformed by being subsumed in a higher mode of consciousness. Thus we have a philosophy of history which avoids seeing history either as a "nightmare from which we cannot awake" or as a completely determined,

7. William James, *The Writings of William James—A Comprehensive Edition*, ed. with an Introduction and Annotated Bibliography by John J. McDermott (New York: Random House, 1967), p. 489. Referred to hereafter as *Writings*.
8. John Dwey. *On Experience, Nature and Freedom*, ed. by Richard J. Bernstein (New York: The Liberal Arts Press, 1960), p. 243.

self-contained, self-justifying iron law of reality. Aurobindo manifests both a sensitivity to Nature and an awareness of the dangers of transgressing it,[9] while simultaneously rejecting any role for man which would reduce him to Nature's passive puppet. *The Human Cycle* is eschatalogical from beginning to end, yet it heightens our awareness of the importance of and necessity for concrete societal structures.[10] Finally, Aurobindo maintains that spirituality is the ultimate goal of humanity, but he strongly criticizes any view which puts this spirituality "at the end of life and its habitat in another world of our being, rather than here in life, as the supreme status and formative power on the physical plane"(153). Aurobindo rejects any such other-worldly view because it "rules out the idea of the kingdom of God on earth, the perfectibility of society and of man in society, the evolution of a new and diviner race" (153–154).

The Human Cycle: Its General Form and Structure

The Human Cycle can be described as the story of human development—past, present and future. It is obvious, however, that this is not a story which fits into any neat category, for it involves literary, philosophical, sociological, political and historical elements. This work can no more be read literally than can Hegel's *The Phenomenology of the Spirit.* An effort must be made to move with its subtle rhythms, grasp its suggestive metaphors and follow its permeating spirit. Hence, it would be fruitless and frustrating to attempt an exact correlation of the various aspects of *The Human Cycle* with specifically identifiable persons, ideas, events or movements. Of course, Aurobindo draws upon a variety of such realities,

9. "Our civilized development of life ends in an exhaustion of vitality and a refusal of Nature to lend her support any further to continued advance upon these lines; our civilized mentality, after disturbing the balance of the human system to its own greater profit, finally discovers that it has exhausted and destroyed that which fed it and loses its power of healthy action and productiveness" (209).

10. Though it is not a central theme of *The Human Cycle*, Sri Aurobindo's concern for the body should be noted here. "If a total transformation of the being is our aim, a transformation of the body must be an indispensable part of it; without that no full divine life on earth is possible." "The Divine Body" in *The Supramental Manifestation*, BCL, 16: 24. See also, "Perfection of the Body" in *The Mind of Light*, Robert A. McDermott (ed.), (New York: E. P. Dutton, 1971), chapter 1.

but these particulars are profoundly transformed through incorporation within his vision or world view. The whole of this work is greater than the sum of its parts and indeed its parts cannot be grasped apart from the whole. Its significance, therefore, lies not in its information about historical details but in its richness of vision, imaginative power and depth of insight into the human condition.

The Human Cycle might be viewed as an ideal microcosm of the actual macrocosmic human cycle; that is, it both describes and is itself a succession of overlapping, upward-spiraling cycles. As in a symphony, Aurobindo sounds his central theme at the outset and then proceeds to articulate, deepen and amplify it in succeeding cyclical movements. Thus, the reader will note that Aurobindo's "story" moves backwards and forwards rather than continuing in a neat, clear and distinct straight line. Further, there are repetitions but they are repetitions of a symphonic nature in which the theme is not mechanically restated but organically transformed into a richer and fuller expression. Aurobindo himself views the development of the world in precisely this fashion, as the following text indicates:

> It is true that the world's movement is not in a straight line; there are cycles, there are spirals: but still it circles, not round the same point always, but round an ever advancing centre, and therefore it never returns exactly upon its old path and never goes really backward. As for standing still, it is an impossibility, a delusion, a fiction.[11]

Succinctly stated, the central and recurring theme of *The Human Cycle* is the processive divinization of the human race. This theme is expressed more fully and concretely in Aurobindo's description of the "ideal law of humanity"—namely, that humanity is

> to pursue its upward evolution towards the finding and expression of the Divine in the type of mankind, taking full advantage of the free development and gains of all individuals and nations and groupings of men, to work towards the day when mankind may be really and not only ideally one divine family, but even then, when it has succeeded in unifying itself, to respect, aid and be aided by the free growth and activity of its individuals and constituent aggregates. (64)

The divinization of humanity involves and is involved in three modes of cyclical development; first, the cycle of the Spirit; second, the cyle of the infrarational-rational-suprarational; finally, the cycle

---

11. Sri Aurobindo, *Ideals and Progress*, BCL, 16: 317.

of the five psychological stages. These do not simply succeed each other but are overlapping and interpenetrating cycles. Thus, the latter two cycles are more concrete and specific expressions of the first, and the third a more refined mode of the second.

Now to describe briefly the general features of these cycles, after which the characteristics and development of the psychological stages will be considered in more detail. For Aurobindo, the end is in the beginning and the beginning is in the end, though, of course, not in identical modes. Thus, the beginning and the end of *all* development, human and other, is the Spirit. Faithful to the spiritual emphasis in the Indian tradition, Aurobindo affirms Spirit in its ultimate and eternal mode as Sachchidananda (Existence-Consciousness-Bliss). As the alpha and omega of all developing entities, Sachchidananda is interiorly (though secretly) present to and infinitely beyond all its "manifestations" (all beings). Evolution, according to Aurobindo, is possible only because of involution—because Spirit has involved itself in the depths of matter, increasingly higher modes of being can emerge in the world. "We are bound then to suppose that all that evolves already existed involved, passive or otherwise active, but in either case concealed from us in the shell of material Nature."[12]

All development, therefore, is the unfolding of the Spirit. Spirit has othered itself in such a way as to take on the appearance "of a Void, an infinite Non-Existence, an indeterminate Inconscient, an insensitive blissless Zero" (158). In the early stages of the development of the material universe it appears to be an Inconscient Energy; this, however, is an "appearance," a "mask," since "this unconscious Energy does at every step the works of a vast and minute Intelligence" (158). Out of this primordial matter there comes forth Life and from Life there comes Mind. Nature is then prepared to bring forth humanity, which is accomplished through a great mental effort to understand Matter, Life and Mind "in their phenomena, their obvious action, their secret laws, their normal and abnormal possibilities and powers so that they may be turned to richest account, used in the best and most harmonious way, elevated to their widest potential aims" (74). But a mere accumulation of phenomena and activities does not constitute the goal of developing reality. As with humanity, these activities are instrumental for and transitional to the emergence of Spirit, that is, the divinization of the material world (234). Summarily, Spirit, having "othered" itself in material Nature, is returning to itself through the effort of humanity, which in turn will in the future transform humanity into a divine race.

The second way of expressing the human cycle for Aurobindo is in terms of three powers: the infrarational, the rational and the suprarational. It is important to note that these three powers "are present, but with an infinitely varying prominence in all our activities" (119). However, depending on the dominance of one of these powers, an age can be called Infrarational, Rational or Suprarational. Hence, an earlier age characterized by instinct and impulse can be designated Infrarational. The present age is a Rational Age since it both "takes up and enlightens the life of the instincts" and "looks up towards the absolute" (119). But, as shall be indicated more fully below, reason is unable fully to satisfy human aspirations and hence it must be transformed by and into that which is beyond it— "suprarationality." When this has been realized, humanity will have entered a "suprarational age," in which it "will develop progressively a greater spiritual, supra-intellectual and intuitive, perhaps in the end more than intuitive, a gnostic consciousness" (173).[13]

In addition to the all-encompassing cycle of the Spirit and the infrarational-rational-suprarational cycle, a third way of describing human development is in terms of the cycle of psychological stages. It should be noted that the term "psychological" has a much richer meaning for Aurobindo than it does for most Western thinkers. It refers to that dimension of human reality of which laws, institutions, rites, customs and the like are but manifestations. In the West "psychological" often connotes at best a restricted if not illusory mode of reality. Though not always explicitly stated, there is an underlying assumption in both sophisticated and unsophisticated thought that psychological reality is deficient when compared with the hard currency of "objective reality." For Sri Aurobindo, however, "psychological" expresses the depth dimension of reality— rather than less real, it is more real. When, therefore, he speaks of "The Psychology of Social Development" (the original title of the work under consideration), Sri Aurobindo is concerned with the evolution of the real world which is presently passing through a human phase.

13. For more on "gnostic consciousness," see *The Life Divine*, Book Two, Chapter 27.

The human phase of cosmic evolution is manifest in those civiliza-tions which constitute history. Drawing upon the terminology of the German historian Lamprecht, Aurobindo maintains that the devel-opment of civilizations goes through five stages: symbolic, typal, conventional, individualistic and subjective. It would seem that Aurobindo means that all civilizations follow these stages but we are given very little concrete historical data or specific chronological periodization to support this. There is nothing, for example, like the specific detailing of civilizations which is found in Spengler or Toyn-bee. I prescind, therefore, from the question as to whether these stages as described by Aurobindo can be found in all civilizations. Indeed, I think that Aurobindo is not concerned with such precise categorizations. He explicitly rejects any classification which sug-gests that human history has developed in a simple, forward-moving straight line. "The psychology of man and his societies is too com-plex, too synthetical of many-sided and intermixed tendencies to satisfy any such rigorous and formal analysis" (2). Sri Aurobindo is attempting something much more ambitious than the construction of a scheme which would correspond to the particular phases of every civilization. His concern is to explain the development of human civilizations considered in their totality, that is, the ultimate meaning of their collective development. Hence, even if each partic-ular civilization did not exactly correspond to the developmental pattern described in *The Human Cycle*, I believe that we are pre-sented with a set of categories which can be most illuminating in our continuing effort to grasp human history as a whole or in terms of its overall significance.

One further point concerning the relation of these five stages to each other. Aurobindo does not intend that these be understood as hermetically sealed stages or ages. An earlier stage shades into a later stage and a future stage will be anticipated in the one which precedes it.

Symbolic, Typal and Conventional Stages

The Human Cycle begins with the description of the "symbolic age"—"an age in which man felt a great Reality behind all life which he sought through symbols"—and concludes with the description of a "spiritual age"—"an age in which it will begin to live in that

Reality, not through the symbol, not by the power of the type or of the convention or of the individual reason and intellectual will, but in our own highest nature which will be the nature of that Reality fulfilled in the condition—not necessarily the same as now—of terrestrial existence" (244). Thus we might describe these two ages —the symbolical and the spiritual—as the past and future poles of history. All human development takes place between these two poles, not in a straight line but in ascending spirals through which man's symbolic experience of ultimate reality is gradually transformed into a direct experience.

The "symbolic age" according to Aurobindo cannot be viewed as a primitive one, pure and simple. Such an age is characterized by a wisdom and experience which must be recovered and transformed in the movement to the spiritual age. Aurobindo seems to suggest that some four thousand years ago (the Vedic period of Indian history) the Spirit miraculously broke through into human consciousness. For those living in this age both humanity and the cosmos are "symbols and expressions of the same hidden Reality"; hence, "everything in society [is] a sacrament" (5–6). But this profound and, in a sense, unsurpassable truth grasped by the Vedic sages was too rich for the general mode of human consciousness at that time. Humanity was not sufficiently developed to hold this truth in its purity and hence inevitably it was lost; or better, this truth receded into the background of human consciousness from which it will reemerge through the later stages of evolution.

In the second, or "typal," stage, the religious and spiritual dimensions of consciousness are subordinated to their psychological and ethical expressions. It is clear that for Aurobindo this is not an advance; nor is it a fall into a totally corrupt stage. The contribution of the typal stage still remains in the great social ideas, particularly that of "honor." The shift here is best illustrated by Sri Aurobindo's interpretation of "the Vedic institution of the fourfold order, *caturvarna*, miscalled the system of the four castes" (4).

In the symbolic stage each of the varnas—Brahmin, Kshatriya, Vaishya and Shudra—symbolizes an aspect of God and also corresponds to one of the four cosmic principles of Wisdom, Power, Harmony and Work. In the typal period, however, these varnas cease to be "the direct expression of the divine Being or cosmic Principle in man." Instead, they become identified with the social ideals peculiar to each of the four classes. When, however, these social ideals lose their inner life and become identified with their external and outward expressions, we have moved into the "conventional stage." This stage tends "to fix, to arrange firmly, to formalise, to erect a system of rigid grades and hierarchies, to stereotype religion, to bind education and training to a traditional and unchangeable form, to subject thought to infallible authorities, to cast a stamp of finality on what seems to it the finished life of man" (8). This stage is most obviously manifest in the caste system of India and in Catholicism of the late middle ages. It inevitably brings forth a rebellion, an effort to break the chains of external forms and to recover an interior truth. When this takes place the "individualistic age" has begun. Aurobindo explains that "it is in Europe that the age of individualism has taken birth and exercised its full sway" (11). The specific historical movements involved are the Renaissance, the Protestant Revolt, and the Scientific Revolution. With this age a new upward movement of the cycle begins; it is a movement from the infrarational stage to the rational. The symbolic, typal and conventional stages constitute the infrarational stage of human development. This stage, particularly in its symbolic mode, is not completely negative; during this period a profound and intimate experience of the Divine was realized. Nevertheless, it is a stage which must be subsumed in a later and higher one.

Individualistic and Subjective Stages

The "rational age" encompasses two substages or ages—the individualistic and the subjective. These shade into and overlap one another and can be viewed as the critical and constructive phases of the broader "rational age." Consequently, "the dawn of individualism is always a questioning, a denial" (12), but eventually man "finds that he can only know himself entirely by becoming actively self-conscious and not merely self-critical" (24). The discovery of and centrality assigned to the individual is the great and irreplaceable achievement of the individualistic age. But such an age needs both a "general standard of Truth" and "some principle of social order" (15–16) if it is to avoid a destructive individualism. While science seems to fulfill the need for these "two supreme desiderata of an individualistic age," it is at the same time a formidable threat to the individual. This threat stems from the attempt, a consequence of the emergence of science, to govern and organize human life on the basis of universal laws determined by "experts who shall know better than ourselves and choose for us our work and quality" (17). This judgment, remember, was made in the second decade of the twentieth century; the danger here noted has become immeasurably heightened in the latter half of this century. A vivid description of this danger is given by Theodore Roszak in his attack upon what he calls "The Citadel of Expertise."

> And here is an effect of scientific progress that has received far too little attention. In a world of experts, what becomes of the imaginative energies of ordinary people? Where everything—*everything*—has been staked out as somebody's specialized field of knowledge, what is the thinking of ordinary people worth? Precisely zero. For what do they know about anything that some expert does not know better? There are even experts on *their* sex life, *their* dreams, *their* relations with *their* children, *their* voting habits, *their* morals and manners, *their* tastes, *their* needs.[14]

But as Aurobindo observed, this threat to the individual has brought forth a renewed concern for human subjectivity which is manifested in art, literature, music and education. This "inward turn" which characterizes the present "subjective age" is fundamentally sound, but Aurobindo makes clear that it is not a danger-free path to paradise. There is both a true and a false subjectivism, and the future of humanity depends upon the ability to develop the one and reject the other. For Aurobindo, the greatest need is to understand that the "ego is not the self." True subjectivism recognizes two truths: first, "there is one self of all and the soul is a portion of the universal Divinity"; secondly, that the individual is "not only himself, but in solidarity with all of his kind" (39–40).

Sri Aurobindo thus reprises the insight of the symbolic stage—"mankind upon earth is one foremost self-expression of the universal Being in His cosmic self-unfolding" (59). This insight is crucial for an understanding of human development, since only if we know man's "future mental and spiritual destiny" can we discover the "ideal law of social development" (56). As was noted above, the ideal law for humanity is to evolve into a divine race by means of the free development of individuals and collectivities.

14. Theodore Roszak, *Where the Wasteland Ends* (New York: Doubleday, 1972), p. 258.

From Barbarism to Suprarational Life

Having stated the goal of human evolution, Aurobindo now takes us on two more detailed spiraling cycles. The first is from barbarism through reason to suprarationality; the second is from the Infrarational Age through the Rational Age to the Spiritual Age. The first of these two cycles begins with a consideration of barbarism; by "barbarism" Aurobindo means the pursuit of the human for its own sake rather than as an instrument to a higher good (73). An earlier physical barbarism has been succeeded by more modern vitalistic and economic barbarisms; but as humanity becomes aware of the priority of the mental, "culture" emerges. Culture can develop along primarily ethical lines (Republican Rome) or with a primacy of esthetic values (Periclean Athens). Great as such cultures are, they inevitably must collapse since "neither the ethical being nor the aesthetic being is the whole man, nor can either be his sovereign principle" (92).

It would appear that reason is this needed sovereign principle and Aurobindo concedes that "reason using the intelligent will for the ordering of the inner and the outer life is undoubtedly the highest developed faculty of man at his present point of evolution" (94). There follows a description of the possibilities and the limitations of reason which leads to a distinction reminiscent of Bergson. Aurobindo maintains that "intellective reason" must be succeeded by "intuitive reason." It is not that he is unappreciative of the necessity for and the contribution of intellect; he recognizes that this faculty transforms the lower powers acting as a "guide, teacher, purifier, liberator." It "strengthens and purifies the hedonistic and aesthetic activities" and "sweetens the ethical will by infusing it with psychic, hedonistic and aesthetic elements." In addition, the intellect judges and legislates by giving rules and systems which enable man "to walk by a settled path and act according to a sure law." More important, "it leads man to the gates of a greater self-consciousness" (105–106).

Having detailed these achievements of the intellect, Aurobindo proceeds to argue that it nevertheless must be surpassed. Since it must function by analyzing the integral whole into parts and making "more or less artificial classifications," intellect is not able to bring man into the full presence of the Absolute (101–103). Intellect has done its task when it has brought man to the awareness that there is a reality which surpasses him.

In spite of the great achievements of ancient and modern rationalistic cultures, therefore, a more ancient ideal lives and remains
unfulfilled—"the old religious and spiritual ideal, the hope of the
kingdom of heaven within us and the city of God upon earth" (116).

Sri Aurobindo then considers the relation of reason to religion,
man's search for Beauty and Good and the human drive and struggle
for Life. In each instance he shows us that only in a suprarational
Beauty, Good and Life can man's deepest yearnings and strivings be
fulfilled. Whether he expresses the goal of human striving as God,
the Eternal, the Absolute or Spirit, Aurobindo is insistent that only
by a radical transformation of the present mode of human consciousness can the human race avoid becoming another dead-end development of cosmic evolution. Sri Aurobindo concedes that

> this is a solution to which it may be objected that it puts off the
> consummation of a better human society to a far-off date in the
> future evolution of the race. For it means that no machinery invented
> by the reason can perfect either the individual or the collective man;
> an inner change is needed in human nature, a change too difficult to
> be ever effected except by the few. This is not certain, but in any case,
> if this is not the solution, then there is no solution; if this is not the
> way, then there is no way for the human kind. (207)

The Spiritual Age

The goal of human evolution having been more explicitly articulated, there begins another spiraling cycle. Starting with "The
Infrarational Age of the Cycle," Aurobindo takes us through an
expanded analysis of the development of the rational age, leading us
once again to the recognition that spiritualized humanity—individually and collectively—is the only future that the human race can
have if it is to have a future.

In those sections of *The Human Cycle* dealing with the infrarational ages of humanity (symbolic, typal and conventional) Aurobindo has described where humanity has been. In those dealing with
the rational age (individualistic and subjectivistic), he describes
where humanity is. The concluding chapters of *The Human Cycle*
present Aurobindo's view as to where humanity is going or at least
ought to be going.

Humanity is on the brink of a spiritual age or it is doomed to
cataclysm and destruction. But this new age will not just happen, it

will require great human effort as well as a difficult bringing together of a number of elements. In particular two conditions must be fulfilled simultaneously—a most arduous undertaking:

> There must be the individual and the individuals who are able to see, to develop, to re-create themselves in the image of the Spirit and to communicate both their idea and its power to the mass. And there must be at the same time a mass, a society, a communal mind or at the least the constituents of a group-body, the possibility of a group-soul which is capable of receiving and effectively assimilating, ready to follow and effectively assimilating, ready to follow and effectively arrive, not compelled by its own inherent deficiencies, its defect of preparation to stop on the way or fall back before the decisive change is made. (232)

Sri Aurobindo acknowledges that much trial and error will be involved in bringing to birth the spiritual age, for in an enterprise of this scope the chances of failure are much greater than the chances of success (232). Nevertheless, Aurobindo condemns those who would *a priori* declare a spiritual transformation impossible. The only way of showing that such a difficult goal can be realized is by continually moving in the direction of this goal. "For by the doing the difficulty will be solved. A true beginning has to be made; the rest is a work for Time in its sudden achievements or its long patient labour" (251).

The spiritual age will not be one which destroys or mechanically replaces those modes of human life which have been formed in an earlier age. Aurobindo insists that the coming age of the spirit will not obliterate man's physical, vital and mental life but it will transform them by subsuming them in a higher mode of reality.[15] It will be an age of unity without obliteration of individuality. Aurobindo repeatedly emphasizes that the realization of Spirit must be achieved through freedom and never through coercion. Freedom and Unity, however, can be realized only if mankind recognizes that it is a manifestation of God—that which is at once the highest self and the self of all creatures (239). This was, of course, the profound intuition of the sages of the symbolic age. A spiritual age, however, will be characterized by the transformation of this insight and symbolic

15. Sri Aurobindo merely alludes here to what is a central theme of his metaphysics, namely, that the transformation must lead to increasingly higher levels of reality. Reason must be converted into intuition, which in turn must rise to overmind in order that it might finally be incorporated into supermind (252).

mode of expression into the lived reality of a new race of beings—
a race of beings who are in intimate union with the ultimate reality,
with Sachchidananda.

Pragmatic Convergences

In *The Human Cycle* Aurobindo focuses on the creative possibilities manifest in human history but, as we have seen, he places this
historical development within a much more encompassing, cosmic
mode of development. His philosophy of history extends backward
to the earlier cosmic development and forward to the future spiritual
realization. One of the features of this philosophy of history which
a pragmatist would find most appealing is that it does not pretend
to be a literal representation of historical development. Aurobindo
does not claim to give a spectator's photographic picture of some
passing parade; he is much too sensitive to the complexity and
richness of human history to make such a claim. *The Human Cycle*
does, of course, present us with a dynamic scheme of human history.
I believe, however, that Aurobindo would agree that his scheme
should be judged not only on the basis of its inner conceptual
consistency but also on its ability to account for the phenomena, to
contribute to our efforts to find meaning and significance in human
history and to expand and deepen our consciousness. No pragmatist
could consistently ask for more from any description or philosophy
of history.

Further, James and Dewey concur with the view of Aurobindo
that human history evolves out of cosmic history and that this
process is by no means terminated with the present form of human
development. For all three, we live in an "unfinished" or "open"
universe in which "something is doing."[16] The human, as a manifestation of this universe, is also unfinished and hence has the possibility of participating in its own transformation. Aurobindo does not
hesitate to declare that "man is an abnormal who has not found his
own normality" (220). Elsewhere he states

---

16. From a letter of James, cited by Ralph Barton Perry in *The Thought and
Character of William James* (Boston: Little Brown and Co., 1935), vol. II, p. 656.

Man is a transitional being; he is not final. For in man and high beyond him ascend the radiant degrees that climb to a divine supermanhood. There lies our destiny and the liberating key to our aspiring but troubled and limited mundane existence.[17]

While he maintains and emphasizes the role of the Divine in human evolution, Aurobindo does not deny the essential contribution of human effort.

Man's greatness is not in what he is, but in what he makes possible. His glory is that he is the closed place and secret workshop of a living labour in which supermanhood is being made ready by a divine Craftsman. But he is admitted too to a yet greater greatness and it is this that allowed to be unlike the lower creation, he is partly an his conscious assent, his consecrated will and ed that into his body may descend the glory His aspiration is earth's call to the supramental

'ꓭꓱꓒ

here alluding to the future emergence of a new is, of course, a central and explicit theme of his n farther than James or Dewey in speculating on us consciousness but there is nothing in the basic views which would have to be rejected *a priori* by a pragmatist. Of course, the pragmatic perspective excludes understanding Aurobindo's future stages of development (intuition, overmind, supermind) as representing already existing ontological levels of reality. A pragmatist, however, will find in Aurobindo an exciting and suggestive set of hypotheses concerning both the possibilities for future development as well as dimensions of reality with which we are related but of which we are only vaguely and sporadically aware. James, for example, was most sympathetic to the view that human consciousness participates in a more inclusive consciousness. "Every bit of us," he maintains,

is part and parcel of a wider self, it quivers along various radii like the wind-rose on a compass, and the actual in it is continuously one with possibles not yet in our sight. And just as we are co-conscious with our own momentary margin, may not we ourselves form the margin of some more really central self in things which is co-conscious with

17. Sri Aurobindo, "Man a Transitional Being" in *The Hour of God*, BCL, 17: 7.
18. *Ibid.*, p. 9.

the whole of us? May not you and I be confluent in a higher consciousness, and confluently active there, tho we now know it not?[19]

As for treating Aurobindo's description of the various levels of
mind as hypotheses, this would not seem to be totally inimical to the
spirit of his thought. As sensitive and sympathetic an interpreter of
Aurobindo as Haridas Chaudhuri does not hesitate to say "that from
the empirical standpoint the . . . theory of higher spirit-worlds is no
more than a hypothesis which can hardly be proved conclusively."
Further, "there is no warrant for hypostatizing such emerging levels
of consciousness as eternally preexistent supernatural planes sustained by a supernatural Deity." Nevertheless, Chaudhuri maintains, and I believe a pragmatist should agree, that "at the present
state of our incomplete scientific knowledge it would certainly be
wise to keep an unbiased and open mind, without slamming the door
upon any possibility, however occult or mysterious."[20]

Whatever differences Aurobindo and a pragmatist might have
concerning any new, higher or wider consciousness, they are at one
in rejecting its achievement by an escape from the "here and now"
world. *The Human Cycle* does not hold out hope for any shortcut
to a higher level of consciousness. Aurobindo does not deny that a
few individuals may, indeed must, be more advanced than most of

19. William James, *Writings*, p. 297. See also, *ibid.*, p. 472, "I firmly disbelieve,
myself, that our human experience is the highest form of experience extant in the
universe." James throughout his life exhibited an interest in psychic phenomena.
He was a founder of The American Society for Psychical Research and participated
in and wrote about a number of psychic experiments. His attitude on such matters
was expressed as early as 1886 in a letter to Carl Stumpf. After lamenting the
scandalous state of scientific opinion concerning psychic phenomena he added: "It
is a field in which the sources of self-deception are extremely numerous. But I
believe there is no source of deception in the investigation of nature which can
compare with a fixed belief that certain kinds of phenomena are *impossible*" (*ibid.*,
p. 787).
20. Haridas Chaudhuri, "Supermind in Aurobindo," *International Philosophical
Quarterly*, June 1972, p. 191. Of course, I think that it is crucial to understand
"science" as itself developing. I would find unacceptable any view which locates the
paradigm for science in the so-called natural or physical sciences. Such a view was
long ago condemned by Dewey, who maintained that "the assimilation of human
to physical science represents only another form of absolutistic logic, a kind of
physical absolutism." *Freedom and Culture* (New York: Capricorn Books, 1963,
first published in 1939), p. 171. The need for a science of man which is not modeled
on physics has been compellingly argued by Ernest Becker. Becker claims to be
following in the steps of Dewey in his efforts to construct an interdisciplinary
science of man. For the most developed statement of Becker's views, see *The
Structure of Evil: An Essay on the Unification of the Science of Man* (New York:
George Braziller, 1968).

not have to go to knowledge to obtain an exclusive hold on reality."[27] In texts such as these, James and Dewey are calling attention to the richness of experience rather than hailing some dark principle of irrationality as the determining feature of human life. I think it fair to say that Aurobindo would join these thinkers in affirming affective, esthetic and religious experience, which cannot be simply identified with knowledge or relegated to some inferior mode of being or human activity.

The richness of concrete life is nowhere more manifest than in the inability of ideas or intellectual schema to express it adequately. "Experience," James notes, "has ways of *boiling over*, and making us correct our present formulas."[28] And in a strikingly similar text, Aurobindo states: "Life escapes from the formulas and systems which our reason labours to impose on it, it proclaims itself too complex, too full of infinite potentialities to be tyrannised over by the arbitrary intellect of man" (100).

Pragmatism is often accused of being anti-intellectual because of its critique of abstract ideas. Neither James nor Dewey, of course, deny the importance and indispensability of theories, categories or concepts. Indeed, they are precious tools or instruments by which human life is directed, developed and expanded. It is only when these ideas are taken as the "really real," when they become the end rather the means in relation to life, that pragmatism becomes critical. Aurobindo joins the pragmatist on this point. It is not enough, he says repeatedly and emphatically, that certain ideas be held, even if they happen to be profound ideas highly favorable to the general direction in which humanity should be going. Indeed, "the holding of an ideal becomes almost an excuse for not living according to the ideal" (247). Aurobindo goes on to say that "we have to enlarge and to deepen the pragmatic principle that truth is what we create, and in this sense first, that it is what we create within us, in other words, what we become" (247). I do not mean here to suggest any simple identification between Aurobindo and pragmatism. A divergence is manifest in Aurobindo's assertion that "undoubtedly, spiritual truth exists eternally beyond, independent of us, in the heavens of the Spirit" (247). Dewey would be highly sceptical, if not deeply antagonistic, to such a claim, while James, as a minimum, would insist upon

27. John Dewey, *The Quest for Certainty* (New York: Minton, Balch & Co., 1929), pp. 295–296.
28. James, *Writings*, p. 438.

substituting "possibly" for "undoubtedly." Nevertheless, both could enthusiastically affirm with Aurobindo that such truth "is of no avail for humanity here, it does not become truth on earth, truth of life until it is lived" (247).

Intuition

It would be misleading simply to assert agreement by Aurobindo and the pragmatists on the issue of life or experience as larger than knowledge. Aurobindo would undoubtedly want this qualified by noting that he means knowledge in its present state of development. As we saw above, Aurobindo concedes that "reason" is "the highest developed faculty of man at his present point of evolution" (94). But the primary thrust of *The Human Cycle* is the necessity for man to transcend reason. Aurobindo maintains that man cannot remain satisfied with reason as it is presently functioning. "For his nature pushes him towards the heights; it demands a constant effort of self-transcendence and the impulsion towards things unachieved and immediately impossible" (102). Aurobindo, as we have seen above, does not deny the great achievements of reason but he concludes that in the end it has not been a success since "it has left the heart of almost every problem untouched" (101). And in a statement which might appear to be lifted from a contemporary counterculture manifesto, he refers to the arrival of a time "when the reason becomes dissatisfied and sees that it is only erecting a mass of new conventions and that there has been no satisfying change" (181).

Sri Aurobindo's resolution for this unsatisfactory situation appears deceptively simple—reason must be immediately supplemented and eventually supplanted by intuition. "If reason is to play any decisive part, it must be an intuitive rather than an intellectual reason, touched always by spiritual intensity and insight" (125). While Aurobindo undoubtedly believes that there is a power possessed by man which enables him to experience reality with a profound depth and immediacy, this power is still in an embryonic form, at least as regards most of the human race. After stating that "the intelligence of man is not composed entirely and exclusively of the rational intellect and the rational will," Aurobindo goes on to say that "there enters into it a deeper, more intuitive, more splendid and powerful, but much less clear, much less developed and as yet hardly at all

self-possessing light and force for which we have not even a name"
(76). A text such as this is stressed because it expresses a position
much more congenial to pragmatism than would be that of a simplistic intuitionism. Again, my concern is not to claim a superficial
identity between the two views. Rather, it is to call attention to the
shared recognition of a dimension of human experience which, however differently interpreted, suggests the possibility for a fruitful
dialogue.

The Absolute

If there is one point on which Aurobindo and pragmatism seem
diametrically opposed, it is the question of the Absolute. Aurobindo
is led to criticize the intellect and to affirm intuition precisely because the latter is the means by which the Absolute is grasped (103).
Pragmatism's critique of "the Absolute" is, of course, well known.
While a fuller consideration of Aurobindo and pragmatism on this
question would recognize a number of important differences, a few
texts from James and Dewey will serve to indicate that the two views
are not completely antithetical.

For historical and polemical reasons, James and Dewey were
deeply suspicious of any claims to know the Absolute. Both believed
that absolutistic philosophies turned human energies away from the
concrete complexities of human experience. This resulted in the
dissipation of crucial and all too limited energy in the pursuit of
abstract perfection rather than the application of such energy to the
task of transforming the world in which we live. Now whatever else
might be said about Aurobindo's doctrine of the Absolute, it must
be admitted that he emphatically rejects any interpretation which
would lead to an escape from the concrete responsibilities of daily
human living. By the same token, it is simply untrue to assert that
James and Dewey were insensitive to a more encompassing reality
which was most intimately present to human experience. Consider,
for example, the following passage from James:

> My present field of consciousness is a centre surrounded by a fringe
> that shades insensibly into a subconscious more. . . . What we concep-
> tually identify ourselves with and say we are thinking of at any time
> is the centre; but our *full* self is the whole field, with all those
> indefinitely radiating subconscious possibilities of increase that we

can only feel without conceiving, and can hardly begin to analyze. The collective and the distributive ways of being coexist here, for each part functions distinctly, makes connexion with its own peculiar region in the still wider rest of experience and tends to draw us into that line, and yet the whole is somehow felt as one pulse of our life, —not conceived so, but felt so.[29]

It is, perhaps, not surprising that James acknowledged the possibility of grasping a reality which transcends human consciousness. After all, he did not hesitate to refer to himself as a "crass supernaturalist" and his famous work, *The Varieties of Religious Experience,* gives ample evidence of his sympathy for those whose experiences take them beyond the limits of the mundane. It is much more significant, I believe, to find in Dewey the recognition of a strikingly similar phenomenon. Consider the following excerpt from his great work *Art as Experience:*

> A work of art elicits and accentuates this quality of being a whole and of belonging to the larger, all-inclusive, whole which is the universe in which we live. . . . We are, as it were, introduced into a world beyond this world which is nevertheless the deeper reality of the world in which we live in our ordinary experiences. We are carried out beyond ourselves to find ourselves. I can see no psychological ground for such properties of an experience save that, somehow, the work of art operates to deepen and to raise to great clarity that sense of an enveloping undefined whole that accompanies every normal experience. This whole is then felt as an expansion of ourselves. For only one frustrated in a particular object or desire upon which he had staked himself, like Macbeth, finds that life is a tale told by an idiot, full of sound and fury, signifying nothing. Where egotism is not the measure of reality and value, we are citizens of this vast world beyond ourselves, and any intense realization of its presence with and in us brings a peculiarly satisfying sense of unity in itself and with ourselves.[30]

Nor is this an isolated text in Dewey as the following illustrates: "Within the flickering inconsequential acts of separate selves dwells a sense of the whole which claims and dignifies them. In its presence we put off mortality and live in the universal."[31]

There is little doubt that Aurobindo would have acknowledged

29. James, *Writings,* p. 296.
30. John Dewey, *Art as Experience* (New York: Capricorn Books, 1958, first published in 1934), p. 195.
31. John Dewey, *Human Nature and Conduct* (New York: The Modern Library, copyright, 1922), pp. 331–332.

that such texts express an insight convergent with his own. It is, of course, not unimportant that Aurobindo would claim an intuitive knowledge of the transcendent while James and Dewey would insist that such experiences are better described in terms of faith than knowledge. Even here, however, a fuller comparison of the two perspectives would show more convergence than is indicated by simply labeling one "intuition" and the other "faith." As a minimum, such a comparison would show that "intuition" for Aurobindo is ultimately a mode of living, while "faith" for James and Dewey is not merely a subjectivistic projection of an illusory reality but a creative act. By means of the activity of faith we move beyond the limited situation in which we now exist, thereby enabling us to participate more fully in that expanding reality with which we are continuous.

Individuality, Collectivity and Freedom

One of the crucial and persistent themes of *The Human Cycle* is the importance and centrality of the individual. It is particularly important to note that Aurobindo's affirmation of the individual is not at the expense of the social or communal. "Human life," he contends, "is moved by two equally powerful impulses, one of individualist self-assertion, the other of collective self-assertion" (147). In some of the most perceptive passages of *The Human Cycle*, Aurobindo exposes the destructiveness which accompanies both a narrow, isolating and enclosing individualism and a smothering, obliterating collectivism. The need is for a community of individuals in which the individual and the communal dimensions will be positively and organically related. "In this view neither the separate growth of the individual nor the all-absorbing growth of the group can be the ideal, but an equal, simultaneous and, as far as may be, parallel development of both, in which each helps to fulfill the other" (53).[32]

A similar call for a movement beyond rugged individualism and totalitarian collectivism is sounded repeatedly by Dewey. He em-

---

32. See also Sri Aurobindo, *Ideals and Progress*, BCL, 16:311. "The salvation of the human race lies in a more sane and integral development of the possibilities of mankind in the individual and in the community."

phatically rejects any view which holds that we must choose either the individual or the collective.[33] Dewey fervently opposes any atomistic individualism which calls for the realization of individuality through isolation from, if not opposition to, the community. It is significant that he finds both "militant atheism" and "traditional supernaturalism" guilty of "exclusive preoccupation . . . with man in isolation."[34]

At the same time, Dewey is critical of the modes of collectivity which have emerged in the modern world. He contends that the major flaw in the present situation is that the "collectivity" or "corporateness" of our time is to a great extent external to the individual. Only when it becomes internalized, that is, when it is realized in thought and purpose, will it become qualitative. "In this change, law will be realized not as a rule arbitrarily imposed from without but as the relations which hold individuals together. The balance of the individual and social will be organic."[35]

Dewey's insistence upon the need for internalization of laws and values might also be expressed as the affirmation of the necessity for freedom. Both James and Dewey strongly reject any form of external imposition or coercion in the realm of human activity because such acts stifle growth and prohibit the creative realization of human possibilities. Similarly, Sri Aurobindo maintains that freedom is inseparable from human development. "Man needs freedom of thought and life and action in order that he may grow, otherwise he will remain fixed where he was, a stunted and static being" (198).[36] A spiritualized society for Aurobindo would be characterized by a multiplicity of individuals unified in the life of the Divine. But neither God nor Unity can be reached by humanity unless we have the possibility of freely transforming our present mode of

33. Cf. Sidney Hook, *John Dewey* (New York: The John Day Co., 1939), p. 149. Hook points out that Dewey "refuses to recognize any validity in the time-worn opposition between *the* social and *the* individual. . . . There is no mind, there is no individual, that measures itself as an independent entity over against society."
34. John Dewey, *A Common Faith* (New Haven: Yale University Press, 1960, first published in 1934), pp. 52–53.
35. John Dewey, *Individualism Old and New* (New York: Capricorn Books, 1962, first published in 1929), pp. 94–95.
36. Cf. Dewey, *Experience, Nature and Freedom, op. cit.*, p. 280. "Our idea compels us . . . to seek for freedom in something which comes to be, in a certain kind of growth; in consequenes, rather than in antecedents. We are free not because of what we statically are, but in as far as we are becoming different from what we have been."

life.[37] Most striking, perhaps, is Aurobindo's refusal to identify free-dom with right or good action. "All experience shows that man must be given a certain freedom to stumble in action as well as to err in knowledge" (216). In this text, I believe that Aurobindo acknowl-edges an experimental feature of the human situation which can properly be called "pragmatic."

Institutions

In both Aurobindo and pragmatism, therefore, we find affirmation of the individual and the community, of individual freedom and an inseparable social context for this freedom. These affirmations can be viewed as expressing a doctrine of institutions. In neither Auro-bindo nor pragmatism do we find a simplistic, pseudo-romantic condemnation of institutions in favor of some abstract realization of an isolated individual self. At the same time both give us devastating criticisms of those attempts to identify human nature with the institutional forms of a particular age. It can fairly be said of both Aurobindo and the pragmatists that, while they affirm the necessity of institutions for the emergence and development of human life, they strongly reject any particular institutional forms as embodying the essence of human nature. It is because they see institutions as concrete articulations of a processive humanity that they avoid either transforming them into idols or suggesting that they can be dispensed with through the creation of some noninstitutional world.

Institutions are modes of human living apart from which human

---

37. I do not wish to suggest that for either pragmatism or Sri Aurobindo "freedom" is nothing more than the absence of coercion or simply the means to some external end. For both, but especially for Sri Aurobindo, freedom is an inner realization and an interior quality of life which constitutes the individual self while simultaneously enabling that self to participate more deeply in an encompassing reality. Here, I believe, Sri Aurobindo has much to teach pragmatism by contributing to its aware-ness of the interiority dimension of the human self. It is in his *The Synthesis of Yoga* that Sri Aurobindo gives his developed view of freedom. The characteristics of this freedom have been succinctly described by Rhoda P. Le Cocq as follows: "For him, freedom is integration, wholeness, mental, emotional and spiritual human being. . . . Sri Aurobindo's freedom is always toward the ever-increasing, unending transfor-mation of the earth and its inhabitants. . . . Sri Aurobindo's radical freedom, therefore, *is* both means and end. It is *process, dynamic eternal change* almost as inconceivable to the human mentality as the concept of Infinity. In fact, no human mind *can* conceive such freedom; it can only be *experienced."* *The Radical Think-ers* (San Francisco: California Institute of Asian Studies, 1972), pp. 176–177.

beings would be an aggregate of characterless and chaotic atomistic entities. At the same time institutions are not ends in themselves; they are the organic means by which values become incarnated and richer modes of human living are brought into existence. This is the crucial insight in Aurobindo's declaration that "man does not actually live as an isolated being, nor can he grow by an isolated freedom." Consequently, society is needed "as a field of relations which afford to the individual the occasion for growing towards greater perfection" (203).

The awareness of both the dangers of institutions and their liberating possibilities suggests that Aurobindo and pragmatism have a unique contribution to make to the contemporary situation. Humanity is in danger of being polarized into two warring camps —those who work for and support the existing institutions as if they were natural or divine necessities, and those who drop out or absent themselves from the monumental task of creating institutions which will enhance and expand human life. It is because Dewey rejected both these alternatives that he insisted throughout his life that his philosophy was not separable from his efforts to transform educational, political and social institutions. Similarly, the Sri Aurobindo Ashram and Auroville are necessary incarnations of Sri Aurobindo's ideals and vision.

Future and Hope

Perhaps the most important similarity between *The Human Cycle* and pragmatism is that they both affirm the reality and importance of a human future. Numerous thinkers have noted that the later half of the twentieth century is characterized by a profound threat of meaninglessness. This despair which seems to grow almost daily is the result of a variety of factors—religious, scientific, political, economic and social. The consequences of the radical changes which have been taking place in each of these spheres over the last several hundred years have brought man to the brink of destruction— psychological as well as physical. The great fear is that humanity may have no future. This fear is no longer restricted to a few isolated and seemingly eccentric individuals but seems characteristic of an entire culture—most immediately Western culture, but the threat already gives signs of extending to all cultures. The testimony of religion, psychology, anthropology and sociology, and art persuasively suggest that neither individually nor collectively can man survive without hope. Only if human beings are energized by a deep sense of expect-ance—by a belief that their activities do count for something beyond themselves—are they likely to make the increasingly difficult effort to bring forth a better, more human world. Because the threat of the continuance of the human race is greater than it has ever been, there is need for thinkers who are capable of illuminating the positive possibilities of our situation—who are able to give us hope.

Sri Aurobindo and the pragmatists resoundingly reject any "tale told by an idiot" interpretation of human life. At the same time they are "tough-minded" since neither suggests that the human condi-tion can be transformed without a sustained effort which inevitably will involve its tragic dimension. There is no attempt to mask or gloss over the numerous evils which have emerged from and are still present in the human situation. Nevertheless, they refuse to make such evils the determining factors of human life. Both believe that humanity has a future and, while the fruitful realization of human potentialities is not absolutely assured, the possibilities for such realization are decidedly real. The need for a philosophy of hope is greater now than it was when Aurobindo, James and Dewey ar-ticulated their visions. We are more than ever besieged on the one hand by apostles of cynicism and despair and on the other by prom-ises of instant salvation. Fortunately, most people are repelled by the first approach and suspicious of the second. Still, there is a growing anomie which profoundly threatens to sap the human energies needed for the continuing effort radically to transform our present condition. This alone would justify a dialogue between the traditions manifested in the thought of Sri Aurobindo and pragmatism. Such a dialogue may not only enrich the respective traditions but might make them more widely accessible, thereby enabling them to con-tribute more fully to the processive realization of the future of humanity.

SIX

THE LIFE DIVINE

Sri Aurobindo's Philosophy of Evolution and

Transformation

by Robert A. McDermott

There is possible a realistic as well as an illusionist Advaita. The philosophy of The Life Divine *is such a realistic Advaita. The world is a manifestation of the Real and therefore is itself real. The reality is the infinite and eternal Divine, infinite and eternal Being, Consciousness-Force and Bliss. This Divine by his power has created the world or rather manifested it in his own infinite Being. But here in the material world or at its basis he has hidden himself in what seem to be his opposites, Non-Being, Inconscience and Insentience. This is what we nowadays call the Inconscient which seems to have created the material universe by its inconscient Energy, but this is only an appearance, for we find in the end that all the dispositons of the world can only have been arranged by the working of a supreme secret Intelligence. The Being which is hidden in what seems to be an inconscient void emerges in the world first in Matter, then in Life, then in Mind and finally as the Spirit. The apparently inconscient Energy which creates is in fact the Consciousness-Force of the Divine and its aspect of consciousness, secret in Matter, begins to emerge in Life, finds something more of itself in Mind and finds its true self in a spiritual consciousness and finally a supramental Consciousness through which we become aware of the Reality, enter into it and unite ourselves with it. This is what we call evolution which is an evolution of Consciousness and an evolution of the Spirit in things and only outwardly an evolution of species. Thus also, the delight of existence emerges from the original insentience, first in the contrary forms of pleasure and pain, and then has to find itself in the bliss of the Spirit or, as it is called in the Upanishads, the bliss of the Brahman. That is the central idea in the explanation of the universe put forward in* The Life Divine.

—*Letters on Yoga, 22:44*

Introduction

SCOPE AND APPROACH

An essay on Sri Aurobindo's *The Life Divine*, particularly one by a young Western academic, cannot but be regarded as work in progress. As philosophy, *The Life Divine* is as demanding as Hegel's *Phenomenology of Spirit*, F. H. Bradley's *Appearance and Reality* or Royce's *The World and the Individual*—each of which it resembles—but unlike even these idealist metaphysical treatises, *The Life Divine* is essentially an intellectualization of a singularly advanced mystical soul. With a keen awareness of the stubborn irreducibility of this mystical-philosophical system, the present essay frequently proceeds on a level obviously below that on which the book was written and intended to be read.

So at the outset it must be emphasized that the more advanced aspects of Sri Aurobindo's spiritual philosophy are simply not available at this interpreter's level of spiritual and intellectual perception. As a result, much of this introductory essay will consist in a pointing to the spiritual experiences of which the philosophical expression is a cool distillation. In philosophical terms, this article will exhibit the peculiar difficulty attending an effort to interpret and evaluate a spiritual or mystical philosophy on the level of intellect. It will do this not by discussing the problem directly, but by attempting to present Sri Aurobindo's vision in terms intelligible to a readership which is willing to see but has not yet been shown. The author counts himself in this group.

In addition to this introductory section, which offers a broad characterization of *The Life Divine* and its dominant themes, this essay consists in six expository sections: Matter and Spirit; Brahman and the Delight of Existence; The Stages of Evolution; The Triple Transformation; Ascent to Supermind; and Supermind and the Life Divine. As these section titles clearly indicate, the two dominant strains in this interpretive exposition are the meaning and structure of evolution and the series of transformations by which the physical, vital and mental levels of existence are raised to a more manifestly divine life. As will hopefully be established in this essay, Sri Aurobindo's theories of evolution and transformation simultaneously reveal the content of his philosophical system and the spiritual experience on which it is based.

Both evolution and transformation evidence the blending of yogic and philosophical elements. There are many points at which these elements interpenetrate, but the most perspicuous is probably the theory of psychic entity, or the inmost self which lies behind the outer, observable self. According to this theory, the surface self, consisting of physical, vital and mental aspects, is a manifestation of the psychic being *(caitya purusha)*, which uses the surface self as an instrument of its own involvement in the evolutionary process. This theory is pivotal for transformation because the awareness of, and increasingly a direct action of, the psychic entity leads to the growth in the spiritual and supramental life; it is basic for evolution because it is the psychic entity which carries with it, from personality to personality through the entire course of evolution, all of the experiences gleaned from the physical, vital and mental aspects of the surface self. The details and rationale for this theory of the psychic entity and its implications for the theories of evolution and transformation will be discussed in the body of the paper, but are introduced here in order to show the experiential basis of the philosophical system articulated in *The Life Divine*. Sri Aurobindo's insistence on the reality of the psychic entity is certainly based on his own yoga experience, but his arguments on its behalf are those of a philosopher—or at least of a profound thinker who knows not only his own intellectual and spiritual experience, but also the intellectual theories which count for and against such experience.

SPIRITUAL EXPERIENCE AND PHILOSOPHY

The first puzzle confronting the interpreter of *The Life Divine* is its author's disclaimer to philosophic training, attitude or intent. Although *The Life Divine* is one of the lengthiest and most profound of metaphysical treatises, Sri Aurobindo insists that its basic ideas were the result of spiritual experience rather than philosophical scholarship. It was his theory that "a Yogi ought to be able to turn his head to anything"; writing *The Life Divine* in monthly installments in *Arya*, a journal founded for his writings by Paul and Mira Richard, did not involve his becoming a philosopher, or doing philosophy, but simply writing down in terms of intellect all that he had "observed and come to know in practicing Yoga."[1] In 1934, fifteen years after completing the first draft of what was to become his *magnum opus* of his thirty-volume corpus of writings, Sri Aurobindo repeated to his disciple, Dilip Kumar Roy, that he had never been a philosopher: "I knew precious little about philosophy before I did the Yoga and came to Pondicherry—I was a poet and a politician, not a philosopher!"[2]

While the great philosophers have presumably experienced periods of greater or less inspiration, Sri Aurobindo would seem to be exceptional in insisting that he could not "write philosophy to order," but could only write when it came to him.[3] By the time he issued the revised edition of *The Life Divine* in 1939–1940, the yogic source of his philosophical creation was all the more prominent. Indeed, all of his writings after 1926 flow from a quite different source, and consequently required a correspondingly different mode of expression.

To a remarkable degree, then, *The Life Divine* is both a systematic metaphysical treatise and a highly personal statement of Sri Aurobindo's spiritual experience. In this respect it most closely resembles *Savitri*, the other work which he revised throughout his life. Both of these works received extensive revision and expansion as a result of his experience of the "descent of the Overmind" in 1926. Obviously, a philosopher's personal experience is to some extent the source of every philosophical system, but in the case of *The Life Divine* Sri Aurobindo's experience apparently reaches beyond the more usual and accessible range of intellectual experience to a level ordinarily regarded as mystical and nonphilosophical. At the outset of an attempt to understand *The Life Divine*, one is faced with the problem of ontological and epistemological levels, the highest of which are not ordinarily acknowledged in academic philosophy.

The prominence of spiritual experience is certainly to be expected in a commentary on the Gita or in a treatise on yoga. It is perhaps less expected in works such as *The Human Cycle* and *The Foundations of Indian Culture*, but the claims in these works are not rendered exceptional or unintelligible because of a spiritual basis. But in *Savitri* and in *The Life Divine*, his two major works, the role of advanced spiritual experience is both pervasive and unavoidable.

1. Dilip Kumar Roy, *Sri Aurobindo Came to Me* (Bombay: Jaico Publishing Company, 1964), p. 33.
2. *Ibid.*
3. *Ibid.*

Indeed, as the interpreter of *Savitri* must explain the peculiar nature of poetic expression in that work, so *The Life Divine* must be rendered intelligible as a quite distinctive and perhaps unique form of philosophizing. Although Aurobindo attempts to establish a theoretical framework for the transformation of human nature, and the ultimate creation of an entirely new stage of existence is characterized by philosophical argumentation, clarity and erudition, many Western interpreters will dismiss *The Life Divine* because its presuppositions and the scope of its concerns reach beyond the ordinarily accepted range of philosophical topics. For some, Aurobindo's philosophical system may appear to be more an exercise in imagination than in philosophical reason. Since he writes as a realized yogi rather than as a professional philosopher, Sri Aurobindo would be neither surprised nor apologetic about this reaction; even though he spent many years working on this philosophical study, he nevertheless insisted that the conceptualization of his discipline and vision—even if it were adequate to the depth and range of his mystical experience—could not be grasped by the intellect alone. So, knowing the inherent limitations of the intellectual level at which this work would be interpreted, Aurobindo proceeded with it in the hope that it would help to create the intellectual climate wherein it would be understood. Since he believed his own experience to be exemplary of intellectual and spiritual realizations which will eventually be more widely shared, he believed that all his works, but *The Life Divine* most particularly, were more a forecast of the future than another philosophical description of the human condition in its present state of development.

Despite its emphasis on the future possibilities, and the accompanying acknowledgment that most interpreters will reject this system as fanciful, Sri Aurobindo nevertheless made a determined effort to base this system on the most credible interpretations of the past and present. His other works bear eloquent testimony to this firm grasp of systematic and cultural studies, and *The Life Divine* evidences his extraordinary grasp of the traditional and contemporary philosophical alternatives of both India and the West. Although he would not consider such mastery to be of any particular significance either concerning his authoritativeness or the reader's task to move from the intellectual to the spiritual aspects of his system, this control of philosophical theories and method well serves his intent to bring the reader through the intellectual to the higher reaches of his vision. He also notes that the sources of such expertise in his spiritual experience are not an insignificant by-product of yoga.

PLACING *THE LIFE DIVINE*

In relation to Sri Aurobindo's other major works, *The Life Divine* is both more basic and more comprehensive. Whereas *Savitri* offers the most complete account of Sri Aurobindo's spiritual experience and its implications for spiritual transformation, and *The Synthesis of Yoga* and *Essays on the Gita* offer systematic accounts of the discipline by which this transformation is effected, and *The Human Cycle* and *The Foundations of Indian Culture* establish the cultural and historical context for the spiritual age, the burden of *The Life Divine* is to establish the theoretical framework by which the discipline and historical vision are rendered intelligible. The root of Aurobindo's vision of gnostic or supramental being is in the human aspiration for perfection, truth, immortality and delight. Similarly, Aurobindo points to the aspiration of each level of existence—physical, vital and mental—as proof that all existence is carried forward by a power or force larger than itself. This force is the power of the spirit to carry each level of existence one level higher. According to this theory, the first three stages of evolution developed because each stage included within it the seed of its own evolution to the next stage. As matter is a form of veiled life, and life a form of veiled mind, so is mind a form of something higher than mind, supermind. Man's aspiration for freedom, truth, immortality and delight is in fact an aspiration for that next stage, the supramental or gnostic stage of evolution. It is with this fourth stage of evolution that the mature and most distinctive parts of *The Life Divine* are primarily concerned.

Within the context of Indian philosophy, Aurobindo's philosophical system is distinctive for its emphasis on cosmic and human evolution, with its clear implication that man and the world are incontestably real and valuable. In contrast to Western process philosophies such as those of Bergson, James, Dewey and Whitehead, for which evolution is the key, Aurobindo's system is perhaps unique in its insistence on the importance of involution and transformation. In relation to evolutionary and spiritual visions expounded by Teilhard de Chardin or S. Radhakrishnan—the contemporary Christian and Indian thinkers with whom Aurobindo is frequently compared—Aurobindo's system is unique in that it is derived from his own spiritual experience and claims that this experience is itself an instrument of the next evolutionary stage. Finally, through the instrumentality of the Mother of the Sri Aurobindo Ashram, Auro-bindo's spiritual vision and discipline have found historical expression in a spiritual community and a utopian city in Pondicherry, both of which are intended as models for the advent of a new age envisioned in Sri Aurobindo's writings on historical and spiritual evolution.

Thus, *The Life Divine* on the one hand bears striking resemblances to major works in the Hegelian and evolutional philosophical traditions, while on the other hand it moves to a level beyond that claimed by any modern Western philosopher. Perhaps the closest parallel to the prominence of the mystical in *The Life Divine* is the *Enneads* of Plotinus. While it is certainly possible to critique both the specific and general points in the Plotinian system, the system itself aims less at Platonic dialectic than at disclosures or exhibition of the author's own mystical experience. In the modern West, the nearest analogue to *The Life Divine* is Heidegger's *Zein und Zeit*, particularly since it is Heidegger's express intent to allow Being to disclose itself. The philosophical content and language of *The Life Divine* resembles the major works of the modern idealists and process philosophers—Hegel, Bradley, Royce, Bergson, James and Whitehead, but unlike these Western philosophers, Sri Aurobindo's system is an expression of his own spiritual or mystical experience. James, Royce and Bergson, the three modern Western philosophers most sympathetically concerned with mystical experience, were nevertheless writing from outside such experience; at no point do these or any other Western philosophers claim to be philosophizing on the basis of their own mystical experience. That Aurobindo makes this claim and insists on the indispensability of such experience for an adequate philosophical system necessarily presents the reader with very serious problems of interpretation. This essay is largely a response to these problems, the most pressing of which are, first, the general character of a spiritual philosophy and, second, an understanding of spiritual evolution and transformation.

Matter and Spirit

In the opening chapter of *The Life Divine*, Sri Aurobindo reveals simultaneously the task of his philosophy and the distinctive character of his own experience: "For all problems of existence are essentially problems of harmony" (2). As is indicated in the title of this keynote chapter, "The Human Aspiration," Sri Aurobindo sees humanity as a phase of evolution seeking a richer and deeper harmony within itself and in relation to other levels of existence. This realization of a general harmony requires "the upward impulse of man towards the accordance of yet higher opposites" (3). Such an inspiration is both natural and rational: "For essentially, all Nature seeks a harmony, life and matter in their own sphere as much as mind in the arrangement of its perception" (2). But the history of philosophy, Indian as well as Western and Chinese, attests to the difficulty of discerning and articulating the harmonious quality of existence. Discordance sets the task for philosophy precisely because it sits at the base of existence; in Sartre's phrase, "There is a worm in the core of Being." Echoing many strains of Indian and Western spiritual traditions, Sri Aurobindo perceives a dissatisfaction at the root of existence, but more than other spiritual philosophers, he emphasizes the positive function of such disharmony.

In sharp contrast to the Christian notion of sin and guilt, and the Hindu and Buddhist emphasis on liberation from the bonds of nature, Sri Aurobindo emphasizes the positive function of all levels of existence. But to be honored, such an affirmation must hold its own against the perceptions of existence which claim greater fidelity to experience or greater philosophical cogency. As philosophy, Sri Aurobindo's positive rendering of both matter and spirit must meet the objection of the materialist, for whom the spiritual is illusory, and the objection of the spiritualist, for whom matter is illusory. In these two positions, as well as in Sri Aurobindo's integral position, intellectual receptivity is as decisive as argument. The ancient quarrel can be decided "only by an extension of the field of our consciousness or an unhoped-for increase in our instruments of knowledge" (20).

The materialist opposes spirit not only because the material or sensible and measurable aspects of experience are sufficiently real and valuable, but because the spiritual is generally affirmed at the expense of the material. As Sri Aurobindo rightly admits, the spiritualist position has traditionally collapsed into "the refusal of the ascetic," a denial as extreme as that of the materialist's. Both positions claim to be preserving a particular value against the incursion of the other, and thereby isolate this value from its necessary complement. It remains to be seen whether Sri Aurobindo's attempt to reconcile these metaphysical polarities can be sustained experientially and metaphysically, but there is no doubt as to the position to which his work is committed:

> The passionate aspiration of man upward to the Divine has not been sufficiently related to the descending movement of the Divine leaning downward to embrace eternally Its manifestation. Its meaning in Matter has not been so well understood as Its truth in the Spirit. The Reality which the Sannyasin seeks has been grasped in its full height, but not, as by the ancient Vedantins, in its full extent and comprehensiveness. But in our completer affirmation we must not minimize the part of the pure spiritual impulse. As we have seen how greatly Materialism has served the ends of the Divine, so we must acknowledge the still greater service rendered by Asceticism to Life. We shall preserve the truths of material Science and its real utilities in the final harmony, even if many or if all of its existing forms have to be broken or left aside. An even greater scruple of right preservation must guide us in our dealing with the legacy, however actually diminished or depreciated, of the Aryan past. (24)

In this text, and throughout his writings, Sri Aurobindo reveals a variety of reasons for his insistence on the equal reality of Spirit and Matter. In philosophy as well as in the spiritual discipline he agrees to preserve the ascetic value as long as necessary: "In practice also the ascetic spirit is an indispensable element in human perfection and even its separate affirmation cannot be avoided so long as the race has not at the other end liberated its intellect and its vital habits from subjection to an always insistent animalism" (24). Similarly, the materialist value must be preserved in order to avoid the world-negating tendency, typified by Advaita Vedanta: "Shankara's wordless, inactive Self and his Māyā of many names and forms are equally disparate and irreconcilable entities; their rigid antagonism can terminate only by dissolution of the multitudinous illusion into the sole Truth of an eternal Silence" (7). In response to the anti-material tendency of most spiritual disciplines and philosophies, Sri Aurobindo argues that the physical universe is rightly described as "the external body of the Divine Being" (6). In the following text, Sri Aurobindo both affirms the value of the material world over against the "ascetic denial" and acknowledges the lofty function of spirit in relation to matter:

> The affirmation of a divine life upon earth and an immortal sense in mortal existence can have no base unless we recognize not only eternal Spirit as the inhabitant of this bodily mansion, the wearer of this mutable robe, but accept Matter of which it is made, as a fit and

noble material out of which He weaves constantly His garbs, builds
recurrently the unending series of his mansions. (6)

For "a divine life upon earth" spirit and matter are equally essential
but not equally divine. Matter is also Brahman—but not in the same
way nor to the same degree as spirit. Matter and spirit function
harmoniously but on separate levels. The harmony which is required
for their individual and collective advance involves all of the levels
of existence.

Basically there are two ways to understand this solution to the
problem of matter and spirit: on the one hand, matter is the lowest
level of existence and ought to be transcended to the spiritual; on
the other hand, matter and spirit are equally real and valuable because they are equally essential components of the one divine reality,
called Brahman or Sachchidananda (Sat-Chit-Ananda; Being-
Consciousness-Bliss). According to Sri Aurobindo's conception of
the Divine, material and spiritual realities are phases of the earth
process; it is only from within the limitations of matter or spirit,
supported by the diverse functions of the intellect, that one or
another of these phases is affirmed or denied. Yet even from within
Sri Aurobindo's integral yoga it appears that spirit, or the various
spiritual levels, is more real, valuable, divine than the "merely"
material. This perception follows from an interpretation of Sri Aurobindo's thought in terms of evolution without sufficient attention to
either of the two complementary processes, involution and transformation.

When understood without reference to involution, the theory of
evolution suggests that matter constitutes the lowest and least valuable level of existence; to the extent possible, all beings aspire to
transcend the material to the vital, mental and perhaps higher levels
of perfection. This idea is indeed valid within this framework. The
theory of evolution, however, describes the process of evolution but
not its rationale. Why do matter, life and mind aspire to the next
level? Why and how is the process possible in the first place? Sri
Aurobindo's answer to this question, partially reminiscent of the
Greek and Christian problem of creation, is the theory of involution.
The world evolves on its several levels because at each level Sachchidananda has already involved itself in each of these levels. Logically prior to evolution, involution is the process whereby Brahman,
or Sachchidananda, seeks its own manifestation through the mul-
tileveled universe.

Similarly, on the far side of evolution, the process of transformation refers to the uplifting of each level by the level immediately above it. Just as the involution of Brahman makes possible its own manifestation at each stage of evolution, the total transformation of terrestrial existence requires the effect of psychic, spiritual and supramental transformations. So although evolution is the most observable part of the Divine Play (Līlā), the processes immediately preceding and following evolution offer a deeper rationale for the process of evolution itself. While the middle process—the evolution from matter to life to mind and to supermind—evidences the genius of natural aspiration, the involution of Brahman into nature and the triple transformation (psychic, spiritual and supramental) evidence the delight which is ultimately the only adequate answer to the question concerning the meaning of involution. Indeed, evolution assumes a quite different significance if once it is granted that the only rationale for the entire process is Ananda or delight. Since it serves as the *raison d'être* for the entire process of creation, the concept of Ananda warrants a detailed account. As is indicated by the term Sachchidananda, a compound synonymn for Brahman or the Absolute, Ananda is an integral component of Ultimate Reality. Consequently, the next section will treat Ananda, or the Delight of Existence, in relation to the Absolute Brahman.

Brahman and the Delight of Existence

As with virtually all of Sri Aurobindo's writings, the two chapters on the problem and solution of the "delight of existence" evidences both classical and contemporary strains. The classical note is sounded in the epigraph of each chapter: Chapter XI, "Delight of Existence: The Problem," is prefaced by the following text from the Taittiriya Upanishad:

> For who could live or breathe if there were not this delight of existence as the ether in which we dwell?
> From Delight all these beings are born, by Delight they exist and grow, to Delight they return. [II.7]

Similarly, Chapter XII, "Delight of Existence: The Solution," is keynoted by a text from the Kena Upanishad: "The name of That is the Delight; as the Delight we must worship and seek after It"

(IV.6). In both texts, Sri Aurobindo identifies Brahman by this one quality, Delight. Brahman not only is blissful—or pure Ananda—but also bestows bliss to those who become united with it. In contrast to the usual Advaitic interpretation of such union, however, Sri Aurobindo contends that a person "must worship and seek after" the Delight of Existence by selfless participation in the creative function of Brahman. In effect, Sri Aurobindo's theory of the Delight of Existence serves as an explanation of human and divine creativity and the ideal relationship between them. Although the individual feels separate from other creative processes, and says of its activity, "This is I," all creative activity is part of the self-manifestation of the Divine. The source, justification and goal of such creativity is Ananda, or the Delight of Existence. In the following text, Sri Aurobindo articulates the analogy between the human and divine modes of creativity or self-manifestation:

> Existence that acts and creates by the power and from the pure delight of the conscious being is the reality that we are, the self of all modes and moods, the cause, object and goal of all our doing, becoming and creating. As the poet, artist or musician when he creates does really nothing but develop some potentiality in his unmanifested self into a form of manifestation and as the thinker, statesman, mechanist only bring out into a shape of things that which lay hidden in themselves, was themselves, is still themselves when it is cast into form, so is it with the world and the Eternal. All creation or becoming is nothing but this self-manifestation. (112)

The significance of this explanation is certainly not limited to the similarity between human and divine creativity, but is due rather to its bearing on the possibility of explaining the cause and purpose of existence in the first place. Sri Aurobindo confronts head-on the most basic question—perhaps so basic as to be unanswerable—of metaphysics: why the world at all? Whereas a naturalistic metaphysics, or any metaphysics which denies the existence of an ultimate reality, must explain the origin and apparent intelligibility of a world which does not owe its existence to a prior or more self-sufficient reality, a metaphysics which affirms an ultimate principle must explain why that self-sufficient and presumably eternal being involved itself in a spatially and temporally limited universe. Explicitly rejecting the concept of necessary creation (or necessary emanation—the logic of the problem is the same whether cast in terms of creationism or emanationism), Sri Aurobindo offers the following response to this time-honored metaphysical problem:

"Why should Brahman, perfect, absolute, infinite, needing nothing, desiring nothing, at all throw out force of consciousness to create
in itself these worlds of forms?" For we have put aside the solution
that it is compelled by its own nature of Force to create, obliged by
its own potentiality of movement and formation to move into forms.
It is true that it has this potentiality, but it is not limited, bound or
compelled by it; it is free. If, then, being free to move or remain
eternally still, to throw itself into forms or retain the potentiality of
forms in itself, it indulges its powers of movement and formation, it
can be only for one reason, for delight. (91)

In support of this theory, Sri Aurobindo utilizes, and partially revises,
two basic concepts: Maya and Lila. He also builds on the positive
relationship between his metaphysics and his spiritual experience.
The entire complex of problems can be illumined by an acceptance
of Ananda, or delight of existence, as a root metaphor for the divine,
the human and natural orders of being. As is always the case in Sri
Aurobindo's thought, the theory—in this case, the theories of
Ananda, Maya and Lila—is derived from his spiritual experience.
Specifically, each person, and indeed every particular in the universe,
can and ultimately must discover one's own delight of existence or
the joy of one's own self-manifestation. In accordance with the
teaching of the Gita and his own integral yoga, Sri Aurobindo
contends that the principle of divine Bliss must be functioning not
only on the level of the Divine, and the level of mind, but equally
in the physical world, "veiled indeed and possessing itself behind the
phenomenon of things, but still manifest in us through some subor-
dinate principles of its own in which it is hidden and by which it
must be found and achieved in the action of the universe" (220).
Thus, one can realize the bliss which one shares with Brahman or
Sachchidananda by minimizing the egoistic motive in one's thought
and action whether on the mental, vital or physical plane.

In effect, this emphasis on the delight of existence on every level
of creation constitutes Sri Aurobindo's response to the Advaitic
theory of Maya, or the conception of the universe as illusory and
unreal. For Sri Aurobindo, the universe, from God to inert matter,
should be experienced and described not as an illusion but as creative
energy (Shakti), as play (Lila) or as joy (Ananda). The world is indeed
"a masked form of Sachchidananda," but it is not for that reason
lacking in reality or value; the world is a limited expression of the
divine Ananda, but Ananda nonetheless. This view of the world, and
its positive relation to Brahman, issues from and further advances a

advances a world-affirming, world-transforming spiritual discipline. While the practical teaching of this world-affirming yoga is articulated in *Essays on the Gita* and *The Synthesis of Yoga*, in *The Life Divine* this yoga is supported by a metaphysical system, one element of which is the theory of Ananda, or delight of existence. On the side of creation and humanity, this theory may be summarized as follows: "To seek for delight is therefore the impulse and sense of Life; to find and possess and fulfill it is its whole motive" (219). On the side of the Divine, the theory contends that "the Absolute can have no purpose in manifestation except the delight of manifestation itself" (834). Further, these theories complement the theories of evolution and the Brahman which Sri Aurobindo develops throughout *The Life Divine*. The theory of evolution will be explained in the next section—suffice it at this point to note that the evolutionary movement falls within the general theory of the delight of existence, and consequently "it can be there only for the delight of the unfolding, the progressive execution, the objectless seried self-revelation" (834). The accompanying theory of Brahman warrants a further explanation.

In the foregoing discussion of Brahman and the delight of existence, the rationale for the existence of the universe has been described as the self-manifestation of Brahman; it remains to explain the logical and ontological relationship between Brahman and the universe. Drawing on his own integral Yogic experience as well as his understanding of the Indian and Christian spiritual traditions, Aurobindo describes the realization of the Divine in terms of three separate aspects of the Divine: the transcendental, the cosmic and the individual, and their harmonization by the supermind. Although his own Yoga and his own carefully articulated theory of the Divine accords a defining function to the supramental link between creation and Brahman or Sachchidananda, Aurobindo nevertheless acknowledges the validity, however limited, of transcendental, cosmic and individual aspects of the Divine. The following text describes the relative value of the individual, cosmic and transcendental realizations, and concludes with Sri Aurobindo's invitation to realize the supramental link between the lower and the higher levels of existence:

> If I realise only the Divine as that, not my personal self, which yet moves secretly all my personal being and which I can bring forward out of the veil, or if I build up the image of that Godhead in my

members, it is a realisation but a limited one. If it is the Cosmic Godhead that I realise, losing in it all personal self, that is a very wide realisation, but I become a mere channel of the universal Power and there is no personal or divinely individual consummation for me. If I shoot up to the transcendental realisation only, I lose both myself and the world in the transcendental Absolute. If, on the other hand, my aim is none of these things by itself, but to realize and also to manifest the Divine in the world, bringing down for the purpose a yet unmanifested Power—such as the supermind—a harmonization of all three becomes imperative.[4]

In addition to the spiritual implications cited here, this harmonization of the three aspects of the Divine also has theoretical implications, the most significant of which is its ability to reconcile the conflicting aspects of the Divine: the cosmic aspect refers to the consubstantiality of Brahman and the world, or the reality of the world as the self-manifestation of Brahman; the transcendent aspect indicates that, although the world is permeated by the Divine, the Divine is not exhausted by, i.e., transcends, the world; thirdly, the individual aspect of the Divine refers to the function of the Divine in each individual, e.g., the awareness of Ananda in each person manifesting the Ananda of Brahman, or Sat-Chit-Ananda. By insisting on these three both individually and collectively, Aurobindo is better able to offer a solution to the age-old problem of being and becoming (or eternal and temporal). In "Reality and the Cosmic Illusion," one of the several chapters in which Aurobindo contrasts his own position with the Advaita Vedanta system of Shankara, Sri Aurobindo both rejects Shankara's conception of the world as Māyā, or illusion, and reveals the attitude toward the world which distinguishes his entire philosophy from Shankara's. Essentially, he insists that the reality and value of the world follows from the dynamic or creative aspect of Brahman—or, conversely, to deny the reality and value of creation is to render Brahman an inert absolute. Hence the significance of Ananda as a rationale for creation: Aurobindo offers a wide variety of arguments against Shankara's position, but the basic reason for his rejection of Māyāvada is simply that it runs counter to his own experientially sustained belief that humanity, the cosmos and the Divine are intimately dependent aspects of the blissful self-manifestation of Brahman. He concludes:

4. *Letters on Yoga*, 23: 510.

> The theory of Illusion cuts the knot of the world problem, it does not disentangle it; it is an escape, not a solution: a flight of the spirit is not a sufficient victory for the being embodied in this world of the becoming; it effects a separation from Nature, not a liberation and fulfilment of our nature. (468)

Characteristically, Aurobindo's most basic metaphysical assertion draws from and points toward spiritual experience. He argues most persistently against the Advaitist position precisely because it is spiritually rich but significantly less rich than his own integral yoga. With the full weight of Upanishadic and Vedantic mysticism lined up against his attempt to establish a world-affirming yoga theory and practice, Aurobindo cannot but acknowledge the spiritual and philosophical power of this tradition: In the area of spiritual illumination, "the theory of Illusionism is in occupation of a very solid ground; for, although it is in itself no more than a mental formulation, the experience it formulates into a philosophy accompanies a most powerful and apparently final spiritual realisation" (469). Aurobindo's intent is not to discredit this realization—since "all truths, even those which seem to be in conflict, have their validity"—but rather to take this realization beyond itself to a liberation and oneness which transforms in the process each level of existence, or each aspect of Brahman involved in the play. For Sri Aurobindo, yoga and philosophy must express the delight of existence which is "the impulse and sense of life." More technically, the particular impulse which characterizes Aurobindo's philosophy and yoga, and clearly distinguishes them from Adwaita Vedanta, is called Shakti, the divine force which progressively bridges the gap between the Divine, human and natural levels of the self-manifestation of Brahman. This concept presupposes the reality of the Avatar as developed in the Gita, and points toward the concept of the Mother as the embodiment of the Divine in its transcendent, cosmic and individual forms, and ultimately as the expression of the supramental manifestation. The concepts of the supermind will be more fully explained below but it requires a preliminary introduction to the levels of evolution and the means of their transformation.

Stages of Evolution

As Sri Aurobindo's theory of Brahman or the Absolute separates his system from most process or evolutionary philosophers, his the-

ory of evolution separates his system from most spiritual philosophers (particularly the Advaita Vedanta school). Yet for Aurobindo
the theories of Brahman and evolution as developed in *The Life
Divine* are logically and experientially inseparable. In "The Teaching of Sri Aurobindo," which is his own brief summary of his teaching written in 1948, Sri Aurobindo presents his theory of evolution
as the second key component of his system, following after the
theory of Being or Brahman. As crisply stated in this summary—and
as explained in the preceding section of this article—"the teaching
of Sri Aurobindo starts from that of the ancient sages of India that
behind the appearances of the universe there is the Reality of a
Being and consciousness, a Self of all things, one and eternal. All
beings are united in that One Self and Spirit but divided by a certain
separativity of consciousness, an ignorance of their true Self and
Reality in the mind, life and body."[5] According to the theory of
involution, it is this Being which has involved Itself in the universe;
evolution is the manifestation of involved Being. In this sense, evolution is essentially the heightening of the force of consciousness of
Brahman through the successive stages of the matter, life and mind.
As Sri Aurobindo explains, evolution is the process by which consciousness, involved in matter, liberates itself:

> Life is the first step of this release of consciousness; mind is the
> second; but the evolution does not finish with mind, it awaits a release
> into something greater, a consciousness which is spiritual and supra-
> mental.[6]

At the outset, it is significant to note that this release of consciousness refers not only to Brahman *per se*, but each stage of evolution
is also a partial release from the preceding stage. But because each
release on the lower level is partial, some force above these levels is
needed to effect a more total release. Since life and mind are bound
to matter, they cannot be entirely liberated from the limitations of
matter. In this scheme, then, evolution in the usual sense of the term
is but one aspect of the complex process which Sri Aurobindo articulates by means of three concepts: involution, evolution and transformation. These processes include the various stages of consciousness
or what Sri Aurobindo refers to as the "sevenfold chord of Being."

5. "The Teaching of Sri Aurobindo," in Robert A. McDermott (ed.), *The Essential
Aurobindo* (New York: Schocken Books, 1973), p. 29.
6. *Ibid.*

Temporarily omitting the principle called soul or psyche, "which comes into manifestation at the nodus of mind, life and body" (263), the seven stages are as follows:

> Existence (Sat)
> Consciousness-Force (Chit)
> Bliss (Ananda)
>
> Supermind (perfect unity in diversity)
>
> Mind (intellect and intuition)
> Life (vital, organic)
> Matter (physical, inconscient)

Although the upper hemisphere, Sat-Chit-Ananda (or Brahman) is ontologically prior to the lower hemisphere, it is the lower to which human consciousness is ordinarily limited—or from which it is generally not yet released. Although some great souls—not only the Avatars such as Buddha or Krishna, but presumably mystics such as Shankara and Sri Ramana Maharshi—have moved beyond the lower levels of existence to a unitive experience of Sat-Chit-Ananda, the bulk humanity as a whole remains at a level which blends physical, vital and mental elements. While Aurobindo emphatically affirms the value of each of these levels, he also contends that, when these lower stages are separated from their spiritual source, they experience what was referred to above as "a certain separativity of consciousness, an ignorance of their true Self and Reality in the mind, life and body." More precisely: "This lapse, this separation creates a state of limited knowledge exclusively concentrated on its own limited world-order and oblivious of all that is behind it and of the underlying unity, a state therefore of cosmic and individual Ignorance" (663).

Thus, neither matter nor life nor mind is independent or an adequate account of reality; each emerges as supreme for a time but when scrutinized in the light of their spiritual source each reveals that it is essentially a manifestation of spirit. Matter, for example, is really Energy, or Sat (Being) involved through its principle of Shakti. Life appears to be all-sufficient when it first emerges as a power over matter, but life too is a function of Brahman, particularly of Chit, or its consciousness aspect. Mind, which of the three has most often been regarded as the highest and altogether sufficient principle of reality, is here described as "a limited and derivative power; it is an outcome of Overmind or it is here a luminous shadow thrown by the divine Supermind" (665).

In addition to the three stages of the lower hemisphere just described, Aurobindo posits a fourth principle, called "psyche," or soul. As matter, life and mind are manifestations of some aspect of Brahman, psyche is a manifestation of the Ananda aspect. The delight of existence which the individual can discover in his own experience is possible because the human soul, or psyche, has reached the stage of manifesting the divine Ananda within its own material, vital and mental being. This aspect of the self, called *caitya purusa*, is one's true self or the central core of one's being which is inaccessible to the person who has not realized the divine or spiritual source of his own existence. It is the psychic or inmost soul which opens to the delight of existence. But the bulk of humanity does not realize the delight of existence, or the delight of Brahman, precisely because the psychic remains inaccessible: "The malady of the world is that the individual cannot find his real soul, and the root-cause of this malady is again that he cannot meet in his embrace of things outward the real soul of the world in which he lives" (221). This contact with one's psyche is one of the goals of Sri Aurobindo's yoga; it is also a prerequisite for the transformation which Sri Aurobindo envisions through the meeting of a psychically and spiritually receptive humanity and the force of the supermind. As the next section explains, future stages of evolution will be effected by a triple transformation—psychic, spiritual and supramental.

The Triple Transformation

In his essay on "The Energies of Men," William James wisely develops the thesis "that as a rule men habitually use only a small part of the powers which they actually possess and which they might use under appropriate conditions."[7] In support of this proposition, James refers to the increased "strength of character, personal power, unshakability of soul" which have resulted from the practice of "the yoga system in Hindustan."[8] While yoga theory and practice surely

7. William James, "The Energies of Men," in John J. McDermott (ed.), *The Writings of William James* (New York: Random House [Modern Library], 1968), p. 674.
8. *Ibid.*, p. 679.

do not need the endorsement of James or any other contemporary philosopher, an essay such as "Energies of Men" [9] articulates the undeveloped human potentiality which Sri Aurobindo so powerfully embodies.

According to the theory and practice of yoga as developed by Sri Aurobindo, the "appropriate conditions" for the full range and development of human potentiality consists in three stages of transformation, the first, or psychic, stage of which seems to meet James' call for "an absolutely concrete study" of the various ways of unlocking the reserves of power exemplified in individual lives. Further, Sri Aurobindo's account of the psychic transformation, in his own case and presumably in a more general way, exemplifies "a program of concrete individual psychology . . . replete with interesting fact, and points to practical issues superior in importance to anything we know."[10] Sri Aurobindo certainly attributes a comparable importance to the "concrete individual psychology" generated by his theory of the psychic entity. This theory of the inmost aspect of the self serves as the cornerstone for the first of the three transformations, the discovery of the soul behind the observable body, life and mind: before the spiritual and supramental transformations can be effected, "there must first be the psychic change, the conversion of our whole present nature into a soul-instrumentation" (891).

Whereas the psychic transformation consists in a movement to the depths of the inmost self, the spiritual transformation is "an opening outward of the inner and inmost being and nature" (908), and the supramental transformation is "a direct and unveiled intervention from above" (922). Although a spiritual or supramental transformation could conceivably be effected without a prior psychic transformation, contact with the jivatman, or the divine element of the self, protects the self against psychic experiences which are variously daemonic or egoistic (908). Indeed, the primary function of the psychic entity is to control "the surface desire-soul which works in our vital cravings, our emotions, aesthetic faculty and mental seeking for power, knowledge and happiness" (220) so as to replace the usual attachment to pleasure by the true experience of Ananda.

9. Delivered as the Presidential Address before the American Philosophical Association at Columbia University, December 28, 1906.
10. From James' address as originally delivered before the American Philosophical Association. *Ibid.*, p. 683n[40].

As is taught by the Gita and virtually every other Yoga treatise, the spiritual seeker must obliterate the distinction between pleasure, pain and indifference; Sri Aurobindo's theory of transformation revises this "view of old philosophies" by contending that when the real soul *(caitya purusha)* breaks through the confines of the desire-soul, it replaces "the egoistic standards of pleasure and pain by an equal, an all-embracing personal-impersonal delight" (224). In short, if the psychic entity can once be contacted and enabled to dominate, the true power or energy of will can be realized:

> If the secret psychic Person can come forward into the front and, replacing the desire-soul, govern overtly and entirely and not only partially and from behind the veil this outer nature of mind, life and body, then these can be cast into soul images of what is true, right and beautiful and in the end the whole nature can be turned towards the real aim of life, the supreme victory, the ascent into spiritual existence. (228–229)

Thus, the psychic transformation prepares the way for the evolution of a spiritual humanity: "It is the psychic personality in us that flowers as the saint, the sage, the seer; when it reaches its full strength, it turns the being towards the Knowledge of Self and the Divine, towards the supreme Truth, the supreme Good, the supreme Beauty, Love and Bliss, the divine heights and largenesses, and opens us to the touch of spiritual sympathy, universality, oneness" (226).

Consistent with his theory of spiritual evolution, Sri Aurobindo insists that the function of the spiritual person is to discover one's spiritual being "and to help others towards the same evolution" (885). This spiritual transformation must eventually encompass the mental, vital and material levels, but their total transformation cannot be effected on the spiritual level, but rather requires the unique capacity of supermind to unify all particulars—whether spiritual, mental, vital or physical—in a dynamic unity (965).

Finally, it should be noted that, although the evolutionary process up to the level of mind seems to have effected a change of consciousness by a change of physical natures, the spiritual and supramental transformations proceed in reverse: it is through human consciousness that the physical organism will evolve in the future (843). In the end, the function of spiritual and supramental transformations is to spiritualize the material universe (918). But the ascent to the supermind, and its subsequent descent into matter (including the human body) involves several intermediary steps which need more precise delineation.

Ascent to Supermind

The psychic and spiritual transformations by which the dominance of the egoistic self is increasingly replaced by the action of divine knowledge, power and bliss are a necessary but not a sufficient condition for the supramental transformation. For this transformation to be fully realized, many individuals will have to take advantage of their spiritual power to achieve a higher than mental mode of knowledge. The line of transition from psychic and spiritual to supramental will not be the same for all, but in general, "the gradation can be resolved into a stairway of four main ascents": higher mind, illumined mind intuition and overmind (938).

The first step above normal intelligence "is an ascent into a higher mind," an ascent into a mode of cognition particularly adept at grasping the relations between large ideas. Higher mind, strikingly similar to a Platonic or Plotinian theory of *nous* (or system of ideas), can conceive of a system of ideas "at a single view" (940). Since higher mind remains limited to cognition or thought—albeit wider and more integral than the normal range of thought—it does not remain satisfied with its ideational achievement but rather seeks a more direct grasp of reality. It moves from a conceptual to a perceptual contact, from higher to illumined mind. This second stage of ascent toward supermind is well summarized as follows:

> A consciousness that proceeds by sight, the consciousness of the seer, is a greater power for knowledge than the consciousness of the thinker. The perceptual power of the inner sight is greater and more direct than the perceptual power of thought: it is a spiritual sense that seizes something of the substance of Truth and not only her figure; but it outlines the figure also and at the same time catches the significance of the figure, and it can embody her with a finer and bolder revealing outline and a larger comprehension and power of totality than thought-conception can manage. (945–946)

Although the definitions of higher mind and illumined mind help to clarify these two levels of insight immediately above mind, neither Sri Aurobindo nor any of his interpreters offer a single example of these levels. His account of intuition is somewhat more precise but in view of the significant literature on this topic, it is again disappointing that he did not explicitly distinguish his concept from those developed by Western philosophers, notably Henri Bergson.[11]

Sri Aurobindo does, however, explain the more salient features of intuition in relation to levels of knowledge above and beneath it. In this respect, his singularly high estimate of the Vedic seers is particularly revealing: Aurobindo contends that the Vedas and Upanishads consist in intuitions rather than rational insights, and as such were too unstable to be sustained against the analytic and organizational functions of reason. As explained in the preceding article, on *The Human Cycle*, the intuitions of the Vedic sages were spiritually so rich that they "receded into the background of human consciousness" until a more advanced stage of consciousness would be ready for them.[12] In one sense, the succession from Vedic intuition to rational metaphysics mixed with Shruti (or revelation) to purely rational philosophizing must be regarded as a devolution of consciousness; when viewed from the perspective of these capacities themselves, however, the appropriation of intuitive insights by reason must be viewed positively because it eventually leads to a greater openness and plasticity of reason itself. The following lengthy passage clarifies the relationship between intuition and reason, and shows how this mutual interpenetration prepares for the more integral knowledge made possible by the overmind and supermind:

> But in our surface being it is not the Intuition, it is the Reason which is organised and helps us to order our perceptions, thoughts and actions. Therefore the age of intuitive knowledge, represented by the early Vedantic thinking of the Upanishads, had to give place to the age of rational knowledge; inspired Scripture made room for metaphysical philosophy, even as afterwards metaphysical philosophy had to give place to experimental Science. Intuitive thought which is a messenger from the superconscient and therefore our highest faculty, was supplanted by the pure reason which is only a sort of deputy and belongs to the middle heights of our being; pure reason in its turn was supplanted for a time by the mixed action of the reason which lives on our plains and lower elevations and does not in its view

11. For Bergson's theory of evolution, see especially *Introduction to Metaphysics* (New York: Random House, 1944), *Creative Mind* (New York: Philosophical Library, 1946) and *The Two Sources of Morality and Religion* (New York: Doubleday, 1956); see also S. K. Maitra, *The Meeting of the East and the West in Sri Aurobindo's Philosophy* (1956) and R. S. Srivastava, *Sri Aurobindo and the Theories of Evolution* (Varanasi: Chowkhamba Publications, 1968.
12. See above, p. 140.

exceed the horizon of the experience that the physical mind and senses or such aids as we can invent for them can bring to us. And this process which seems to be a descent, is really a circle of progress. For in each case the lower faculty is compelled to take up as much as it can assimilate of what the higher had already given and to attempt to re-establish it by its own methods. By the attempt it is itself enlarged in its scope and arrives eventually at a more supple and a more ample self-accommodation to the higher faculties.(68)

Thus, reason tinged with intuition is better able to receive "the higher faculties." In effect, the descent of the overmental and supramental consciousness represents the reversal—and the fulfillment—of the complex process by which Vedic intuitions were appropriated by reason so that reason could ascend to intuition.

The descent of both the overmind and the supermind enables reason and intuition to receive, each in their respective ways, these higher forces and modes of knowledge.[13] It remains to describe, however inadequately, the implications of the overmental and supramental descents.

Supermind and the Life Divine

According to Sri Aurobindo's experience of the overmental descent and his subsequent account of its implications, the overmind can bridge the division between Knowledge and Ignorance—i.e., between the unity of reality (or Brahman) and the partial manifestation of Brahman in evolution. The overmind, then, is the highest stage of knowledge immediately below Knowledge—or, the highest stage within Ignorance. It seizes the unity of Brahman and is consequently part of Knowledge, but since it cannnot hold this knowledge in a permanent realization, it is still within the limits of Ignorance. It would remain partially an instrument of Ignorance were it not for the unifying and stabilizing power of supermind.

The overmental descent, which Sri Aurobindo experienced in his "day of siddhi" (November 24, 1926), enables a self which has

---

13. Some sense of the contrast between a later work such as *The Life Divine* and earlier works such as *The Human Cycle* with respect to Sri Aurobindo's ascent to the supermind can be derived from his reference in *The Human Cycle* to "a deeper, more intuitive, more spelndid and powerful . . . light and force for which we have not even a name" (quoted above, pp. 152–153, from *The Human Cycle*, p. 76).

achieved higher and illumined mind to make contact with cosmic or global consciousness. In a passage which could only have been written after the 1926 experience of the overmental descent, Sri Aurobindo explains:

> When the Overmind descends, the predominance of the centralising ego-sense is entirely subordinated, lost in largeness of being and finally abolished; a wide cosmic perception and feeling of a boundless universal self and movement replaces it: many motions that were formerly egocentric may still continue, but they occur as currents or ripples in the cosmic wideness. Thought, for the most part, no longer seems to originate individually in the body or the person but manifests from above or comes in upon the cosmic mind-waves: all inner individual sight or intelligence of things is now a revelation or illumination of what is seen or comprehended, but the source of the revelation is not in one's separate self but in the universal knowledge; the feelings, emotions, sensations are similarly felt as waves from the same cosmic immensity breaking upon the subtle and the gross body and responded to in kind by the individual centre of the universality; for the body is only a small support or even less, a point of relation, for the action of a vast cosmic instrumentation. In this boundless largeness, not only the separate ego but all sense of individuality, even of a subordinated or instrumental individuality, may entirely disappear, the cosmic existence, the cosmic consciousness, the cosmic delight, the play of cosmic forces are alone left: if the delight or the centre of Force is felt in what was the personal mind, life or body, it is not with a sense of personality but as a field of manifestation, and this sense of the delight or of the action of Force is not confined to the person or the body but can be felt at all points in an unlimited consciousness of unity which pervades everywhere. (950–951)

Thus, the overmental descent brings the soul to a larger experience of the delight of existence, and dramatically reduces the role of the desire-soul in such an experience. But although it reduces the action of the "separative mind" in favor of a more universal mode of knowing, "it cannot lead mind beyond itself":

> For it is the Supermind alone that is the supreme self-determining truth-action and the direct power of manifestation of that Transcendence. If then the action of evolutionary Nature ended here, the Overmind, having carried the consciousness to the point of a vast illumined universality and an organized play of this wide and potent spiritual awareness of utter existence, force-consciousness and delight, could only go farther by an opening of the gates of the Spirit into the upper hemisphere and a will to enable the soul to depart out of its cosmic formation into Transcendence.(953)

In short, the overmind represents the highest stage of nature and mind, while supermind represents the gradual but permanent and comprehensive transformation of mind, life and the human body.

Ultimately, overmind and all of the levels of Ignorance below it will be transformed by the force of the supramental descent:

> The supramental consciousness and force would take up the transformation directly into its own hands, reveal to the terrestrial mind, life, bodily being their own spiritual truth and divinity and, finally, pour into the whole nature the perfect knowledge, power, significance of the supramental existence. The soul would pass beyond the borders of the Ignorance and cross its original line of departure from the supreme Knowledge: it would enter into the integrality of the supramental gnosis; the descent of the gnostic Light would effectuate a complete transformation of the Ignorance. (955)

This text emphasizes the supramental transformation of Ignorance into Knowledge, but this transformation is accomplished by—and ultimately identical with—the transformation of all levels within Ignorance, namely, the material, vital, mental levels of existence.

In this sense, the supermind harmonizes each of the conflicts which lie at the root of every metaphysical system. In Sri Aurobindo's system, the supermind harmonizes matter and spirit, the many levels of existence from sticks and stones to Sachchidananda, and the cosmic, individual and transcendent aspects of the Divine. In each such conflict, the opposing constituents are reconciled by exhibiting their capacity to express the Divine in their nature. The last, and most difficult, such reconciliation of an ontological conflict is that between Matter and Spirit. This reconciliation is the ultimate task precisely because it was the first conflict to occur; the descent of Spirit (or Brahman) into Matter (or Inconscience) was the initial fall from spiritual perfection and consequently will be the last to be restored. But because of the supramental descent, the ascetic's "refusal" of the physical would no longer be necessary, for the supermind would make possible "a free acceptance of the whole of material Nature in place of a rejection" (986). Once the supermind descends, all levels of existence, including matter, will be seen more immediately as the manifestation of Brahman. Thus, there would develop a sacramental reverence for matter such as taught by the Vedas and the Gita:

> As in the Gita the act of the taking of food is spoken of as a material sacrament, a sacrifice, an offering of Brahman to Brahman

by Brahman, so also the gnostic consciousness and sense can view all the operations of Spirit with Matter. The Spirit has made itself Matter in order to place itself there as an instrument for the well-being and joy, *yogaksema*, of created beings, for a self-offering of universal physical utility and service. The gnostic being, using Matter but using it without material or vital attachment or desire, will feel that he is using the Spirit in this form of itself with its consent and sanction for its own purpose. There will be in him a certain respect for physical things, an awareness of the occult consciousness in them, of its dumb will of utility and service, a worship of the Divine, the Brahman in what he uses, a care for a perfect and faultless use of his divine material, for a true rhythm, ordered harmony, beauty in the life of Matter, in the utilisation of Matter. (187)

In joyfully following the lines of the divine play, the gnostic being proceeds in perfect freedom: "In gnostic life, therefore, there is an entire accord between the free self-expression of the being and his automatic obedience to the inherent law of the supreme and universal Truth of things" (999). Here again Sri Aurobindo moves beyond a traditional antinomy—freedom and determinism—by reference to the harmonizing function of supermind.

In his own life Sri Aurobindo clearly regarded himself as a gnostic being; he was convinced that his sadhana (yoga discipline), by virtue of the overmental descent and his near ascent to the supermind, did indeed remove the "play of a separative ego" and enable him to "be one with the will of Ishwara" (1005). His thought and action were not fully supramental or gnostic, but he did approach this state on its essential points: he lived "in and for the Divine in himself, in and for the Divine in the collectivity, and in and for the Divine in all beings" (1030). In short, he exemplified the early stages of the first three perfections generated by the supermind. But by his own admission it was to be the Mother of the Sri Aurobindo Ashram (his spiritual collaborator who is regarded by thousands of disciples as co-Avatar with Sri Aurobindo) who would experience—indeed, be the instrument of—the supramental descent.

All of Sri Aurobindo's writings—most notably the claim in *Savitri* that the Mother's task is to help achieve physical immortality—point toward the creation of communities such as those over which the Mother presided for nearly fifty years. Both the Sri Aurobindo Ashram and Auroville[14] aim to express Sri Aurobindo's call for a

14. For a description of the Sri Aurobindo Ashram and Auroville, including the Mother's role in their creation and development, see *The Essential Aurobindo*, pp. 219–246.

community of gnostic individuals who would form "a new common life superior to the present individual and common existence" (1031). The effort at collective Yoga has gained in force due to the Mother's account of her experience of the supermind in 1956,[15] but the most extraordinary import of the Mother's spiritual power, and the one with the most fundamental philosophical implications, is the Mother's attempt to transform her own body.

As explained in the introduction to "Notes on the Way," the Mother's serialed account of her attempt to initiate the process of transforming the cells of her body, her experiences and reflections "are like landmarks on the way of Transformation: they were chosen not only because they illumine the work under way—a yoga of the body of which all the processes have to be established—but because they can be a sort of indication of the endeavour that has to be made."[16] Although the supermind was not experienced until 1956—six years after his death—Sri Aurobindo apparently foresaw the nature of the Mother's work for physical transformation. Given the order of evolution from matter to supermind, and the order of transformation from supermind to matter, it is entirely appropriate that as the unification of matter and spirit was his earliest yogic and philosophical concern, it was also his last. As *The Life Divine* opens with the human aspiration toward "God, Light, Freedom and Immortality," and the complementarity of matter and spirit, it closes with the actual spiritualization of matter in the present age. The last paragraph of *The Life Divine* begins with a conditional, but the previous one thousand pages sought to establish that the claims of this concluding statement are in fact the case:

15. For the Mother's account of the supermind, see K.R. Srinivasa Iyengar, *Sri Aurobindo: A Biography and a History* (1972), II, pp. 1368–1373, and *The Essential Aurobindo*, p. 237.
16. *Bulletin of the Sri Aurobindo International Centre of Education* (Sri Aurobindo Ashram), Vol. 17, No. 1 (February 1965), p. 77. These "Notes," for which Satprem, author of *Sri Aurobindo or the Adventure of Consciousness* (1968), served as amanuensis, have been published in most issues of the *Bulletin*, date from October 7, 1964 until March 10, 1973, several months before the Mother's death. Understandably, the disciples have sought to clarify for themselves and others the extent of the Mother's transformation prior to her "departure from the body," and the implications of her effort for the larger task of spiritualizing all material existence. The most significant of these statements is that by Nolini Kanta Gupta, the Mother's successor as head of the Sri Aurobindo Ashram; see Nolini Kanta Gupta, "The Mother and Ourselves," *Mother India* (A Monthly Review of Culture published at the Sri Aurobindo Ashram), March 1974, pp. 165–168.

If there is an evolution in material Nature and if it is an evolution of being with consciousness and life as its two key-terms and powers, this fullness of being, fullness of consciousness, fullness of life must be the goal of development towards which we are tending and which will manifest at an early or later stage of our destiny. The self, the spirit, the reality that is disclosing itself out of the first inconscience of life and matter, would evolve its complete truth of being and consciousness in that life and matter. It would return to itself—or, if its end as an individual is to return into its Absolute, it could make that return also,—not through a frustration of life but through a spiritual completeness of itself in life. Our evolution in the Ignorance with its chequered joy and pain of self-discovery and world-discovery, its half fulfilments, its constant finding and missing, is only our first state. It must lead inevitably towards an evolution in the Knowledge, a self-finding and self-unfolding of the Spirit, a self-revelation of the Divinity in things in that true power of itself in Nature which is to us still a Supernature. (1069–1070)

Such is Sri Aurobindo's vision of the Life Divine.

NOTES ON CONTRIBUTORS

THOMAS BERRY, a historian of Indian and Chinese culture, is Associate Professor of Asian religions in the Graduate School of Fordham University. He did his advanced study at Catholic University of America under Dr. Friederich Engel-Janosi who introduced him to the thought of Giambattista Vico, whose *The New Science of the Nature of the Nations* became the subject of his dissertation. His books include: *The Historical Theory of Giambattista Vico, Buddhism,* and *Religions of India.* His articles include: "Oriental Philosophy and World Humanism," in *International Philosophical Quarterly* (1961), "The Spiritual Form of Oriental Civilizations," in *Approaches to Asian Civilizations* "The Problem of Moral Evil and Guilt in Early Buddhism," in *Concilium* (1970), and "Traditional Religions in the Modern World," in *Cross Currents* (1972). He is founder and director of The Riverdale Center for Religious Research in New York, and is a member of the Executive Board of the Teilhard Association for the Future of Man. He is presently completing a full-length study of contemporary spirituality.

JOHN E. COLLINS is Assistant Professor of Religion at Wake Forest University. He has studied at the University of Tennessee (B.S. and M.S. in Physics, 1960, 1962), Southeastern Seminary (B.D., 1965), and Princeton University (M.A., Ph.D. in History of Religions, 1967, 1970). He teaches in the area of history of religions, phenomenology of religion, and religion and science. His dissertation, *The Integral Vision of Sri Aurobindo* was a study of the religious symbolism of *Savitri.* He has written other articles and presented papers on Sri Aurobindo to various professional organizations. His primary research interest continues to be related to Aurobindo's use of religious symbols.

191

EUGENE FONTINELL is currently Professor of Philosophy and was formerly Chairman of the Department of Philosophy at Queens College, CUNY. He pursued graduate studies at Fordham University, where, under the mentorship of Robert Pollock, he wrote a dissertation on Josiah Royce (Ph.D., 1957). He is an associate editor of *Cross Currents* and the author of *Toward a Reconstruction of Religion: A Philosophical Probe.* He has written for a variety of journals and has contributed to a number of collections of essays in the area of the philosophy of religion. His interest in Sri Aurobindo's thought centers on its evolutionary aspects particularly as it compares and contrasts with the process features of American pragmatism.

THOMAS J. HOPKINS received a B.S in Mechanical Engineering from M.I.T. in 1953 and a concurrent B.S. in Physics from the College of William and Mary; at Yale University he received a B.D. (1958) in Religion and Culture and an M.A. (1959) and Ph.D. (1962) in Comparative Religion. His publications include "The Social Teaching of the *Bhāgavata Purāna*" in *Krishna: Myths, Rites and Attitudes,* edited by Milton Singer, and an introductory textbook, *The Hindu Religious Tradition;* he is currently working on a source-book on the Hindu tradition. Since 1961 he has taught at Franklin and Marshall College, where he is now Professor and Chairman of Religious Studies and Director of the Central Pennsylvania Consortium India Study Program at the University of Mysore. For the past several years, he has served as Group Leader on a project to improve undergraduate teaching in Indian Religion and Philosophy sponsored by the Council for Intercultural Studies and Programs and the National Endowment for the Humanities. His householder life is centered around his wife, Fran, their four children, and their 60-year-old row house in Lancaster, Pa.

J. BRUCE LONG is currently Assistant Professor of Asian Religions at Cornell University. He received his graduate training at the University of Chicago under the direction of Mircea Eliade and J. A. B. van Buitenen. After earning the M.A. (1963) in Theology and Literature, he received a Ph.D. (1970) in History of Religions and Indology. His publications include *Judaism and the Christian Seminary Curriculum* (ed.), "Śiva and Dionysos: Visions of Terror and Bliss,"

Numen; "Festival of Repentance: A Study of Mahaśivarā-tri," *Journal of the Oriental Institute, Baroda;* and "Life Out of Death: A Structural Analysis of the 'Churning of the Ocean' Myth," in *New Essays in Hinduism* edited by Bardwell Smith. He is currently engaged in preparing a complete annotated bibliography on the Mahabharata.

ROBERT A. MCDERMOTT is Associate Professor and Chairman, Department of Philosophy, Baruch College, CUNY. He was trained in philosophy at Emory University (M.A., 1965) and Boston University (Ph.D., 1969), where he wrote a dissertation on "Radhakrishnan's Comparative Philosophy" under the direction of John Lavely.He was secretary of the American Academy of Religion (1969–72) and is active in the Society for Asian and Comparative Philosophy. He is the editor of *Radhakrishnan* (Dutton, 1970), Sri Aurobindo's *The Mind of Light* (Dutton, 1971), *The Essential Aurobindo* (Schocken, 1973), and with V. S. Naravane, *The Spirit of Modern India* (Crowell, 1974). He visited India while on a Fulbright grant in 1966 and visited the Sri Aurobindo Ashram in 1970.

BIBLIOGRAPHY

Sri Aurobindo Birth Centenary Library (1970–1972)

Guide to Further Reading

Anyone seriously interested in Sri Aurobindo's writings will want to use the
thirty-volume Sri Aurobindo Birth Centenary Library (hereafter BCL) described
above. Many of the volumes in this edition, including the six works discussed in
the present volume and such other major works as *The Upanishads, Sri Aurobindo
on Himself, The Mother,* and *Letters on Yoga* (3 volumes), are also available
individually in an inexpensive offset edition. Volumes cited in this guide which are
part of the offset edition of the Birth Centenary Library are followed by the volume
number of the BCL edition and the publication date of the offset edition. Volumes
marked by an asterisk are paperback. The BCL, the offset edition and several
hundred additional works by and about Sri Aurobindo are available from Matagiri,
a Sri Aurobindo ashram in upstate New York.

GENERAL

Sri Aurobindo's writings on philosophy, yoga and historical vision, including
selections from *Savitri, Essays on the Gita, The Synthesis of Yoga* and *The Life
Divine,* have been collected in Robert A. McDermott (ed.), *The Essential Aurobindo* (New York: Schocken Books, 1973*). This anthology includes the editor's
introductions, an annotated bibliography and selections from the Mother's writings
on education and Auroville.

There are countless books, most of them by disciples, which offer a broad
introduction to Sri Aurobindo's life, teachings and influence, the most useful of
which are the following: R. R. Diwakar, *Sri Aurobindo Mahayogi* (Bombay: Bhara-
tiya Vidya Bhavan, 1967*); Jesse Roarke, *Sri Aurobindo* (1973); and K. R. Srinivasa
Iyengar, *Sri Aurobindo: A Biography and a History* (2 vols., 1972*), a massive work
which is clearly the most authoritative secondary source on virtually every aspect
of Sri Aurobindo's life and work.

As a result of the centenary of Sri Aurobindo's birth celebrated in 1972, many articles have been collected in symposia volumes, the most significant of which are V. M. Reddy (ed.), *Towards Eternity* (1973) and Kishore Gandhi (ed.), *The Contemporary Relevance of Sri Aurobindo* (Delhi: Vivek Publishing House, 1973).

LITERATURE

Sri Aurobindo's literary works include *Savitri* and BCL, 5–9; of these, *Savitri* (BCL, 28–29; 1970), *Collected Poems* (BCL, 5; 1972) and *The Future Poetry* (BCL, 9; 1972) are available separately.

The most useful studies of Sri Aurobindo's poetry are the letters on *Savitri* by Sri Aurobindo (BCL, 29: 727–816) and the following works by disciples: K. D. Sethna, *Sri Aurobindo: The Poet* (1970); Iyengar, *Sri Aurobindo: A Biography and a History* (1972*); and Roarke, *Sri Aurobindo* (1973)

HISTORY AND CULTURE

Sri Aurobindo's writings on historical and cultural topics are contained principally in a one-volume trilogy: *Social and Political Thought* (BCL, 15; 1971), which includes *The Human Cycle*, *The Ideal of Human Unity* and *War and Self-Determination*. Sri Aurobindo's political career and social philosophy are capably treated by both Diwakar and Iyengar, but the foremost authority on this aspect of Sri Aurobindo's thought is Sisir Kumar Mitra; see especially *The Liberator: Sri Aurobindo, India and the World* (Bombay: Jaico Publishing Company, 1970*) and *India: Vision and Fulfillment* (1972).

INTEGRAL YOGA

The indispensable complement to *Essays on the Gita* (BCL, 13; 1970) and *Synthesis of Yoga* (BCL, 20–21; 1971) is the three-volume collection *Letters on Yoga* (BCL, 22–24; 1971). Useful anthologies of Sri Aurobindo's writings on integral yoga include Satprem, *Sri Aurobindo or the Adventure of Consciousness* (1968*; New York: Harper and Row, 1974*), a presentation of brief passages by Sri Aurobindo with extensive commentary by one of Sri Aurobindo's most accomplished disciples, and *A Practical Guide to Integral Yoga* (1971).

For secondary sources, see Haridas Chaudhuri, *Integral Yoga* (1965; Wheaton, Ill.: Theosophical Publishing House [Quest Books], 1974*). Nolini Kanta Gupta, the newly appointed head of the Sri Aurobindo Ashram, is the author of a significant six-volume study entitled *The Yoga of Sri Aurobindo* (1950–1972).

PHILOSOPHY

Sri Aurobindo's writings in philosophy include *The Life Divine* (BCL, 18–19; 1970); *The Human Cycle* (BCL, 15; 1971), which articulates his philosophy of historical evolution; and his commentary on the Upanishads (BCL, 12; 1972), which reveals his novel interpretations of the philosophical claims in these most profound of spiritual-philosophical texts.

The Mind of Light, which was written by Sri Aurobindo in 1949 just before his death, well summarizes his philosophy and can be read as a popularization of *The Life Divine;* see *The Mind of Light,* Introduction and Annotated Bibliography by Robert A. McDermott (New York: E. P. Dutton, 1971). There are also two anthologies which are primarily philosophical: P. B. Saint-Hilaire [Pavitra] (ed.*), *The Future Evolution of Man* (1963* and Wheaton, Ill.: Theosophical Publishing House [Quest Books], 1974*) and Rishabhchand and Shyamsundar (eds.), *The Destiny of Man* (1969*).

For an excellent study of Sri Aurobindo's philosophical system, see Beatrice Bruteau, *Worthy Is the World: The Hindu Philosophy of Sri Aurobindo* (Rutherford, N.J.: Fairleigh Dickenson University Press, 1971). Haridas Chaudhuri, *Sri Aurobindo: Prophet of the Life Divine* (1950) has recently been reissued with a foreword by Robert A. McDermott, by the Cultural Integration Fellowship (San Francisco, 1973*). Eight essays on Sri Aurobindo's philosophy were collected in the *International Philosophical Quarterly,* XII (June 1972). Finally, S. K. Maitra is the author of two excellent studies on Sri Aurobindo's philosophy: *An Introduction to the Philosophy of Sri Aurobindo* (1965*), the best brief (70-page) introduction, and *The Meeting of East and West in Sri Aurobindo's Philosophy* (1956*), which offers revealing comparisons between Sri Aurobindo and Plato, Plotinus, Hegel, Bergson and Whitehead.

BIBLIOGRAPHY

For a comprehensive listing, with cross references, of writings by and about Sri Aurobindo, see H. K. Kaul, *Sri Aurobindo: A Descriptive Bibliography* (New Delhi: Munshiram Manoharlal, 1972). Annotated bibliographies by Robert A. McDermott have been published in *The Mind of Light,* pp. 120–128 and in *The Essential Aurobindo,* pp. 250–254. Perhaps the most useful description of available works by and about Sri Aurobindo is the *Sri Aurobindo Booklist* 1974–75, available free of charge from Matagiri, Mount Tremper, New York 12457.